THE DILEMMA OF THE COMMONERS

One of the classic problems in social science is known as 'the dilemma of the commons', in which land, water, and other resources held jointly by social or economic segments tend to be depleted sooner and to a greater extent than privately held assets. During the eighteenth and nineteenth centuries, many aspects of western European society changed fundamentally, including the abolition of common-property rights, which in itself was related to social, political, and economic shifts in that same society. This book intends to put the debate on commons, commoners, and the disappearance of both throughout early modern and modern northwestern Europe in a new light, through new approaches and innovative methodologies. Tine De Moor aims to link the historical debate about the long-term evolution of commons to the present-day debates on common-pool resources, as well as touching upon various disciplines within the social sciences that work on commons issues.

Tine De Moor is Professor of Institutions for Collective Action in Historical Perspective at Utrecht University. She has published in various top journals on a variety of topics in social and economic history, but most extensively on commons in northwestern Europe. She has won several prizes for her research, including the prize for the best dissertation in the category 'Medieval and Early Modern Period' of the International Economic History Association. She is also currently President (2015–2017) of the International Association for the Study of the Commons and the co-founder, former editor-in-chief, and member of the editorial board of the *International Journal of the Commons*.

POLITICAL ECONOMY OF INSTITUTIONS AND DECISIONS

Series Editors

Stephen Ansolabehere, Harvard University
Jeffry Frieden, Harvard University

Founding Editors

James E. Alt, Harvard University
Douglass C. North, Washington University of St. Louis

Other Books in the Series

Alberto Alesina and Howard Rosenthal, *Partisan Politics, Divided Government and the Economy*

Lee J. Alston, Thrainn Eggertsson, and Douglass C. North, eds., *Empirical Studies in Institutional Change*

Lee J. Alston and Joseph P. Ferrie, *Southern Paternalism and the Rise of the American Welfare State: Economics, Politics, and Institutions, 1865–1965*

James E. Alt and Kenneth Shepsle, eds., *Perspectives on Positive Political Economy*

Josephine T. Andrews, *When Majorities Fail: The Russian Parliament, 1990–1993*

Jeffrey S. Banks and Eric A. Hanushek, eds., *Modern Political Economy: Old Topics, New Directions*

Yoram Barzel, *Economic Analysis of Property Rights, 2nd edition*

Yoram Barzel, *A Theory of the State: Economic Rights, Legal Rights, and the Scope of the State*

Robert Bates, *Beyond the Miracle of the Market: The Political Economy of Agrarian Development in Kenya*

Jenna Bednar, *The Robust Federation: Principles of Design*

Charles M. Cameron, *Veto Bargaining: Presidents and the Politics of Negative Power*

Kelly H. Chang, *Appointing Central Bankers: The Politics of Monetary Policy in the United States and the European Monetary Union*

Peter Cowhey and Mathew McCubbins, eds., *Structure and Policy in Japan and the United States: An Institutionalist Approach*

Gary W. Cox, *The Efficient Secret: The Cabinet and the Development of Political Parties in Victorian England*

Gary W. Cox, *Making Votes Count: Strategic Coordination in the World's Electoral System*

Gary W. Cox and Jonathan N. Katz, *Elbridge Gerry's Salamander: The Electoral Consequences of the Reapportionment Revolution*

Raymond M. Duch and Randolph T. Stevenson, *The Economic Vote: How Political and Economic Institutions Condition Election Results*

Jean Ensminger, *Making a Market: The Institutional Transformation of an African Society*

David Epstein and Sharyn O'Halloran, *Delegating Powers: A Transaction Cost Politics Approach to Policy Making under Separate Powers*

Kathryn Firmin-Sellers, *The Transformation of Property Rights in the Gold Coast: An Empirical Study Applying Rational Choice Theory*

Clark C. Gibson, *Politicians and Poachers: The Political Economy of Wildlife Policy in Africa*

Daniel W. Gingerich, *Political Institutions and Party-Directed Corruption in South America: Stealing for the Team*

continued after the Index

THE DILEMMA OF THE COMMONERS

*Understanding the Use of Common-Pool Resources
in Long-Term Perspective*

Tine De Moor

Utrecht University, The Netherlands

CAMBRIDGE
UNIVERSITY PRESS

32 Avenue of the Americas, New York, NY 10013–2473, USA

Cambridge University Press is part of the University of Cambridge.

It furthers the University's mission by disseminating knowledge in the pursuit of education, learning, and research at the highest international levels of excellence.

www.cambridge.org
Information on this title: www.cambridge.org/9781107022164

© Tine De Moor 2015

This publication is in copyright. Subject to statutory exception and to the provisions of relevant collective licensing agreements, no reproduction of any part may take place without the written permission of Cambridge University Press.

First published 2015

A catalog record for this publication is available from the British Library.

Library of Congress Cataloging in Publication Data
Moor, Tine de.
The dilemma of the commoners : understanding the use of common-pool resources in long-term perspective / Tine De Moor.
pages   cm. – (Political economy of institutions and decisions)
1. Cooperation – Europe – History.   I. Title.
HD3484.A4M56   2015
333.2–dc23   2014048656

ISBN 978-1-107-02216-4 Hardback

Cambridge University Press has no responsibility for the persistence or accuracy of URLs for external or third-party Internet Web sites referred to in this publication and does not guarantee that any content on such Web sites is, or will remain, accurate or appropriate.

For Kaat

Under what conditions will cooperation emerge
in a world of egoists without central authority?
This question has intrigued people for a long time. And for good reason.
We all know that people are not angels,
and that they tend to look after themselves and their own first.
Yet we also know that cooperation does occur and that our civilization is
   based upon it.
But, in situations where each individual has an incentive to be selfish,
how can cooperation ever develop?

(Axelrod 1984, 3)

Contents

List of Figures and Tables .... *page* xi

Preface xiii

Acknowledgments xvii

Introduction 1

1 The emergence of commons and other forms of institutions for
collective action in western Europe from the late Middle Ages
onwards 18
  1.1 An institutional revolution in western Europe? 18
  1.2 Historical development: the rise of commons and guilds from
    1000 to 1300 24
  1.3 Distinct institutions for collective action 31
  1.4 The design of institutions for collective action 34
    1.4.1 Exclusive 34
    1.4.2 Self-governed and relatively democratic governance
       structure 38
    1.4.3 Protectionist 40
    1.4.4 Local 44
    1.4.5 Features of the governance model versus features of succesful
       institutions 46
  1.5 Explaining the origins of institutions for collective action in western
    Europe 48
    1.5.1 Motives for collective action: potential advantages of
       cooperation 49
    1.5.2 Motors of institutions for collective action: stimulating factors
       to form collectivities 52
    1.5.3 Conditions for collective action: weak family ties, tolerant
       states, and legal recognition 55
  1.6 Conclusions 58

2 Common land and common rights in Flanders 61
  2.1 Description of the area 61
  2.2 The nature of common land 67

ix

Contents

2.2.1 Common waste	68
2.2.2 Common arable land	71
2.3 The evolution of the legal basis of common land	73
2.4 Management of common land in Flanders	84
2.4.1 Boundaries of common land	88
2.4.2 Regulation of the use of common land	91
2.4.3 Managers and monitors of common land	93
2.5 Conclusions	97

3 From rules to practice: case description, sources,
and methodology 100
    3.1 Case study: the common of the Gemene and Loweiden in the
villages of Assebroek and Oedelem, Flanders 100
        3.1.1 The rights and duties of the *aanborgers* 103
        3.1.2 Historial sources on the case of the Gemene and
Loweiden 107
    3.2 Methodological framework: the functioning of a common captured
in a three-dimensional approach 113

4 The choices of the commoners: understanding utility,
efficiency, and equity on the commons through the behavior of
commoners 121
    4.1 The commoners' changing participation in use and management
of the common 124
    4.2 The effect of changing power balances on the management of the
common 139
    4.3 Dealing with over- and under-exploitation 143
    4.4 Keeping it in common: the choice between collective and private
property 148
    4.5 Conclusions 149

5 Dealing with dilemmas: conclusions 152

Epilogue: The revenge of history? The return of the homo cooperans
in present-day western European countries 161

References 169

Archival references 183

Index 191

x

Figures and Tables

Figures

1 Conditions, motors, and motives for institutions for collective action to emerge . . . . *page* 58

2 Flanders, with indication of sandy area and indication of case study (gray dot) 64

3 The Gemene and Loweiden as presented on the detailed maps of Count Ferraris, 1777 101

4 Example of part of a page from the first *hoofdboek* of the Gemene and Loweiden (1515–1622), showing how several members were registered in July 1622 108

5 Overview of the debates on the resource, institution, and users of commons 116

6 The three-dimensional approach to commons: commons as common-pool resources, common-pool institutions, and common-property regimes 118

7 Illustration of an invitation to a general meeting of the commoners to be held on 22 June 1860 129

8 Evolution of the average participation intensity per 20 years, 1680–1860 132

9 Average age at subscription compared to average marriage age in the area 134

10 Percentage of categories of cattle owners according to the total number of cattle units in their possession 142

11 Exploitation level of the common, 1699–1840, in terms of cattle units 145

12 Evolution of the balance of accounts, 1699–1900 149

xi

List of Figures and Tables

Tables

1 Overview of features of commons in the western versus eastern part of Flanders 86
2 Features of closed versus open types of commons 97
3 Total number of persons registered as members of the Gemene and Loweiden, in absolute numbers and as average per year (with registrations) 106
4 Subdivision of ways (economically or functionally) in which *aanborgers* were active, 1700–1900 131
5 Evolution per half century of the percentage of farmers, farm laborers (including servants and day laborers), and laborers among the *aanborgers*, 1700–1900 137

Preface

Some projects keep growing long after they have been initiated. This book is the result of several projects that have taken place at various universities in Flanders and the Netherlands. Part of this book originated from a study taken up as a PhD project (which I defended in 2003) back at the University of Ghent. But most of the book, which was developed over the past few years, is based on new insights about the similarities between institutions in the historical context – such as commons and guilds – as well as between such historical institutions and those that result from what some would call the 'institutional revolution', which Europe has been witnessing for the past decennium, with many new forms of institutions for collective action being developed, both in town and in the countryside, and in many different sectors. In a way, taking time to finalize this book has allowed for opportunities to embed the historical evolutions and what we have learned about the way in which citizens collaborated in the past into the broader perspective of the role institutionalized forms of collective action can play in our present-day society. Ten years ago, the commons were for most citizens simply a reflection of an old era, long gone; however, the societal developments that have speeded up quite a bit since the economic crisis (2008 and onwards) have put these institutions back on the agenda. Sometimes the concept of the commons has been interpreted too broadly, giving the impression that resources managed in the form of a common were accessible to all, and could be used by all. Commons sometimes have been used to refer to 'all that we share', but that, arguably, is a far too broad definition for anyone with prior historical knowledge. With this book, the conditions for the functioning of a common in historical Europe may become clearer again, and the detailed description of how such a common really worked can be used as a framework for further research on present-day commons. Bringing together in a coherent manner the common as a concept, the

Preface

historical context, and in-depth research on a specific case is the main challenge of this book, but by doing so I believe the debate on the future role of institutions for collective action, which is also touched upon in the epilogue, can be moved a few steps forwards.

Several colleagues have contributed – each in his or her own way – to this book. Jan Luiten van Zanden has been a *compagnon-de-route* throughout the projects that are the basis of this book; for more than fifteen years now, he has offered his very valuable advice and critique whenever it was needed (and even when it wasn't needed!). It was during a conference/coffee-break talk back in 1998 that we first met and he introduced me to the work of Elinor Ostrom, which later would prove to be vital for my own course of action. On various topics, including that of the commons, Jan Luiten and I have talked again and again over the past few years. He critically revised most of the material in this book at some point during those years, while also challenging me to build 'the bigger picture', to go beyond the historical case study and connect historical insights to present-day developments. This has directly influenced the structure of the book, which, as I will explain, starts from a very broad institutional framework, then narrows to a specific case study, and finally widens the perspective again at the close of the book, ending with reflections on present-day issues. Without his support, I would never have had the courage to 'think big' and write this book. Such out-of-the-box thinking is a fundamental and cherished feature of the way in which the Social Economic History research group at Utrecht University – to which we both belong – works. For more than ten years, this group has been in many different ways a real 'home' for me, away from my 'natural habitat' in Flanders. In addition to Jan Luiten, I would like to thank my colleagues Bas van Bavel, Joost Dankers, Maarten Prak, and Keetie Sluyterman for their important contribution to making our group such a great place to work and more than that.

Using methods and insights from other disciplines is often a big endeavor and not always applauded within traditional historiography, but thanks to the support of my colleagues at the other faculties of Utrecht University and the International Association for the Study of the Commons (IASC), combining the insights from different disciplines and from different time periods has become for me a natural way of doing research and engaging in the public debate. In particular, I want to thank Vincent Buskens, Ivo Giesen, Stephanie Rosenkranz, and Erik Stam – all connected to the Strategic Theme 'Institutions' at Utrecht University – for creating such a stimulating interdisciplinary research environment in Utrecht. The IASC played an equally important role for my research, not in the least because the disciplinary boundaries were entirely absent within this large group of commons enthusiasts.

xiv

Preface

Specifically, I would like to thank Ruth Meinzen-Dick, Leticia Merino, Susan Buck, and Marco Janssen for their role as fellow board members over the past few years. Among all the members of the IASC, however, is one person who has served as an example, both as a scientist and as a 'cooperator', to me and to many others. Lin Ostrom, an excellent scholar, opened my eyes as a historian to a field much wider than I could have ever expected and also showed me what kind of person one can attempt to become in the often very competitive world of academia.

The institutions for collective action research team I started to build in 2009 has become a sort of research hub for both historical and present-day issues related to cooperation and collective action, and consists of a wonderful group of dynamic and highly motivated researchers. I would like to thank past and present team members for enduring the returning complaints about my lack of time to finalize the book. Among them, my very special thanks goes to René van Weeren, who has contributed a great deal to making this into a publishable document but has, besides this, also been an enormous help to me and all other team members. All mistakes in agenda management are mine. I would also like to thank the members of the Gemene and Loweiden, the case study that appears very frequently in this book, and in particular their *hoofdmannen* who at the beginning of my research on this common showed a lot of confidence in a young scholar to use their precious archive and dive into their collective past. I hope that by bringing together their heritage with that of many other commons Europe once had, they will value their own history even more than they already do.

Finally, I would like to thank my partner Hans for enduring even more complaints about my slow progress and for being one of the first – by now many years ago – to direct me to commons as an alternative way of dealing with the world's resources. Both of us have been involved in many initiatives that resembled the organizations that are discussed in this book. I sincerely hope our daughter Kaat wasn't suffering too much from my enduring procrastination while writing this book. And I hope she will – one day – get some inspiration from this book about what makes cooperation with others successful – or not – and will manage to make it work for herself. It is a challenge, but it makes life richer in many different ways.

Acknowledgments

The research for this book was made possible with funding from the Flemish Foundation for Scientific Research and the European Research Council, the latter under the European Community's Seventh Framework Programme (FP7/2007–2013/ERC agreement no. 240928) as part of the project '"United We Stand": The Dynamics and Consequences of Institutions for Collective Action in Pre-Industrial Europe' (2010–2014).

Introduction

For its one hundred twenty-fifth anniversary in 2005, the journal *Science* considered the question 'How did cooperative behavior evolve?' to be one of the top twenty-five issues for scientists in the future to solve (Kennedy and Norman 2005, 75; Pennisi 2005, 93). This question has puzzled scientists from many disciplines for ages, including Charles Darwin. Darwin himself was intrigued by his discovery that, although humans seem to be 'programmed' to fight other humans to survive, humans *do* search for cooperation with others, precisely as part of this survival strategy.[1] Thus, cooperation should be considered one of the distinctive features of humankind. What is more, humanity needs cooperation to survive. Clearly, this was a conundrum for Darwin. His confusion becomes even more understandable in its contemporary context: his *On the Origin of Species* (1859) was written during a period when liberal thought received broad political recognition. The individual became the central unit of society; in European-wide political and intellectual circles, private property was increasingly considered the most ideal way of governing natural and other resources. During the eighteenth and nineteenth centuries, many aspects of western European society changed fundamentally. One of those changes was the abolition of (legally recognized) common-property rights, which in itself was related to fundamental social and economic shifts in society.

Darwin was living at a time when the rights of communities were gradually (and sometimes rather abruptly) replaced by more rights for the individual, though not necessarily for all individuals. Whereas most villages had held at least part of their land in common for centuries for its use by villagers, national governments now decided that these lands were to be

---

[1] This conclusion has meanwhile been confirmed by the many cooperation experiments conducted by both economists and sociologists (see for instance Jager et al. 2000).

Introduction

sold and split up into separate units. This was to benefit the nation as a whole, since the establishment of private property on these previously commonly held lands was expected to encourage villagers to invest more time, money, and effort in their land, presumably leading to a rise in land productivity. Witnessing a dramatic increase in population and industrial development, governments welcomed growth in their country's agricultural output. Despite this theory behind the politics, in practice most of the land ended not in the hands of industrious and hard-laboring farmers, but in those of wealthy investors who lived in nearby urban centers.[2] But even they, working with the best and most expensive fertilization methods, often could not achieve the desired increased productivity. Apart from the few commons that had survived the liberalization wave that swept through Europe during the nineteenth century, most villagers were left empty-handed. They lost not only a means of income, but also part of their community and the invisible bonds that working together from generation to generation created among community members. Commons had, as will be explained, a primarily economic function, namely, that of sharing the risk of relying on a resource for which the production – and thus the income – was unreliable. Besides this, however, the commoners also found in the common a social welfare system – albeit not for everyone – and a source of social capital.[3] The long-standing history of many commons in Europe shows that cooperation and reciprocity were the binding agents for those who used the common. Without cooperation, the common land was bound to be over-exploited; the commoners were very aware of this and showed this awareness in their daily and long-term commons management. It cannot be denied, however, that formerly enthusiastic participants can cease to cooperate, or that non-entitled users may try to encroach on the resources of others. To prevent this, commoners started to devise autonomously a body of instruments and mechanisms to enable their common usage system to work. Some of those tools were used to prevent abuse of the use-rights; others were implemented when the harm was already done (i.e., to punish abusers). These instruments were not always used correctly, nor should we present the commons as a paradise-like pasture, but in many ways the common represents the drive for cooperative behavior, with its own peculiar twists and turns.

Over the past decades, scholars have shown that owners of collective resources were capable of limiting the behavior of others to achieve a better common output. The historical commons that are the core example of

---

[2] See, e.g., the dissolution process in the Campine area of Belgium (see, e.g., M. De Moor 2002; 2003a).

[3] The word 'commoner' in this chapter is used as a reference to a person who has use-rights on a common, not as a reference to 'common folk'.

Introduction

institutions for collective action in this book demonstrate a high degree of such self-governance by rules that were self-restrictive and self-sanctioning if such rules were not followed correctly. To some extent, self-governance was – in the absence of a well-functioning state and market – the only type of governance to which farmers had recourse. Considering the present-day condition of both state and market, and the urgent need for new governance models to safeguard the world's natural resources, the historical commons can provide us with inspiration on future governance models for natural and other resources.

What is more, the longevity of commons as institutions for collective action assures us of the means to study successes, crises, and failures of institutions for collective action, and can help us to understand which changes in society affected the commons and how commoners reacted to these changes. The history of the commons offers an opportunity to study such dynamics of cooperation over very long periods of time. Cooperation is not just a single act; it can also consist of a large number of repeated acts among many people, often over different consecutive generations. People can thus exert their commitment over time, which can result in resilient institutions that are sufficiently robust to deal with shocks and crises in several domains of society. Such resilience can ensure stability in societies, which in turn can create good environments for social and economic progress. In order to adjust and adapt to change in society – be it of an economic, social, or political nature – the repertoire of instruments and mechanisms of those cooperating must have been considerably large and adapted to local circumstances. Every historical common was a local institution, usually not larger than a few hundred hectares (depending on the region), meaning that whatever decision was taken, it had to reflect local conditions. Thus, rules needed to reflect local needs of both resources and users.

The beginnings of European commons are to be found in the second half of the Middle Ages. At that time, from about 1000 AD, Europe went through a remarkable social and economic development, and one of its key characteristics was the institutionalization of collective action. What is remarkable about the late Middle Ages in Europe is that, rather than solving problems exclusively within the family or within the clan, people started to make alliances with others who followed a similar course in life, mainly people with the same occupation. The household, rather than the family, became the central unit of decision making. Elsewhere, beyond the borders of northwestern Europe, the family remained the most important unit of decision making in various spheres of life. During this period and in this particular area, the idea of an interest group was born and spread among

Introduction

different strata of society, in the countryside as well as in urban settlements. This development and its practical implications for everyday life were remarkable for several reasons. First, it was remarkable from a global history perspective with western Europeans starting to follow a divergent path from the rest of Europe, and, by extension, from the rest of the world. The formation of commons was merely one form of collective action that could be found in Europe. In addition to the commons in the rural areas, guilds, fraternities, and communes developed in the urban areas as examples of this new trend. Outside of Europe, such alliances also developed, but often much later and at a much slower pace.[4] Such a parallel development of different types of collective action shows that these were part of a large wave of collective action that swept through Europe. Like the wave of liberalization that swept through Europe in the nineteenth century, the same area had gone through a process of institutionalizing collective action in a much earlier period. These developments are not necessarily antithetical to one another; both are part of the emancipation of the individual: first from the family ties, and later from other collectivities. Taking into consideration Darwin's conclusion that humans are essentially social animals in need of one another[5] and the present--day institutional revolution, it seems that the collectivity will always remain a functional and necessary form of organization in human societies.

Moreover, the formation of institutions for the use and management of common property may seem remarkable and unusual from a present-day perspective, in particular given the current primacy of private property. After centuries of common property practice, the functioning of commons was questioned as early as the middle of the eighteenth century. The need to feed the increasing population required greater land productivity. It was believed that commons halted development. The same rhetoric was applied to other institutions, such as the guilds: they were supposed to halt the development of new technologies and economic growth. For centuries, despite some conflicts, the common-property arrangement had in general been considered a good and satisfactory way to manage natural resources. Under the changing circumstances, the future of the commons became uncertain. This privatization discourse is still alive, and it has been and continues to be translated into various political reforms we have witnessed

---

[4] See, e.g., the work by Christine Moll-Murata on the development of Chinese guilds. These were not consolidated until the seventeenth century and reached their full development by the nineteenth century, a period when Europe had already eliminated guilds (and commons) in favor of the rule of private property and the market.

[5] The idea that humans are social animals starts already with Aristotle and his novel idea of 'political animal' (*zoon politikon*) (Kullmann 1980, especially pp. 425 ff.).

Introduction

throughout the 1990s.[6] At the moment this course still affects our view of communal resource management in a negative sense. The simultaneous rise and demise of commons, guilds, and other forms of collective action shows that recognition by the higher authorities is of essential importance to the good functioning of institutions for collective action.

Being a historical study, this book focuses mainly on a historical period, one when the drive for continuity by the commoners conflicted with the desire for change by local and national authorities. For centuries after the origination of commons, the commoners lived more or less in accordance with the rulers over the division of the use of the common, whereby local lords reserved some of the resources for themselves – such as the right to hunt on the common land – and left the daily use of the land for pasture, peat digging, or for wood (as building material and as fuel) for the commoners. The period 1700–1900 starts off with relatively few internal or external changes, thus giving us an idea of how the common may have functioned in the centuries before that more turbulent age, starting from the middle of the eighteenth century. From then on, governments began gradually to impose legislation on the commons, and with the introduction of the new civil code book in 1815, the government – both on the local and the national levels – also started claiming the land as municipal property. In the area where the case study of this book is located – ruled first by the Austrians, then the French, and then the Dutch, before Belgium became a nation state in 1830 – the government tried to dissolve the commons in a nonaggressive way, but after achieving little success, new and more aggressive techniques were used to turn what was collective into private plots of land. By studying the common's history, covering over two hundred years, we can see the effect of societal and political change on the common, and how a group of commoners adjusted its governance system to these changes. Many changes that affected the composition of the group of commoners will be taken into account here – not just changes in the government, but also population change, economic change, and changes in the social structures –, as all factors may have induced change in the common's management and use.

Although the effects of the liberalization wave in Europe will also be discussed, the core of this book is devoted to understanding long-term cooperation on another level, from within the institution: that is, from the perspectives of those who were involved in the daily functioning of the commons. As was noted in the extract from Axelrod in the epigraph, cooperation is not necessarily a given for people, who are – so it is

---

[6] See, e.g., the works by Stiglitz (2002) and Easterly (2006).

Introduction

believed – essentially selfish. There must be good reasons to share property, to work together towards a common goal. In order to understand the motives for cooperation or defection, it is possible to follow different research strategies. One would be to compare the reactions of people to different situations in an experimental situation, a method often applied in experimental sociology, psychology, and economics.[7] In the past, such research has revealed important aspects of human behavior towards cooperation – for instance, about the importance of group identity. These experiments have revealed, among many other things, that subjects are more willing to cooperate in a group if they are identified as members of that group. A sense of belonging thus seems to influence the degree of reciprocal behavior. Another avenue for understanding cooperation is through field research and analyzing in situ the behavior of individuals, in particular those who are part of groups that have a common objective, for example, cooperatives or village communities that have land in common.

None of the approaches – from field study to experiment – is applicable to historical research that goes back more than a century while one of the central issues that researchers on cooperative behavior are trying to solve is exactly how to achieve durable cooperation over long periods of time. Many examples can be found in Europe and elsewhere of institutions for collective action that have lasted for several generations, surviving in many cases for centuries, thriving on cooperation and reciprocity. In European history the commons in all their varied forms can serve as an excellent example of resilient institutions. Those commons, in particular the commoners who managed and used the land collectively, form the central subject of this book. Notwithstanding the large body of literature on the Enclosure movement in Great Britain (see, e.g., Neeson 2000; Shaw-Taylor 2001a; Shaw-Taylor 2001b; Tan 2002; Winchester 2002; Hoyle 2010)[8], surprisingly little has been written on the actual functioning of commons in historical perspective. And even more surprisingly, the lessons learned from other disciplines on the basis of experiments or field research have only recently and gradually been incorporated into historical studies on the commons (Lana Berasain 2008; Rodgers et al. 2011, 11–3 and passim). None of the methods mentioned thus far is possible if we want to study cooperation and collective action over the long term (i.e., for several decades or even centuries). But that does not mean that conclusions drawn

---

[7] For an overview see Van Laerhoven and Ostrom (2007), and for many other examples see Poteete et al. (2010, 141–214).

[8] A clear and concise description of the (often confusing) concept of enclosures and the process it entails can be found in Hoyle (2010).

Introduction

from these research methods (group identity, role of the individual, etc.) cannot be integrated into studies using methodological means for long-term studies.

A great advantage of historical research is related to the dilemma mentioned in the title of this book, which refers in the first place to a social dilemma as the core concept, in various forms, in commons studies and any study that deals with individuals who are weighing short-time private/individual interests against long-term collective/group interests.[9] Although such dilemmas contain an essential 'historical' component – whereby the collective interest is far away in time from the individual benefits – most studies dealing with social dilemmas concentrate on the *hic et nunc* choice behavior of individuals, and cannot, usually due to the nature of the methodology they employ, offer any certainty to the individual participant (e.g., in experimental studies) that the future collective outcome, whether positive or negative, will really take place. As much of the studies on contemporary commons and social dilemmas focus on the level of the individual actor, I will also present detailed research on the level of the individual commoner (in particular through a detailed case study), but can, thanks to the historical approach, unravel the incentive structure that was put in place by the commoners to solve social dilemmas over a longer period of time.

However, the methodology used by disciplines outside of history often does not allow inclusion of circumstantial factors, which go beyond the individuals' immediate wishes and needs, that may have influenced the choices commoners made. The difference between historical research and the many other methods that can be applied for the study of contemporary commons is the possibility to relate – post factum – the broad contextual developments to changes on the individual level of the commoner, and to unravel the effects of decisions that were taken by commoners as a reaction to changes in, for example, agricultural techniques on the individual lives of commoners. In many cases, the effects of decisions will not appear until many years later. As mentioned, the concept of a social dilemma, which is often taken as the starting point for experimental research, in itself implies that the impact of short-term decisions will only be apparent in the long term.

One of the reasons for the relatively small body of literature on historical commons – at least in comparison to the very large number of studies on contemporary commons that have taken place over the past twenty years[10] – is

---

[9] A social dilemma refers to a situation in which individual goal-directed behavior may lead to a collectively suboptimal outcome (see Raub, Buskens, and Corten 2014).

[10] See Van Laerhoven and Ostrom (2007) for an overview of studies on commons outside of the domain of history.

Introduction

the lack of sources that can be used for this subject. And whenever there are sources, it is always extremely labor intensive to construct data sets that come somewhat close to what can be done in experiments or field research. Contrary to the urban forms of institutions for collective action, such as guilds or fraternities, documents on the commons and commoners are difficult to find. Charters showing how the commoners reached an agreement with the local lords on management and use of the common are primarily prescriptive and give us only a partial – though important – idea of the daily functioning of the commons. The charters contain rules for use and management and pre-scribe sanctions for those who would infringe on those rules, but they do not disclose to what degree these rules were followed or when sanctions were imposed when rules were broken. But luckily, for some cases more information than this has been preserved.

The central case study of this book is such an example, for which a large body of interesting sources has survived. It is situated near the city of Bruges, in the heart of Flanders (during the ancien régime). Just outside Bruges' city walls, in a village called Assebroek, a name that refers to 'a meadow where horses graze', was and still is a common called the Gemene en Loweiden. Originally, the two main pastures that made up this common were managed separately, but over time they were brought together under the same name and management. In close proximity to this common were several other commons: the Beverhoutsveld, the Sijseleveld, the Bulskampveld, and other cases that will be referred to throughout the book. We analyzed this rich historical archive and inter-preted the results in light of the research on both historical and present-day commons.

The approach applied in this book is a serious attempt to bridge disci-plines, but in doing so, the bridges and gaps between the disciplines also become quite apparent. It is, for example, impossible to repeat experiments with commoners from the past, simply because they are no longer there; but it is nevertheless, to a certain degree, possible to become a field researcher of the past. As far as the sources and time permit, it is possible to reconstruct the daily functioning of a common, and to approach the historical commoners closely in their activities in the village and on the common. It is important to keep in mind, however, particularly when trying to use the results of experimental studies for historical research, that commoners did not (and still don't) live in a laboratory: they were part of an economic and social reality that stretched beyond their own homes and beyond their own village, even if they never went any further than the neighboring village. Therefore, data that sketch the social and economic reality of the eighteenth- and nineteenth-century villager will

Introduction

also be used here to explain what happened on and around the common, and the decisions the commoners made will be put in wider social, economic, and political perspective. It will be made clear that the commoners' backgrounds, and the shifts in these due to external changes, are fundamental to understanding their behavior towards the common's management and use. Rather than looking at commoners as guinea pigs in a laboratory, we should consider the historical situation itself as a laboratory.[11]

Having stressed the potential pitfalls the sources and methods applied in this book might produce, it is also worthwhile to point to the potential benefits. It would be possible, in a more traditional historiographical way, to give a chronological overview of the ways commoners organized their resource use and management. But using new insights based on nonhistorical research will open new ways of interpreting the actions performed by the commoners that previously may have been neglected as important findings. Why were commoners forced to attend the commons meetings, on penalty of a fine? Or were limitations on access to the commons set only to exclude others? And what was the importance of participation, or the opposite, of not being involved? In many cases we can guess what the answers to these questions were, but comparison with the behavior of others in similar situations today might offer more enlightening interpretations. In this book, comparisons are made with case studies in northwestern Europe, but the main focus is on a case in an area in the heart of northwestern Europe: Flanders. Elsewhere in this book (see 2.1) this area will be described in detail, as well as the differences the area has regarding density of commons compared with elsewhere in Europe. The challenge of this book – to provide a very detailed level of commoners' behavior and to reconstruct individual motives for specific choices in relation to the common they were entitled to use – and the extremely high labor intensiveness this entails in archival research and the analysis of a great number of detailed records, keeps us from taking into account more than a single case. Not only has the participatory behavior of the commoners during the eighteenth and nineteenth centuries been reconstructed in detail for the case of the Gemene and Loweiden, we also have information for a very large number of commoners, such as when they were born, which commoners they were related to, when the important events in their lives (such as marriage) took place, the number of livestock they had, and the occupations they held at various times. Such detailed information is particularly important to reconstruct the motivations of commoners for participating in

---

[11] See also Van Bavel (2014) on this topic of the role of history in the study of institutions.

Introduction

the commons' activities, to obey the rules or to defect, to favor privatization or not. However important this kind of information may prove to be to understand the evolution of this particular commoners' community, such an insight into the daily lives of commoners is also fairly unique, making opportunities for comparison sometimes limited.

Methodologically, most of this book is based on a detailed case study, though using a much wider theoretical and interdisciplinary perspective. To some extent, history has already made a pre-selection of cases that were not fit for long-term survival, which may have silently disappeared from the historical records, making it hard to disentangle the real reasons for success behind the surviving cases. That unsuccessful cases may not have been chronicled is a factor we can, in historical studies, not deny, but this is a difficulty with which nonhistorical studies are not confronted because only those cases that exist at a certain point in time are included in studies. This again creates the disadvantage that long-term changes, possibly leading to the disappearance of a common, are as such left out of nonhistorical commons anyhow. Unfortunately, the ideal historical case does not exist.

Considering all this, some might claim that the case examined in this book is an exceptional one, because of the rather well-preserved archives and because it managed to survive until today, although its function and form has altered quite substantially in the meanwhile. Most commons in Belgium disappeared during the nineteenth century at the latest, either by force or because their members were no longer interested in being an active user of the common or could no longer fulfill the conditions of active membership. Elsewhere in the country, such as in Wallonia in the southern part of present-day Belgium, and elsewhere in Europe, common rights are still recognized and actively practiced today, though not always in the same way as before. The fact that the common studied in this book managed to survive is to a large extent due to the exceptional efforts of a local priest, canon Andries, who also had had legal training and defended the commoners in court against the local authorities who tried to put their hands on the common (see further in this book). Without this, the Gemene and Loweiden would likely have suffered the same fate as most other commons in Flanders, with as a sure consequence the loss of the archival documents as well. As will be demonstrated in the book, the common was in terms of design or functioning not exceptional at all. The rules that were designed to limit free riding and overuse were similar to other commons of the so-called closed type (see conclusions of Chapter 2). Its size – both in terms of surface and members – was not exceptional, nor was its management strategy markedly different from that of other commons in Flanders at the time.

Introduction

Although very few commons have survived until today in northwestern Europe, they were very important and widely available during most of the early modern period, contributing significantly to the survival of households. Those that are still left today provide some additional resources or recreation, but on the whole this is a marginal contribution to the household economy for most users. However, in many third world countries, resources held and used in common still offer an ecological and economically viable way to manage natural resources. But, as was the case in eighteenth- and nineteenth-century Europe, the advantages of common-property regimes are often not understood or simply ignored by the supra-local organizations. This book aims at contributing to our understanding of why and in which circumstances cooperation among collective owners of the same resource comes about and how this worked in practice. The fact that the common we study still exists today allows us to start from a positive point of view, both in terms of resource use and management, as well as in terms of the long-term viability of institutions: we see that they can work, that collective action is not necessarily doomed to lead to over-exploitation, and that institutions for collective action can deal with change, both external (linked, e.g., to changes in the economy and society at large) and internal (linked to the changing needs and abilities of the commoners). It allows us to look at the factors that may bring success, instead ruin, as in Hardin's story (1968, see further).

The book starts (Chapter 1) with an explanation of the motives behind cooperation, or more specifically institutionalized forms of collective action, in a broad historical perspective. That commons were a much more complex institution than we originally thought and that they were frequently able to avoid Hardin's tragedy is an issue that others – such as Elinor Ostrom – have already shown. What is novel about this book is the long-term, historical approach, that is, the possibility of expanding Ostrom's insights with a time dimension that looks at change and adaptation within the common. In order to do so we begin in the first chapter with sketching the 'bigger picture' in which the commons in early modern Europe evolved. I will show how in certain parts of Europe institutions for collective action developed more rapidly, and how this can be explained. By including not only the commons but also other forms of institutions for collective action, such as guilds, in this historical overview, the perspective of the commons-researcher will be broadened, and new ways of studying the emergence, evolution, and dissolution of such institutions are made available. Apart from a few exceptions,[12] commons by and large were rural

---

[12] See, e.g., an urban common in Ghent (Heirnis).

Introduction

phenomena, concentrating on agricultural activities. And although a rural variant can be found,[13] guilds were primarily an urban phenomenon. Looking at two such widespread and similar forms of institutions for collective action through the same lens shows us how important the collective solution to social dilemmas was in early modern Europe, at a time when solutions offered through the market or by state intervention were not available or at least not yet sufficiently reliable. We will see the conditions of cooperative strategies and outcomes that may have been better than solutions offered by the market or the state. Cooperation is only one potential outcome of collective action, which itself originated as a reaction to particular problems or dilemmas. Essential in this chapter, and the book, is that cooperation is a motivated choice that – and Darwin understood this correctly – is not the default behavior of most people, except possibly for the few true altruists among us. Nor is the emergence of commons – and likewise guilds – a natural outcome of a long-term evolutionary process, as suggested by some historians. In this sense, the history of commons must be seen as that of the many small, daily, seemingly unimportant choices of individuals, which became a collective choice for cooperation: they had a choice either to cooperate or to defect. Their choices may seem straightforward once analyzed, but this collective behavior certainly did not remain unquestioned by contemporaries. At the time Darwin was wondering why humans cooperated (and why they did so successfully), his contemporary thinkers – economists, philosophers, political philosophers – wondered why on earth anyone would opt to be a co-owner of a common if private property could be so much more advantageous, not only for the individual but also for the society as a whole. A century later Hardin, in his seminal article 'The Tragedy of the Commons' (1968), and others claimed that common property in combination with population growth would definitely lead to ecological degradation of the resources held in common. Hardin claimed that everyone who had access to a collective resource would react in the same way: each individual would think of his or her own benefits in the short run, rather than the collective benefits in the long run. His main concern with this was that population growth in the future (from his 1968-perspective) would lead to excessive harvesting of the world's resources and eventually to tragedy. He demonstrated this with a common pasture that could be used by everyone. As long as natural and demographic disasters would now and then decimate cattle and farmers, pressure on the pasture's resources would remain under the critical level. However, in times of increasing prosperity, population would grow and the number of cattle

---

[13] See, e.g., the article about central European rural guilds by Joseph Ehmer (2009).

Introduction

might rise accordingly, and this, in turn, would lead to an excessive use of the common pasture land. He assumed that individuals would be unable to communicate and organize to prevent overharvesting the resources; he also assumed that human nature is such that greed and selfishness will always lead to free riding and, subsequently, excessive exploitation. Although since its publication the metaphor 'the tragedy of the commons' has been extremely popular in various scientific disciplines and with policymakers, many researchers have given proof of the opposite: individuals, commoners, and others are capable of preventing free riding by institution building.[14]

The initiatives of villagers to manage their land in common in an institutional way led to developing bodies of rules that allowed commoners to give the use of the common a more permanent character. Permanent in this sense does not, however, mean static. The commoners formed a framework that regulated access to the common, the use of natural resources, the managerial structure of the organization, the decision-making process, and the way conflicts should be dealt with. These small communities developed the necessary flexible instruments and methods to induce reciprocity among their members on their own and thus avoided free riding, also taking into account changes in the social, economic, and political environments. Analysis of the structure of these institutions forms the central goal of Chapter 2, providing an impression of the institutional basis of the commons. The focus in this chapter is mainly on Flanders, where the case study is situated, but there will also be references to other parts of Europe. The chapter is also intended to provide a more 'practical' and historical, and less theoretical idea of how commons originated and developed.

But rules were only the skeleton of the common; the daily encounters of commoners with problems, meetings with others not entitled to use the common, commoners' reactions to this, and the eventual consequences for both parties formed the 'flesh' of the institution. Social control and participation were essential instruments of the commoners to secure good daily use of their resources. By creating a responsible community, they promoted the functioning of their rules. Hence, intensive active

---

[14] See the digital library of the Commons for a mass of publications demonstrating the resilience of common-pool institutions: http://dlc.dlib.indiana.edu/dlc/. For some descriptions of successful historical cases, see http://www.collective-action.info/_CAS _COM_New; for some present-day successful case studies, see: http://www.iasc-com mons.org/impact-stories. Hardin was in fact not the first to express his concerns on this topic; see, among others around the same time, *The Logic of Collective Action: Public Goods and the Theory of Groups* (Olson 1965). And in the century before Hardin, see the lectures of William Foster Lloyd (1833).

Introduction

participation of commons' members was essential to making the commons work. It enhanced the identification of the commoner (and thus also of infringers), it sharpened the sense of community, and it discouraged potential free riders.

Chapters 3 and 4 are based on the case study. The third chapter gives a detailed description of the case study itself, which sources are available, and how these will be processed. It also presents a conceptual framework, based on a very general summary of the existing commons literature, that will help us to interpret the results of the sources – in particular, to understand how the decisions made among the commoners interact with the changes in the local economy and society. In Chapter 4, participation of the commoners will be taken as the point of departure, focusing on both qualitative and quantitative variations in this participation, which can help explain the actions taken by the commoners. By zooming in on the background of participants and of those who remained remarkably passive as members, we can offer explanations for those variations in participation. Most studies on common property have been centered on Hardin's assumption that a combination of common property and population growth will lead to the depletion of natural resources. They focused on the number of commoners. Whenever free riding, either by members or nonmembers, is studied, it is usually assumed that the free rider will take more than his or her share and thus 'injure' the common resources. In Chapter 4 it will become clear that the difficulty was not only to limit the number of commoners – there are cases of non-entitled users on this common – but to regulate that number in order to achieve a constant demand for the common. The common turned out to be as vulnerable, not only as a natural resource, but also as an institution, to insufficient use as to the feared excessive exploitation. The commoners of Gemene and Loweiden developed original methods to keep this under control; they could not, however, prevent their institution from changing rapidly and drastically under pressure of the growing group of passive members, members that no longer had any cattle to put on the common and thus had more interest in selling the common.

These changes became visible around the beginning of the nineteenth century and were accompanied by drastic alterations in the juridical basis of commons. The changes to the common made it subject to the new privatization laws. At that point the commoner showed a combative spirit. This changing situation is explained by contrasting the eighteenth-century sustainable use of resources with the situation in the nineteenth century, when pressure on the commons and commoners rose to such an extent that the collectivity nearly collapsed. But the commoners of the Gemene and

Introduction

Loweiden, over the centuries having become experts in finding compromises, managed to survive this crisis and those that followed.

Such a 'bottom-up' study, which allows us to envision commoners herding their cows on their common pasture, requires an intensive and detailed micro-study. In this sense this book can be read as a monograph on the life of a particular common close to the famous city of Bruges. But there is more to it: linking this study to the earlier analysis of cooperation and formation into institutions, and the comparison with other cases, brings us closer to an understanding of why people cooperate and what their prime motives can be for doing so, and for continuing to do so, often by passing on the tradition of cooperation from one generation to another. This book is not an attempt to explain cooperation in all situations, but aims at contributing to the understanding of the collective use of natural resources within local communities in the European past and to show that we need to look beyond the commoner as a user. Commoners – at least in historical Europe – were also part of the wider community, usually also had land in lease or property, and performed all sorts of different functions in the community.

The conclusions are summarized in Chapter 5, and the Epilogue also serves as a look ahead, which is rather unusual for a historical study. Oddly enough, the commons are currently picked up again by contemporaries to create new institutions for collective action, where self-governance is absolutely key to achieve the set goals. A new 'institutional revolution' is currently taking place in northwestern Europe, which can be considered as a reaction to the 'institutional poverty' of present-day societies, with only the market and the state as widely accepted governance systems.

It has now been ten years since the special *Science* issue put the spotlight on the importance of the quest for the foundations of human cooperation. Since then, many new studies have followed, and the field of cooperation studies received even an extra boost by the Nobel prize awarded to Elinor Ostrom in 2009. Meanwhile, many developed countries – mainly the countries of Europe and the United States – have also witnessed a huge renewed interest of its citizens in self-governance and the formation of new institutions for collective action. This new development takes place in practically every field of the economy and society – energy, care, infrastructure, finance, food, etc. – and can be considered as a response of the ordinary citizen to the demise of public services offered by governments in combination with a private market failing to offer an affordable and qualitative alternative. In the epilogue to this book, 'The revenge of history?', the story of the Flemish common is linked to this present-day

Introduction

revival of institutions for collective action, demonstrating at the same time that the conditions underlying the 'silent revolution' as described in the first chapter may be very similar to what we are witnessing in these first decades of the twenty-first century. The worldwide economic crisis that began in 2008 has led to major social problems, but has also opened many eyes and provides new approaches to resource governance, leading to the emergence of institutions that bear striking similarities with their historical predecessors. It is a cliché, but to some extent history repeats itself. The challenges are bigger, but the facilities and opportunities to communicate among commoners and reach effective and efficient decisions have increased as well. Given that Europe has a rich history in collective action, it is probably wise for those involved in this new movement to learn from the past.

The descriptions of the chapters already tell the reader that behind this book are multiple ambitions: bringing together disciplines, widening the time frame of studies on commons, demonstrating the similarities in development and functioning of similar institutions, paying attention to both the individual as the context. In addressing all these goals, several conceptual overviews will be given, although the reader should not expect a magic formula on how to build long-lived, resilient institutions for collective action. The local variations in commons – both in the types of resources they govern as in the way they do this – are too diverse to do so. Given that the commons are built by the users themselves and that the combinations of people and resources will differ from place to place, the outcome with be different from place to place as well. None of the commons in the area and outside of the area I will give examples of in this book were exactly the same in institutional design, as each adapted to the very local conditions.

In order to achieve all the mentioned ambitions, this book takes the reader on a rather unconventional journey which, if one would want to picture it, has the looks of an hourglass: broad at the ends, narrow in the middle. It starts with a very wide perspective, situated in a distant historical period, and places commons among its fellow institutions for collective action, encompassing institutions that developed in both town and countryside. For the reader this might be an unusual perspective, especially for a book on a type of institution intended for the management of natural resources. But as will be demonstrated, it is a perspective necessary to understand the broader context of institutional change, with a role more prominent than ever before for citizens and villagers. After starting with a very wide conceptual and geographic perspective in the first chapter, the

Introduction

book moves to a more regional scope – that of commons in Flanders – in the second chapter. Chapters 3, 4, and 5 deal with the very local level of the case study, in particular the commoners and the resources they governed.

Whereas the first and second chapters deal with a very long period in time, detailing the inception and early phase of the commons, the in-depth case study that is presented in Chapters 3 and 4 concentrates on a much shorter period of only two centuries: the eighteenth and nineteenth centuries. These centuries are not only interesting because of the multitude of sources available, but also because they cover an important period of change, both among commoners and in society as a whole, in the end leading to the dissolution of most western European commons, in particular through nationwide legislation that was executed in between 1750 and 1850. As will be explained towards the end of the first chapter, however, the opinions on the origins of commons and their capacities for agricultural productivity, poverty reduction, and sustainable resource use are closely connected. Being aware of the connections between explicit views on one aspect of the functioning of the commons and what this implies for other aspects, offers those interested in commons some guidance in the vast amount of literature that has been written about them over the past two (nineteenth and twentieth) centuries.

Although the privatization process of the eighteenth and – in particular – the nineteenth centuries seemed to have eradicated this type of governance model entirely in some western European countries, the developments during the so-called second wave at the end of the nineteenth century and the present-day developments in many European countries that were the first to abolish commons in the eighteenth and nineteenth centuries demonstrate a return of the cooperative spirit among its 'ordinary' citizens.[15] The other side of the hourglass – the Epilogue of this book – takes a very broad perspective, both in time and space, and considers the current developments in western Europe, where citizens again are taking up that prominent role in designing 'new' institutions for collective action. With this Epilogue we thus finalize the book with a broad perspective, including also a bit of a daring look into the future.

---

[15] For more on this second wave of institutions for collective action, see T. De Moor (2013).

1. The emergence of commons and other forms of institutions for collective action in western Europe from the late Middle Ages onwards[1]

1.1 An institutional revolution in western Europe?

During the late Middle Ages, European villagers and townsmen alike formed an unprecedented number of alliances with each other. These were not (primarily) based on kinship or blood ties, but on other common characteristics such as occupation. In the urban context, organizations such as guilds of merchants and craftsmen can serve as examples. For the countryside, this was the period when communal land tenure arrangements, or simply 'commons', were increasingly formed and institutionalized. It is not the formation of such types of collective action that is striking, nor their institutional characteristics that make the area of northwestern Europe in this period so exceptional. Elsewhere and in other times (e.g., Roman times), craftsmen and merchants also formed guild-like institutions.[2] It was the intensity of new units of such collective action that makes this movement striking enough to refer to it as 'a silent revolution'. It was a revolution in as much as this was a movement that started from below, among stakeholders with a common cause, and because it may have had important long-term consequences for the course of European history; it was 'silent' because this movement was primarily based on at first tacit and later explicit written agreements among powerful rulers and demanding subjects, villagers, and townsmen. These agreements were largely formed on a peaceful basis. The silent development of the forms of collective action described here has meant that for a long time the revolution remained

---

[1] This chapter is based to a large extent on a previously published article entitled 'The silent revolution: a new perspective on the emergence of commons, guilds, and other forms of corporate collective action in western Europe' (T. De Moor 2008), published as part of a special issue of the *International Review of Social History* on the topic of 'The return of the guilds'. Substantial changes and additions, however, have been made to the original publication.

[2] The so-called *collegia* (see Black 1984).

The emergence of commons

unnoticed. Most attention in historiographical collective action research has gone to the short-lived collective demands for change in the form of riots and protest demonstrations as motors for democratization and political change. In this chapter I argue that the silent revolution to a large extent created the institutional infrastructure for socio-political change – for other forms of collective action – that became characteristic for western Europe and which came to be considered a vital aspect of preparing western Europe's exceptional economic head start. By explaining when the commons originated and why and which other similar institutions also did so around the same time – and how all these different types of institutions for collective action went through similar stages of development – it will become easier to understand which factors influenced the internal functioning of such institutions, which is important for understanding the rest of the book.

It would be an exaggeration to claim 'discovery' of the revolution described here. Several authors have pointed to similar trends, either in the countryside (e.g., Blickle's *Kommunalismus*)[3] or in the cities (e.g., Greif 2006b). Apart from the work of Greif ('Family structure, institutions, and growth' [2006a]), most scholars have missed the co-evolution of these developments, and by doing so, they have not been able to identify the major forces leading to this revolution. Although the literature has already identified both merchant and craft guilds as well as commons as institutions that function according to the 'law' of collective action, these institutions have always been treated separately, without linking their simultaneous emergence, their parallel development, or their similarities in structure, functioning, rise, and decline (see Greif, Milgrom, and Weingast [1994] for merchant guilds, and Ogilvie [2004] for craft guilds). I suggest that there are links between these new institutions (both in the countryside and in the cities) and the specific developmental trajectory of the European economy from 1100 to 1800.

The only historian so far who has brought together the development of different types of cooperative institutions, and has done so for both town and countryside, is Susan Reynolds in her *Kingdoms and Communities in western Europe* (published in 1984) for the period 900–1300. According to Reynolds, lay society and government during that period depended

---

[3] In Blickle's view '*Kommunalismus*' expresses 'the mutual dependency of independent labor organizations of burghers and peasants on the one hand, and communes with state functions on the other' (the commune imposed itself as a horizontal principle within the socio-political system from the thirteenth century). These two complementary factors challenged and altered the wider political regime by means of representation and resistance, establishing 'communalism' as a fundamental organizational principle between medieval and modern times (Blickle 1998, 12).

'in a mass of different ways on the collective activities of a wide range of people ... as a matter of course in support of government, as well as in opposition to it' (Reynolds 1984, 332). She stresses that the homogeneity of the set of values that combined inequality and subordination with a high degree of voluntary cooperation laid the foundation of the new gulf of institutions that could be seen in the late Middle Ages, and which is the central issue of this chapter.[4] At the same time, it is possible to detect later on a reverse, but equally parallel demise of these institutions at the end of the eighteenth century, when both types of institutions had gone through a long period of criticism, fuelled by very similar arguments. The bottom line was the belief that these institutions were the enemies of innovation and economic progress. Were these not remnants of a feudal, medieval, and backward past that limited the development of the nation's economy and the population's growth? Didn't they restrict implementation of the free market and the ambitions of the individual mind? This kind of rhetoric used to attack these organizations in the eighteenth century, most prominently expressed by the Physiocrats, is to a large degree applicable to any other type of institution for collective action which existed at that time.[5] In these periods of legal reform (towards the establishment of absolute, private property) and growing individualism, the raison d'être of commons, guilds, and other forms of institutionalized cooperation was clearly at stake.

The Physiocratic economic theory originated in France in the middle of the eighteenth century. Physiocrats, whose most famous representatives were François Quesnay (1694–1777) and Anne-Robert Jacques Turgot (1727–1781), believed that economy should follow the presumed laws of nature, and politics, therefore, should focus mainly on 'the state of the population and of the employment of men' as the 'principal matter of concern in the economic government of states' (Quesnay [1958, 502] as quoted by Steiner [2003, 63]). In his *Tableau économique* (first published in 1757), Quesnay states that society should be divided into three classes: the productive class (farmers), the possessing class (landowners and sovereign rulers), and the sterile class (merchants and industrials) (Quesnay 1972, xxxviii–xli). According to Physiocratic theory, natural wealth

---

[4] Similar arguments to those of Reynolds, but for the development of merchant guilds, can be found in the chapter on merchant associations in pre-industrial Europe in Meir Kohn's upcoming book (also available as working paper, Kohn 2003, 142).

[5] On the discussion about the abolition of the commons in western Europe, see the European chapters in Demélas and Vivier (2003). On Belgium, see M. De Moor (2003a). On the new ideas about property, linked to the abolition of common property, see Congost (2007). On the abolition of the guilds in the Low Countries, see De Munck, Lourens, and Lucassen (2006, 61–4).

The emergence of commons

would circulate between those three classes in a natural way along unchanging channels. According to Quesnay *cum suis*, natural wealth was the sole base of a country's economic progress, hence agricultural produce and human labor should be highly valuated.[6] In the Physiocratic theory, private property of land was considered to be an essential condition for economic progress, since it was thought that only those who would really own the land securely, and therefore had the guarantee of benefiting personally and directly from the agricultural produce, would be willing to invest in their land. Consequently, Physiocrats considered the most important class to be the landowners, not the farmers. Land that was not held as private property, as in the case of the commons, was considered to be a hindrance to agricultural progress because those using the commons did not own the land privately and therefore were regarded to be less willing to invest in driving up land productivity. The Physiocratic movement received attention from government officials and politicians in France and Belgium (and, although to a lesser extent, also in other countries such as Austria) who were seeking for ways to improve the economic situation of their countries by cultivating the commons.[7]

To a certain extent, this view has been taken over by historiographers, but has changed recently, mainly as a result of a more careful assessment of the economic effects of guilds and commons, and the greater importance attributed to institutions for economic development. In particular, advocates of New Institutional Economics, such as Greif (2006b),[8] see the formation of merchant guilds in the late Middle Ages as a distinguishing moment in European economic development. Guilds underpinned the 'community responsibility system' according to which communities (i.e., towns) would threaten to boycott each other if individual members of these communities did not honor their obligations (e.g., if they

---

[6] Some of the Physiocrats had a more nuanced view, however. In contrast to his fellow Physiocrats, Turgot indicated in his *Réflexions sur la formation et la distribution des richesses*, first published in 1766, that this progress was not without limits: improvement of agricultural techniques would lead to increased produce, but not an exponential increase; instead, according to Turgot, an increase of produce would diminish, until a final point at which innovations would not yield any further produce increase (Turgot 1977, 109–13).

[7] For more information on the Physiocratic theory, see among others Steiner (2003); on the economic motivations of the Physiocrats, see Fox-Genovese (1976); for the influence Physiocratic thought had on the commons dealt with in this book, see M. De Moor (2003a), especially pp. 127ff.

[8] Some historians, however, remain pessimistic about the contribution of guilds to economic growth. See most prominently on this perspective Sheilagh Ogilvie (2004). Although Ogilvie nuances the possibilities to generalize the Württemberg case (see p. 331 of her article), her overall negative view of the impact of institutions such as guilds on the economic development of early modern Europe remains intact, as is also demonstrated in a later article by her hand (Ogilvie 2007).

21

The Dilemma of the Commoners

defaulted on their debts).[9] This laid the foundation for the institutional development of western Europe in later periods as well. Others have stressed the role that guilds played in the transfer of technology (Epstein 1998; Prak 2004; J. L. Van Zanden 2005). More generally, recent social and economic-historical historiography has seen a remarkable return of the guilds, thanks to detailed work on the operation and development of these institutions (Prak et al. 2006). Similarly, recent work on commons has tended to alter the formerly negative view on the functioning of commons. Allen (1992), for example, has compared the agricultural output of enclosed villages – which supposedly invested more in crop rotation and innovation – to open-field villages and concluded that land productivity was not greater in the former. His rather pessimistic view of the potential contribution of enclosures to the increase in agricultural productivity following industrialization contrasts with the previously stated claims by McCloskey (1972) (see also McCloskey [1975; 1989], Turner [1980; 1982; 1986], Yelling [1977], and Dahlman [1980]) of productivity rises of even twenty-five percent after enclosure. At the same time, the institutional adaptability of the commons has been considered by several researchers (e.g., Congost and Lana Berasain [2007], Lana Berasain [2008], T. De Moor [2009]) as an asset in times of rapid social and economic change.

This chapter contributes to the discussion about the role of (craft) guilds and commons in the developing market economy. By analyzing their institutional design, I intend to demonstrate that both types of institutions should be considered reactions to the risks and uncertainties of the new market environment that aimed to stabilize social and economic relationships and adapt economic strategies to this new environment. Because of their omnipresence in northwestern Europe from the late Middle Ages onwards, guilds and commons are the most suitable cases of institutions for collective action for studying this silent revolution; moreover, I will concentrate on the Low Countries, a region that saw a strong, early development of these institutions, especially in its southern half – Flanders, which is also the region in which the case study later in this book can be situated. Other types of institutions that are part of the 'silent revolution' include the

---

[9] See also Greif, Milgrom, and Weingast (1994). Greif also looks beyond guilds: 'Although the late medieval European institutions differ in forms from later ones, many of the elements and features of modern, welfare-enhancing Western style institutions were already present or in the process of emerging during the late medieval period: individualism, man-made formal law, corporatism, self-governance, and rules reflecting an institutionalized process in which these who were subject to them had a voice and influence. To the extent that the Rise of the West is due to its underpinning institutions, the roots of this rise may have begun to take hold as early as the late medieval period' (Greif 2006b, 379).

The emergence of commons

fraternities – brotherhoods with a mainly religious character – and the beguinages, where women chose to live together independently as a religious group, but without belonging to a religious order or convent.[10] In some literature, the beguinages have even been described as the female versions of guilds, though this was primarily because beguines were often involved in the crafts business, primarily in textiles (e.g., Simons 2001, xi; T. De Moor 2014, 15). Though I will not involve these institutions in the discussion, for future studies it might be worthwhile to consider them from the perspective of such a form of collective action in order to understand how common it was in the early modern period to solve problems of various kinds via collective action.

This chapter begins with a brief definition of *craft guilds* and *commons*, and a sketch of their genesis in the high Middle Ages. The focus then switches to identifying the peculiarities of this movement of collective action and its distinctive features. The second part offers an analysis of the factors behind these processes of collective action, subdivided into conditions that were necessary for the European silent revolution to arise, the motors that encouraged individuals to form new institutions, and the motives or incentives on the individual level for those who became members. Analyzing and comparing the problems that collective action tried to solve requires sufficient abstraction of the structure of such a problem. A concept that helps in achieving this is the 'social dilemma': not only does it capture the issues at stake in social problems with conflicting interests between individuals and society, research has in the meantime also revealed those qualities that collective actors should adhere to in order to solve their problems effectively and efficiently.[11]

---

[10] I have dealt with the motives behind the beguinage movement that took place in the same period as the development of guilds and commons (starting around the twelfth century) in a number of articles (De Moor and Van Zanden 2006; 2010; and T. De Moor 2014). Just like guilds and commons, beguinages were able to develop in western Europe because of the loose family ties, the European marriage pattern, and changes in the labor market, which allowed women – including single women – to secure their own income, while still in need of protection when living as single women in the medieval and early modern towns. In principle one could compare beguinages and guilds: some of the women who became beguines did so because the dowry that had to be paid to a normal convent had become too high. In this sense, single women managed to stay out of the religious 'market', but by demanding official recognition from the church they did manage to stay within the religious community. However, as is demonstrated in T. De Moor (2014), the main driver behind the formation of beguinages as institutions for collective action was the need of women to protect themselves, and this could be most easily achieved by uniting forces among them.

[11] Collective action is, of course, not the only change that took place in this region during this period. Elsewhere I have described the changes in the family structure and its consequences for the labor and capital markets (De Moor and Van Zanden 2010). For capital market development in this period, see also Zuijderduijn (2009).

23

The Dilemma of the Commoners

1.2 Historical development: the rise of commons and guilds from 1000 to 1300

Commons were institutions for the collective use and management of land and other natural resources. Although the history and typology (and naming) of commons is quite different on the continent, the English term has become widely used to indicate, for example, the German *Genossenschaften* and the Dutch *meenten* and *markegenootschappen* – all being institutions set up to regulate collective use and management of natural resources, ranging from woodlands to riversides, and sometimes even the river itself.[12] Overall, it is possible to distinguish two types of commons. The first type is comprised of land that is only temporarily – usually after the harvest – open to a group of people (members of the local community) to reap the remaining grain and/or to graze cattle on the stubble left behind. This type of land is generally designated 'common arable' (and is often not formally organized, and therefore not included in this overview, but see 2.2.2 for a more specific discussion). The other type relates to land that is open to a group of entitled users – which can be a group defined differently from the rural community – throughout the whole year (except, perhaps, for specified periods that should allow the commons' resources to regenerate). These commons can be divided into common woodland, common pasture, and common waste – the last usually being poor land – and would be open for pasture and other activities during most of the year. Rights were assigned to groups, in some cases comprising the entire local village and sometimes more than one village; in other cases, use-rights were limited to only those who met certain qualifications (ownership of certain farms, payment of a certain fee, etc.; see 2.4.1.1 for a more detailed explanation).[13]

In the past, two main explanations for the origins of commons have been given in the literature. Elsewhere in this book I distinguish these as the evolutionary explanation and the causal explanation (see 3.2, and more extensively M. De Moor [2003a]). The evolutionary explanation considers the existence of commons as part of a long evolution towards private property, dating from Germanic times when only movables could become individual property and all nonmovables belonged to the family/clan/tribe (Gilissen 1981). Common property could be seen – as Marx (1867), Engels (1884), De Laveleye (1894), and many other nineteenth-century authors claimed – as the primitive form of property. Over time, this common

---

[12] For a discussion of the various terms used for commons in Flanders, the Netherlands, Germany, England, and Scandinavia, see De Moor, Shaw-Taylor, and Warde (2002a).

[13] Further details on this typology of the commons can be found in De Moor, Shaw-Taylor, and Warde (2002b). An explanatory glossary can be found in De Moor, Shaw-Taylor, and Warde (2002a), p. 261.

The emergence of commons

property would evolve into private property. Clearly Marx and Engels did not favor this evolution, but others such as De Laveleye stressed that this was only a natural course, a gradual development:

> When jurists want to account for the origin of such a right, they fly to what they call the State of Nature, and from it derive directly absolute, individual ownership – or *quiritary dominium*. They thus ignore the law of gradual development, which is found throughout history, and contradict facts now well-known and well established. It is only after a series of progressive evolutions and at a comparatively recent period that individual ownership, as applied to land, is constituted.
>
> (De Laveleye 1891, 3–4; author's translation)

In the opinion of De Laveleye, all property, in the long run, would evolve into private property. This way of reasoning not only fails to explain the origins of commons in non-Germanic areas,[14] but it is also at odds with the establishment of new common rights on large plots of land in the Middle Ages and the foundation of many more commons in the period thereafter, when property systems had already evolved further.[15] According to Slicher van Bath (1978), the formation of *marken* and *meenten* (both forms of wasteland commons) went back no further than the twelfth or thirteenth century, although defenders of the Germanic theory, such as Heringa (1982), have contested this. Heringa saw a long, continuous history during which the writing down of rules for the use of the common in charters was the only change. Although the origins of commons have not yet been thoroughly studied, it is clear that large numbers of commons as identifiable institutions appeared during the late Middle Ages in many parts of Europe, and that these did not necessarily stem from previously established collectivities of users. Especially during the twelfth and thirteenth centuries, the first 'corporate' commons – with a clearly outlined institutional basis – appear on the scene in the Low Countries (Godding 1987, 203–4). Certainly there was cooperation among villagers before that time, but what we witness in this period is a formation of collectivities or alliances based not primarily on kinship but by mutual agreement regarding the use of the resources between lords and villagers as well as among the villagers themselves. These rules were discussed among the commoners, written down, confirmed, reviewed from time to time, and, most importantly, self-enforced

---

[14] For many examples of such commons, see the chapters on southern Europe and Latin America in Demélas and Vivier (2003).

[15] Similar to the expansion of common-property rights over land is the growth of guilds – in the form of the foundation of new guilds – long after the Middle Ages. In the Dutch Republic, for example, the number of guilds was about 564 around 1560. By the end of the seventeenth century, the number had grown to approximately 1,300 (Lourens and Lucassen 1997).

The Dilemma of the Commoners

by the commoners. In many cases, these agreements should be read as settlements of conflicts that arose between the lords and the village inhabitants on the usage of some of the resources that officially fell under the local lord's power. This in turn should be seen in light of the Great European Reclamations taking place in the tenth to twelfth centuries, which was a consequence of the increasing population and the related increasing demand for food stuff.[16] As will become clear in a later section of this chapter, these agreements can be considered forms of risk avoidance as well as a way to benefit from advantages of scale in the management of natural resources that are necessary, or even vital, to the agricultural system, but which cannot be commercialized in itself as products and thus cannot simply be bought at the market. The background of these agreements is population growth and the related changes and intensification of land use.[17] Commons were a way to keep the agricultural system in balance with limited risks and thus also costs – whereby costs and risks were at least lower than the alternative, being privatization – while also offering some advantages that could not be achieved in an open access or private governance model. Although the latter advantages so far have not received much attention in the literature, the risks that could be avoided have, as in the studies that point towards the 'prudence' of the commoners (e.g., McCloskey 1991; Allen 1992).

In general terms much of the above can also be claimed for the urban counterparts of the commons: the guilds. Following Lourens and Lucassen (1997, 43–4), craft guilds are defined here as 'organizations that – with the agreement of the local authority – unite members of the same occupational group, with as their most important goal the furthering of their economic interests, but not without taking into account the general well-being of their group as well' (translated from original). The lack of sources often makes it

---

[16] In a similar fashion, Blickle considers the introduction of more complex agricultural methods to reach a higher output as the stimulus for collective decision making:

> 'The thirteenth century, ... witnessed a remarkable change in agricultural production ... economic activities underwent considerable change: more and more crops were planted, using a field rotation system, arable land was separated more clearly from pasture, and neighbouring villages defined their respective territories much more explicitly. All this provides clear evidence for a more intensive use of rural resources in the face of rising population . . . . [T]he comparatively complicated new rotation system ruled out individual choices of crops and demanded a process of collective decision-making involving all peasants. To settle the inevitable disputes, some form of local conflict resolution had to be found, while rules and regulations were necessary to keep the peace among neighbours who now lived in much closer proximity. The result was the emergence of village autonomy, village jurisdiction, and village legislation as autogenous rights of the inhabitants'
> (Blickle 1998, 2–3).

[17] Such as the increasing application of three-field rotation from the eleventh and twelfth centuries onwards in northwestern Europe (Slicher van Bath 1960, fn. 99).

The emergence of commons

impossible to determine whether the late medieval guilds perfectly fit this definition from the time they were actually founded. Guilds may have developed from relatively informal institutions into formal ones, recognized by local authorities. They were mainly urban institutions, but in some cases the densely populated setting in which they developed was not yet a 'city' in legal terms. In the Low Countries, the number of rural guilds and, conversely, urban commons was small (although many medieval towns did have their common pastures and fields to bleach linen, for example).[18]

Given their urban character, guilds clearly had their origins during the process of urbanization that occurred in western Europe from 900 to 1300, which in turn clearly has a close connection with the earlier mentioned process of population growth that affected the formation of the commons. Obviously, one of the prime prerequisites for the emergence of guilds was a certain concentration of members of the same occupational group in the same location (see also Persson 1988, 50–4), and achieving a certain level of critical mass was linked to population growth. For the Netherlands, for example, Lourens and Lucassen (1997) claim that around the year 1400 a city needed to have reached a population of at least 2,500 inhabitants to include one craft guild; small towns of 500 inhabitants or fewer usually did not have craft guilds. Although there are exceptions to this, a certain threshold population seems to have been necessary for guilds to develop. There was also an upper limit to the number of guilds per urban center: there seems to have been a maximum of about fifty guilds per city. Cities such as Amsterdam, with a population much larger than average, had only one guild per 4,000 inhabitants (by 1670, there were fifty-two craft guilds per 200,000 inhabitants), but each of these organizations had on average many more members.[19]

The literature offers two interpretations of the rise of merchant and craft guilds in the centuries from 950 to 1300. The first constructs a link with the *collegia*, guilds that developed during the Roman period; although these proto-guilds disappeared in western Europe, they continued to be important in Byzantium, even though by the thirteenth century they had gradually disappeared.[20] Most guilds (including the Roman *collegia*) were closely supervised and monitored by the state, which contributed to undermining the 'serviceability of the guild system' (Maniatis 2009, fn. 342 and 368). Via southern Italy (the typical Byzantine city of Amalfi is mentioned as the first site of a modern merchant guild in the tenth century), the model

---

[18] For a more detailed description of the rural guild, see Ehmer (2009).
[19] For the evolution of the number of guilds in the Low Countries, see also De Munck, Lourens, and Lucassen (2006).
[20] On the evolution of the guilds in Byzantium, see Yildirim (2009).

The Dilemma of the Commoners

spread to western Europe. Hickson and Thompson (1991, 137–8) describe how the guild model reached the French and Flemish cities from the south, where the merchants with whom the Italians traded at the Champagne fairs lived. This was followed by a spread to western Germania and England in the twelfth century, Spanish trading centers around the middle of the thirteenth century, and afterwards, in the late thirteenth and fourteenth centuries, to the east. This approach to the origins of the guilds is in line with the ideas of De Laveleye *cum suis* about the origins of the commons (see earlier in this chapter).

The alternative view is that guilds developed from informal groups of merchants or other social groups, which in northwestern Europe were organized spontaneously in the ninth and tenth centuries, some of the first examples being Saxon *gegildan* known from tenth-century England (Epstein 1991, 39–40), or the famous Frisian merchant guild of Tiel, known from an early eleventh-century reference by Alpertus van Metz (Akkerman 1962). The organization settled disputes between merchants and established mutual exchanges of credit, in combination with the obligatory drinking and feasting.[21] Though the guild in Tiel was only short-lived, elsewhere, in the southern part of the Low Countries, new guildlike associations would be established, with the merchant guilds developing faster and earlier than the craft guilds.[22] Their dates of origin are often difficult to trace, but by the thirteenth century a considerable number of guilds had already been established in the larger towns of Flanders, especially in textile centers such as Bruges, Ypres, and Ghent.[23] The Northern Netherlands' guilds were slower to develop. In their analysis of the number of new craft guilds in towns having more

---

[21] Tiel is a small Dutch town in between the rivers Waal and Linge, southwest of Arnhem. Tiel took over the position of Dorestad as a leading commercial town in the area. Dorestad had been repeatedly plundered and burned down by Vikings, and after the reinforcements of the dikes along the river Rhine, the trade moved to the nearby cities of Utrecht, Deventer, and also Tiel. During the tenth to twelfth centuries, Tiel was an important international port and trading place, where the river trade met the sea trade. Part of the wealth of Tiel at that time can also be explained by the privileges this town could obtain as a consequence of being frequently visited by the German emperors of this period. In the writings of the same period can be found a merchant guild, set up by the *mercatores Tielenses*, as they were referred to in the writings of the monk Alpertus of Metz. The merchants managed to obtain an unusually powerful position, supported by close relationships with the emperor. Alpertus's mentioning that the guild had obtained the right to hold their own jurisprudence, that they had yearly festivities, and that they had their own moral, adjusted to the living circumstances of merchants, had been considered sufficient evidence that the organization found in Tiel was de facto a merchant guild (Akkerman 1962, 414–7; Lourens, Lucassen, and De Munck 2005, fn. 34 and 35).

[22] See Van der Vleuten and Van Zanden (2010), esp. 60–4.

[23] Lourens, Lucassen, and De Munck (2005) mention the following figures: approx. twenty-five craft guilds in Leuven by 1267, fifty-two in Bruges around the same time, fifty-two by the beginning of the fifteenth century in Ypres, and at least twenty-five before 1400 in

The emergence of commons

than 2,500 inhabitants in 1784, Lourens, Lucassen, and De Munck (2005, 32–73) show that about 41 percent of the well over 1,000 craft guilds in the Southern Netherlands for which the period of establishment is known, originate from the period 1100–1399. In the Northern Netherlands, not even 8 percent of the guilds (in total 1,374 by 1784) would have already existed. The majority would come into being in the period from 1400 to 1669, when about three-quarters of all the new guilds before 1784 were established.[24]

It is not unlikely that the craft guilds were actually modeled after the merchant guilds. But what these merchant groups still missed was a formal institutional structure, as supplied by the concept of a legal body, and therefore a degree of persistence and continuity, as well as a governance structure that became characteristic of late medieval guilds. From these very early and tentative beginnings in tenth-century Europe – thus possibly via two roads, one originating from the elitist state structure of Byzantium, the other developed out of or parallel to the merchant guilds[25] – a broad movement developed, which by 1300 would give western Europe many hundreds, if not thousands, of craft guilds.[26] In the Low Countries, particularly in Flanders, guilds reached the apex of their political power in the years after 1300, or, to be more precise, in 1302, when they played a chief role in the famous Battle of the Spurs, when Flemish urban citizenry – with a glorious role granted to the weavers' guild – defeated French nobility.[27] This revolt of the guilds, which would take control of the Flemish cities, became a truly international phenomenon; revolutionary bands, anticipating later revolutionary periods in European history, 'exported' the revolt of the guilds to other places (e.g., the center of the Northern Netherlands, Utrecht, where a similar revolutionary city government controlled by the guilds was installed in the early fourteenth century) (Prak 2006). Apart from demonstrating the power that institutions such as guilds could dispose of, the role of the guilds in these

---

Ghent. Also relatively small towns such as Sint-Truiden and Lier already had organizations of textile workers in the thirteenth century, which clearly indicates that the presence of textile manufacturing was often a cause for setting up a guild (see also Wyffels 1951, 159). Apart from that, a number of activities have been mentioned by Van Uytven that might be indications of urban groupings of craftsmen (Van Uytven 1982, 210).

[24] In the period 1400–1559 Lourens, Lucassen, and De Munck (2005) recorded 478 guilds (or 35 percent of the total in the period 1100–1784), and in the period 1560–1669 no less than 561 guilds (Lourens and Lucassen 1997, 44–51); see also the regional overview in De Munck, Lourens, and Lucassen (2005).

[25] See also the article by Van Vleuten and Van Zanden (2010), esp. 60–4.

[26] See J. L. Van Zanden (2008a) for an analysis of the context that allowed for this spectacular development of this 'bottom-up' movement.

[27] On the role of guilds in local politics, see Prak (2006). On the Battle of the Spurs, see Tollebeek (2002), and for its relation with the 'guild revolutions' that followed, see Slokker (2010).

The Dilemma of the Commoners

battles also demonstrates that the institutionalized forms of collective action and the more contentious ones are often closely knit together. In the next part (1.3) it will be demonstrated that, although they are indeed often linked, there are also some clear differences.

As mentioned earlier, guilds were becoming an omnipresent phenomenon in the most urbanized areas or early modern Europe. Whenever there was enough critical mass, professionals would get together and join forces. For commons, however, it is difficult to provide an overview of their quantitative importance in western Europe similar to that for the guilds. Thus far, little work has been done on making an inventory that would allow us to estimate the number of associations among farmers to join forces in using the (waste) land or the surface that they controlled for the whole of Europe. In many cases, making an overview of such rural institutions is also markedly more difficult than for the urban setting, where, especially in the late Middle Ages, the presence of notaries and other literate individuals, who could play a role in putting decisions and book keeping on paper, would be more likely, and where the facilities for record keeping were in general better. However, various studies demonstrate clearly that from the thirteenth century, bylaws setting the rights of commoners regarding the use and management of their land can be found in increasing numbers.[28] Slicher van Bath (1978, fn. 242) provided an estimate of the number of *marken* or *meenten*, two regularly used terms to indicate common land in the provinces of Drenthe, Overijssel, and Gelderland in the Northern Netherlands, that were mentioned in written sources before 1500 and came to a total of nearly 300.[29] The majority of the *marken* counted by Slicher van Bath were found in sources dating from as early as the fourteenth century (127 out of 286). For the period before, he counted thirty-seven references, though some might have been overlooked, as they had not taken on a name (such as *marke*) that made them easily identifiable as a common (Slicher van Bath 1978, fn. 243). Similar counts for other regions, such as the one studied in this book, are not available, and hence it remains unclear how popular the common as a governance regime really was in the late Middle Ages. Though we experience similar problems in trying to quantify commons elsewhere in Europe, the situation at the end of the ancien régime also makes clear that commons throughout northwestern Europe had become widespread institutions to govern natural resources; they were even the dominant forms of resource management in some regions.

[28] See, e.g., Shaw-Taylor (2002) on southern England: Shaw-Taylor notices that the number of surviving bylaws increases over the thirteenth and fourteenth centuries, but that the most complete and informative bylaws appear especially in the period after 1500.

[29] The place names *meent* or *marke* can still be frequently found in the Netherlands.

The emergence of commons

1.3 Distinct institutions for collective action

As demonstrated, the power of the guilds and commons in medieval Europe should not be underestimated. Historical literature, however, when looking at collective action, has mostly focused on short, often sudden rises of collective discontent in the form of popular uprisings and mass movements, rather than on the effects of the long-enduring power relations of institutions for collective action. Charles and Louise Tilly (Tilly and Tilly 1981), as well as Douglas McAdam, Sidney Tarrow, and Charles Tilly (2001), considered collective action mainly as large-scale mass movements that often only make their point through riots, demonstrations, or forms of mass violence (e.g., peasant revolts). Charles Tilly justifies the use of the term 'collective action' (rather than 'rebellion') by pointing to the many methods of action (other than rioting or demonstrating) that were used by groups to get their message across and change their fate. For Tilly, therefore, collective action 'consists of all occasions on which sets of people commit pooled resources, including their own efforts, to common efforts' (Tilly and Tilly 1981, 19). Though this definition is broad enough to cover the type of collective action dealt with in this book, Tilly does not include any reference to guilds, commons, or other examples of institutionalized collective action in his description of the various types of collective action.[30] Over the past decades, the debate on Tilly's kind of collective action has also merged with the 'contentious politics' debate, thus moving even further away from the silent and institutionalized version of collective action.[31]

The most prominent forms of collective action in the revolution referred to in this chapter are of a more long-lasting type. It was not unusual for members of such organizations to be also involved in protest movements (the other type of collective action), as, for example, in the Flemish Battle of

---

[30] This evolution of the collective action debate encouraged by Tilly and Tilly should not be surprising: in their studies they have always stressed the ways of expression of the collectivities that drew their attention, and these are what gave immediate cause to the contention with governments. Charles Tilly does mention the guilds, but only as an organization that had forms of collective expression:

Its [collective action's] most dramatic recurrent forms were the food riots, concerted resistance to conscription, organized invasions of fields and forests, and rebellion against tax-collectors. Less visible, but in some ways more influential, were established public festivals and rituals during which ordinary people voiced their demands or complaints, and stated assemblies of corporate groups – communities, guilds, religious congregations, and the like – which produced petitions, lawsuits, condemnations, and occasionally even deliberated acts of rebellion.

(Tilly and Tilly 1981, 20)

[31] See, e.g., the work by McAdam, Tarrow, and Tilly (2001). In 1996, a new journal (*Mobilization: An International Quarterly*) was set up to offer a forum for the debate on contentious politics.

The Dilemma of the Commoners

the Spurs. Though they were composed of more than only guild members, many revolts in cities (e.g., the *Bürgerkämpfe*) in the fourteenth and fifteenth centuries led to the establishment of their formal representation in city councils, albeit not everywhere as effectively.[32] In a similar way, many commoners were actively involved in protests and riots against enclosures in England, France, and elsewhere.[33] In short, there are a number of varieties of collective action, and in some cases they may reinforce each other in pursuing and achieving their goals.

The concept of institutions for collective action relied on the idea that a group of people could form a legal body – a *universitas* –, an idea developed during the legal revolution of the twelfth and thirteenth centuries.[34] But what made such institutions markedly distinct from collective action in general is their degree of formal regulation, or institutionalization. The group formation process was accompanied by the design of a set of rules, which would usually be written down and revised regularly in order to make collective action also work in changed circumstances. Guild members created charters in which acceptable and unacceptable behaviors were precisely specified, accompanied by sanctions for infractions. Commoners kept similar records and updated them on a regular basis.[35] In some cases regulations were regularly added to a book, to which the managers of the commons could easily refer in case of disputes. In the eastern Netherlands many extremely detailed *markeboeken* have been well preserved and provide us with a multitude of rules for a common, giving us spectacular insight into how groups of users could manage resources.[36] The frequent changes in the documents provide clear indications that commoners constantly had to take into account new internal and external circumstances.

Another difference from the goals of short-term collective action is that those involved in uprisings aimed at change, but did not necessarily see an active role for themselves in achieving that change – neither in the short or long term – except perhaps for those who cherished the ambition of a

---

[32] These revolts were concentrated especially in the German areas and in the Southern Netherlands; they only sporadically appeared in the Northern Netherlands and were completely absent from England and France. According to Prak, the degree of urbanization cannot explain these differences (Prak 1994, 22–3).

[33] See, e.g., Wayne Te Brake's chapter about the protest against the enclosures of commons in the Eastern Netherlands (Te Brake 1981, 59–66).

[34] Berman (1983, fn. 393) describes a corporation (*universitas*) as a 'body of people sharing common legal functions and acting as a legal entity'; for a further elaboration on the importance of the idea of *universitas* for economic development, see J. L. Van Zanden (2009b).

[35] See Winchester (2002) and Rodgers et al. (2011).

[36] The Common Rules project, coordinated by Utrecht University, gives a unique insight into the regulation of commons from the late Middle Ages onwards until their disappearance for specific areas in the Netherlands, Spain, and England. Results can be found at ht tp://www.collective-action.info/_PRO_NWO_CommonRules_Main.

The emergence of commons

leadership role. Linked to this is the fact that riots and other such activities aimed at forming large groups (the more the merrier – and more convincing), and these groups were essentially formed by anonymous individuals. In principle there was no need for the individuals taking part in such actions to identify themselves, as long as they all pursued the same goals. The institutions that emerged during the silent revolution, on the other hand, could not exist without identifying those involved, and required that anyone who wanted to join the club identify himself to the other members. This makes these institutions almost always exclusive organizations, although this does not necessarily mean inaccessible by the less wealthy.

Due to the exclusiveness, members could be identified, and this encouraged the reciprocity and mutual control that was needed for the long-term survival of the group (see 1.4).[37] Similarly, the size of the group of members would also have been more limited, since more members made it more difficult to reach consensus.

The degree of institutionalization that typifies the silent revolution is the clearest difference from more short-term collective action. Revolts, riots, uprisings, and demonstrations are largely a response to an immediate provocation, though the underlying causes may have been long-standing.[38] Such actions are supposed to give immediate relief, whereas the institutionalized form of collective action is intended to build organizations for particular goals that do not primarily aim at immediate relief, but rather at constant relief (see also the point on longevity), and some of it not until the distant future. The participants realize that some of the personal contributions they make to benefit the institution, and thus the whole group, may not lead to immediate individual benefits, and that others might benefit sooner than themselves. The time lag in the trade-off between short-term investment and long-term benefit is the most central feature of a social dilemma,[39] and solving such a dilemma demands dedication of its members, reciprocity, and trust. Although it is the subject of many studies, trust still remains an elusive concept to capture, let

---

[37] Jager (2000, fn. 16) considers identifiability as one of the group factors that influences behavior in a dilemma in a positive sense. Jorgerson and Papciak (1981) found that cooperative behavior is promoted if the other people can observe one's personal-choice behavior, and has a similar effect as communication on cooperation, being the promotion of 'social control'. Due to high visibility there is more social control, and this in itself encourages participants to work harder and free ride less than in an anonymous setting. Group size also plays a role in the identifiability of behavior: the larger the group, the more anonymous one is (see Jager 2000, fn. 16)

[38] Many causes of collective resistance and rebellion have been given: inequality, governmental reform, class conflict, social disintegration, conflicting religious values, relative deprivation, and many others. See the works of Tocqueville, Marx, Durkheim, Tönnies, Weber, and Gurr.

[39] See also T. De Moor (2012).

alone measure, especially in a historical context. Several features of institutions for collective action did directly contribute to enhancing trust among the members of these institutions. These features together form the common denominator of the institutions for collective action that were formed during the silent revolution – though in fact, and as I will demonstrate in the Epilogue, they can even be considered general features of such institutions in a present-day context as well. This gives us an idea of the framework within which these institutions operated: the boundaries they set for their own behavior and that of others, both members and nonmembers. As I will also illustrate, however, reality did not always conform to the rules, and in time rules often had to be adjusted to changed circumstances (see further points 2.3 and 2.4 in Chapter 2 and the case study in Chapters 3 and 4).

1.4   The design of institutions for collective action

1.4.1   Exclusive

Individuals taking part in guilds and commons could not remain anonymous; in many cases they even had to swear an oath before they could become a member, which also made them visible and identifiable to the rest of the group. The anonymous crowds that participated in riots, as much as these may have had a deep and long-lasting effect on society, have had entirely different objectives and applied other methods and organizational models than the individuals that formed institutionalized organizations such as guilds and commons. It is known from sociological research that the degree to which participants in collective action know one another influences the potential success (in terms of reciprocity) of that group (Jager 2000, fn. 16–8). The practice of swearing an oath when becoming a member of a guild therefore makes these organizations fundamentally different from revolts and riots, in which the group members were often very diverse and anonymous. The willingness of group members to cooperate in the future lies in the potential benefits that participants may obtain and the security this provides (see, e.g., Olson 1965 and Ostrom 1990).[40]

This 'willingness' has been at the center of sociological/behavioral research on collective action. Cooperative behavior within a group – of

---

[40] In sociological literature this has also been referred to as a 'temporal dilemma' or the choice between investing in today's personal advantage or safeguarding future generations' survival. See Jager (2000, fn. 16).

The emergence of commons

craftsmen or commoners – and respect for the resources of the group were expected from contemporary members of these organizations. In several charters it was made clear that the members were working for the well-being of the institution and future generations, thus implicitly ascertaining the importance of sustainable management of their resources. Keeping in mind Mancur Olson's quote that 'rational, self-interested individuals will not act to achieve their common or group interest' (Olson 1965, 2), the ambitions of our medieval ancestors sound highly unrealistic. Their method of solving a social dilemma was to set up institutions for exclusive groups: institutionalization should secure continuity, while exclusion should secure feasibility by only allowing access to those with at least a minimal interest in keeping the institution going. Whereas sudden, short-lived collective action benefits from attracting as many participants as possible, sustained collective action tries to limit the number of participants via setting clear access rules. Both guilds and commons wanted to distinguish insiders from outsiders and set limits to group size and the use of resources through a set of rules that could (according to the needs of the moment) be expanded or reduced. Rules could include limitations on access to the group by means of several requirements (e.g., financial requirements or a waiting period as in the case of apprenticeships), a set maximum of production to restrict overproduction, and specifications to guard the local market against competition from others (farmers in case of commoners, members from other guilds or non-guild artisans in the case of the guilds).[41]

Nevertheless, under certain conditions, these organizations did honor the requests of ineligible persons. Guilds were closed organizations, but to a certain degree they were also open to nonmembers, as they sometimes also derived income from nonmembers. Those living outside the city but of the same profession could in some cases practice their profession temporarily in the city, but they were obliged to pay redemption money to the guild (Van Genabeek 1994, 78). The same applied to commons: in times when the members themselves could not provide sufficient livestock to graze the commons, nonmembers were allowed to graze their animals there.[42] Their exclusion was officially strict, but in practice rather flexible. This can easily be explained: letting foreign merchants (guilds) or

---

[41] For an overview of the regulation of guilds, see, e.g., De Monté Verloren (2000). For an overview of the commons regulation on access, see T. De Moor (2009).

[42] See an example of such practice in T. De Moor (2009). See also Chapter 4, paragraph 4.3 of this publication.

The Dilemma of the Commoners

non-commoners take advantage for a short while of the benefits that were offered in return for payment did not mean that the outsiders could also make use of the other facilities (social welfare, etc.). In principle, these temporary guests would cost scarcely any money; on the contrary, they could help fill the gaps in the institution's budget (see point 4.3 for an example).

Several aspects of guilds' and the commons' regulations and daily practices show that although these institutions were set up primarily for their own members, their concern also included nonmembers, especially the needy members of the village or town where they were active, and even to future generations. Many references can be found about charitable obligations members had to respect. The members of the Eloy guild (smiths and weapon makers) in Utrecht held regular bread distributions among the city's poor, and in fact continued to do so until the twentieth century (Rommes and Van der Spek 2004, 114–6). But likewise, the commoners were aware of the needs of those excluded from their resources. The commoners in the case study to be discussed in depth in this book regularly allowed a widow or another person in need to graze their cattle on the common. Elsewhere, on other commons, we find similar references to rights of widows.[43] This is another similarity with the guild system, where widows of guild masters often had the right to continue the workshop of their husband temporarily (Bull 2004).

Although in most of the literature they are considered primarily economic associations that regulated access by means of occupational grouping, guilds could also take other forms, and thus use other access rules. In the pre-corporate period, guilds were primarily religious groupings, also referred to as fraternities. Later, with the parallel development of cities, access rules became intertwined with citizenship. In the Low Countries, for example, guild membership required the person to be a *poorter*, which denotes someone in possession of full citizenship rights, which could be obtained through certain rules. Without these rights, it was most advantageous to marry the daughter of a *poorter*, which, considering the surplus of women in Dutch cities, was not a very challenging task. Compared to other countries, the third option – namely, buying city rights – was

---

[43] For example, the regulation of Marke Het Gooi (a common in the province of North Holland, the current Netherlands) of 3 May 1442, states that 'a widow or widower, who will continue to live at their home and land, will be allowed to keep a full share ; but if they are living together with someone, they will not be allowed to have their full share, unless they have a separate household' ['Een weduwer ofte weduwe, die sitten bleeff in zijn huys ende goet, sal moegen houden een schaer, mer indien zij mit yemant inwoenen, alsdan sullen tselve nyet mogen genyeten, tenware zij hair eygen cost dair hielden'] (Enklaar 1932, 386).

The emergence of commons

relatively cheap (Lourens and Lucassen 1997, 52–3; Panhuysen 1997). Other factors, such as the comparatively short period of apprenticeship, indicate that guilds in the Dutch Republic were more inclusive and open than elsewhere. But the guilds still had limited entry. Membership to a certain extent depended on family relations: sons of masters often paid only half the access fee external candidates had to pay, and women only occasionally could obtain the right to become a master, but such cases were rather rare. If strangers married a master's daughter or acquired the necessary fee, they still needed to work several years with a master before being allowed to become a member. This requirement was not in place when the guilds were founded; in most cases it was only introduced later, often from the sixteenth and seventeenth centuries (Panhuysen 1997, 135).

It is difficult to say whether their main concern was related to the fate of those who would benefit in the future or, as in the case of commons, to the sustainable use of the resource itself. Some documents that provided the rules to arrange succession within the common show at least a concern with the continuation of their institution. In some cases, access rules included an inheritance clause: guilds where members/masters needed to inherit the right from their fathers, commons where the right to use the land could only be inherited from family members. But even more convincing are references to the intentions of commoners in regulation documents. To name just one example, that of the regulation of the common Aard van de Zes Dorpen in the Campine area, in 1521, the commoners mentioned how they created new rules that year to control abuse and promote the conservation of the common, clearly indicating a concern for sustainable use and management for the future.[44] There could be several reasons why institutions were set up for 'eternity': the cost, in terms of coming to an agreement with the local ruler, was relatively high; if a person had obtained the right to membership, he would not easily let go of it; and participants may have realized that it would take time before they would really benefitted from the institution. The survival rate of the guilds in the Low Countries shows that they managed to keep their guilds functioning for long periods of time: of the 1,033 guilds that were established in the Southern Netherlands before 1784, only 19 percent had disappeared by that time; a similar figure of 21.5 percent has been found for the Northern Netherlands

---

[44] Original text : '…gemaeckt ende gesloten dese ordinantie (om te schouwen voers. mesbruyck ende tot oorbaerlijcken conservatien der voers. vroonten…' (Aard van de Zes Dorpen, see Paepen 2004).

The Dilemma of the Commoners

(Lourens, Lucassen, and De Munck 2005, 32–73). About 62 percent of the originally founded guilds in the Netherlands survived for more than 150 years, while more than 90 percent of the *markegenootschappen* in the provinces of Overijssel, Gelderland, and Drenthe survived much longer, and easily passed the 150-year mark.[45]

1.4.2 Self-governed and relatively democratic governance structure

In the context of institutions for collective action, self-governance refers to the regulation, including sanctioning, of stakeholder behavior; this includes those directly involved in using the resources governed by those same stakeholders. Self-governance means that those involved not only set up the rules of the game but also had to live up to those conditions, and if they failed to do so, they could punish one another and be punished, in the previously designated way of sanctioning and fining. From a present-day perspective, with governmental bodies setting the rules in society, and juridical bodies applying the legislation, self-governance is not a straightforward choice; from an early modern perspective, however, with a less or no centralized government, such an approach might in fact have been the most obvious choice. Rather than relying on external bodies to control the use of resources, the stakeholders became self-help groups with a specific goal, and though they operated rather autonomously, they did usually have good relations with local authorities.

The fact that people formed groups is not in itself striking, but that they regulated and controlled the execution of these rules (including punishment) themselves is a less obvious practice. To make their collective project work, guilds and commons both relied heavily on group norms (as opposed to formal legal enactments) as enforcement mechanisms. They designed most of the rules themselves, with or without the involvement of the local authorities.[46] Rules were usually made or changed in general meetings, unless very urgent measures had to be taken. To achieve maximum involvement in the rule design and awareness of changes and new rules, commoners and guild members were more or less forced to attend meetings:

---

[45] With thanks to Miguel Laborda Pemán for the calculations based on the files created in the framework of the NWO-Middelgroot project 'Data Infrastructure for the Study of Guilds and Other Forms of Collective Action', see http://goo.gl/qvR12H (short url, commons) and http://goo.gl/nvgo9x (short url; guilds).

[46] This should not be surprising: sociological research shows that involvement in the design of rules offers a better guarantee of success (Jager et al. 2000), as will also be demonstrated in the case study discussed in this book.

The emergence of commons

compulsory attendance, at the risk of being fined in the case of absence, was a normal part of the regulation of both institutions. Guild masters were usually obliged to attend the usual meetings of the guild and the more ceremonial meetings such as funerals of guild masters, and had to confirm their presence by means of a specific coin, in which their name or number was engraved. When the meeting was announced by a messenger of the guild, each guild master received his coin, which had to be handed in at the meeting. If it was not, the guild master would be fined for absence (Van der Steur 1974). Commoners who did not attend the meetings of their common would often lose their right to obtain a share of the profit at the end of the year.[47]

Internally, enforcement of the regulation depended on social control and on the willingness to report another member for breaking the rules. Regulation of both commons and guilds include many clauses that are intended to enhance social control, and that gave commoners the power to limit free riding. There are examples of commoners designing rules to encourage reporting abuses, often with the promise of receiving part of the fine or, in the contrary, by the threat of fining a commoner who fails to report an abuse. Such liability rules were not found, but their existence does indicate that, if needed, commoners were willing to go a long way to prevent free riding on the common, even if this meant sanctioning their neighbors. A liability clause is defined here as any rule that is not primarily aimed at the perpetrator of rules of the common, but at the member of the common who allows other persons (either entitled or not entitled to access and/or use the common) to infringe on the rules laid down in the regulation of the common. Three types of liability can be discerned: a) active participation of the common member in the committed offense (e.g., a common user accepts

---

[47] The regulation of the Gemene and Loweiden dating from 1514, for example, states in article 14: '... als den opperhooftman die principaelic tlast heeft omme te waeren ende onderhouden de rechten ende vryhenden van de voorseide weede, belieft vergaderinghe te houdene ende te gebieden ten zekeren daghe te Fernand coutere, omme den oirboir ende prouffit vande voorseide weede, dan zullen commen versamen de selve ambortighe op de peyne van onbekent gerekent te syne naer costume; mits daer af by kerckgeboden sondaghs te vooren de kennisse te doene indiversche prochie kercken ontrent Brugghe, daer men es dat ghecostumert gheweest van doene van ouden tyden' [Trans.: '... if it pleases the chief *hoofdman*, who has the designated task to guard and maintain the rights and liberties of the aforementioned common [of Gemene and Loweiden], to have a meeting summoned, to be held at a determined date at Fernand coutere, for the good standing and benefit of the aforementioned common, the same *aanborgers* will be held to attend this meeting, and failing to attend will be sanctioned by having this commoner to be regarded as "unknown" in accordance with customary law, on the condition the meeting has been announced at the Sunday before this meeting at several parish churches near the city of Bruges, as has been common use for ages'.]

horses from non-entitled users and has them graze as if they were his own [Hannink 1992, 162]); b) passive participation by common members (e.g., a common user allows non-entitled users to wash their sheep in the waters belonging to the common [Hannink 1992, 138–9]); c) a common user fails to report stated offenses to the officers in charge (e.g., not reporting the grazing of sheep on off-limit land [Hannink 1992, 81]).[48]

In addition, commoners were often burdened with compulsory monitoring tasks, at the risk of being fined if the job was not fulfilled properly. Also, those with the function of manager or monitor were often sanctioned much more severely than ordinary commoners for the same offense, which gave more weight to their position within the common.[49] All in all, commons and guilds were very demanding towards their members, but can be considered to have been relatively democratic organizations with regular opportunities for the members to influence the policy of their organization and to determine who would be nominated as board members in charge of daily management and relationships with external parties. Whether power relations within the village also affected relations regarding the daily management of commons, the daily practice of managing the common and the role commoners of various backgrounds would have differed from place to place and so require an in-depth study. Further in this book I will present such an analysis and reflect on the power relations within the common.

1.4.3 Protectionist

Commoners and guild members tried to regulate the behavior of fellow members through the many rules and regulations designed to discourage free riding. Members of these institutions for collective action, both guilds and commons, developed methods to protect their organization and to safeguard at least part of the production market from the functioning and forces of the free market.

It has often been assumed that guilds even tried to control the whole market by striving towards a complete monopoly, but in practice that was not necessarily so.[50] Notwithstanding the strict regulations in writing, in

---

[48] See also Van Weeren and De Moor (2014).

[49] Examples can be found, e.g., in the regulation of the *markegenootschappen* in the eastern part of the Netherlands. In the regulation of the marke Rozegaarde, it is mentioned that sworn members who refuse to perform their task will be fined and appointed again next year. They were fined three times higher than other uncooperative members (J. Van Zanden 2005).

[50] For a critique on the claim that guilds were monopolistic, see Hickson and Thompson (1991, 128–9).

The emergence of commons

practice there were many, and often some radical, exceptions to the guild regulation that prevented any form of monopoly from being established (Panhuysen 2000, 79 and 276; Prak 2006). Strategies were designed to give the master tailors control over the most profitable parts of the trade, but those master tailors were willing to compromise on what were seen as peripheral activities. In attempting to master product markets, guilds started to form cartels.[51] The number of conflicts over the right to form cartels demonstrates the importance of mastering product markets for the guilds, which was true until just before the guilds were abolished. Although guilds managed to protect the market substantially, market protection was not complete nor could they build monopolies (Prak 1994, 19). The question here is whether it was necessary for the guilds to have complete control over the markets. Would protection of the market have been an objective of a small-scale organization that aimed primarily at securing the income of its members, who had particular skills and wanted to distinguish themselves from the poorly skilled workers in the countryside? Is there much advantage to be gained from a putting-out system when the capital to invest in such a system is lacking?

Peasants also tried to limit the influence of the market on their common and its members. The background to this was a continuous struggle to prevent the excessive exploitation of their common, although nonhistorians such as Hardin (1968) *cum suis* believed that commons were traditionally always overgrazed. Regulation of the use of the common and rules to prevent, or at least restrict, the commercialization of commons goods were devised. Overall, there were two methods to regulate use of the resources: by setting numerical limits to the amount of resource units per person, and by implementing a price mechanism that adjusted prices to the foreseeable pressure on the commons (e.g., payment per head of cattle). Depending on the resource involved, different types of rules that limited the influence of the market were used. In general, the amount of produce a commoner was allowed to take was limited to a specific number of resource units. In some cases the surface of the common was expressed in terms of the number of units of cattle the common could feed. For example, in the Wijkerzand common in Central Netherlands, the number of 180 shares and their size in the grazing rights of the common appear to have been laid down in the fifteenth century, and they are still present today (Hoppenbrouwers 2002). Often, limitation on the shares of commoners

---

[51] Although we could question, whether guilds, based on the way they tried to regulate the market, could be considered cartels. For the discussion, see Persson (1988).

The Dilemma of the Commoners

was not restricted to the capacities of the common, but to the factors directly related to aspects of the subsistence (not to the commercial economy) of the commoners. Another set of rules explicitly prohibited selling produce from the common (e.g., timber, or milk from the common's cows) outside the village borders. This helped to protect the most valuable assets of their common against commericalization and excessive exploitation. Protecting members from the free market is not the same as being against the free market: besides their activities on the commons, commoners could still have participated in the free market.

Furthermore, commons also developed mechanisms to offer resources at a uniform price, intended to create more equality within the organization.[52] For the commons, the prices of the resources that could be harvested were uniform and equal for all members. If nonmembers were allowed to purchase resources from the common, the price to be paid by those outsiders could be higher (this will also be demonstrated in the case study in later chapters).[53] Moreover, this does not mean that prices for products were stable; they were adjusted, not to the prices of the market, but to the situation of the common. Evidence can be found of commons that used an 'internal market' to regulate the use of resources: when demand (from members) for the resources was high and threatened to become too high compared to what was available on the common, the prices per individual head of cattle were raised, leading to a reduction in demand for cattle on the common (see also point 4.3) (M. De Moor 2003b).

Guild functioning was similar. The members of the guilds aimed to offer their products on the markets for uniform prices, thus also promoting, though not necessarily achieving, a maximum average income among their members. Prak (1992, 170–2; 1994, 21) notes, however, that the great social differences among members of the guilds indicates that there must have been other factors at work that turned that optimal average into a minimum wage. Neither the commons nor the guilds used the laws of supply and demand to set and change their prices; they used an internal, autonomously defined, quality standard.[54] Products of the same quality were to be sold for the same uniform price. By offering products of the same quality, they created a medieval form of quality label. This not only made trade easier, but it also prevented internal conflicts from arising. Gustaffson considers quality control a key organizing principle of medieval guilds. The variability of quality as conditioned largely by the individual

---

[52] For a similar argument on guilds, see Van Genabeek (1994, 72).

[53] In some cases nonmembers could ask to obtain some resources (M. De Moor 2003b).

[54] For an elaboration on the role of the guilds in determining price and quality, see also De Kerf (2010), chapter 2.

The emergence of commons

craftsman's skill would change only with the Industrial Revolution, when the quality of products was determined by machines and hence given a more uniform and homogenous character (Gustaffson 1987, 21). In the meantime, guilds were necessary to solve the quality problem for traders in the emerging market economy. Gustaffson sums up several methods the guilds used to control quality: scrutiny of raw materials, scrutiny and regulation of production processes, the setting of standard and compliance inspections for end products, and the use of markings to indicate a specific quality. By controlling quality, guilds achieved a competitive advantage over the free market produce: traders no longer had to carefully check the merchandise as this was already done by the guilds (Gustaffson 1987, 111).

The goal of offering products produced at uniform prices had a similar effect for the guilds as on the common: those who complied with the rules were assured of an income. This was probably not the best possible price they would have received on the free market, but it did assure them of income continuity. Those guild members who decided to ignore the quality standard and make goods of a lesser quality, offering them at a lower price to the consumer, threatened the income of all the suppliers of quality goods. Richardson describes how the members of the guilds depended on one another to achieve the required income level: 'they had a common theme. Guild members acted to increase their incomes, and their efforts required action in concert. Members had to cooperate. Each had to do his part for the guild to attain his goals' (Richardson 2005, 145).[55]

Ignoring the quality standards of a guild was much like overusing the resources of the common for personal or commercial use. In both cases members abused their membership to a privileged group. Commoners could try to put more cattle on the common, thus abusing their legitimate presence on the common. Whether or not their abuse would be discovered depended on the functioning of the commoners' (social) control mechanisms. In the same way, guild members could abuse their reputation as a respected guild member by offering lower-quality products on the market under the pretense that the products were of guild quality. Records exist of manufacturers – guild members – who preferred a low-quality product strategy, which conflicted with the guilds' general strategy (Dyer 2002, 315; Merges 2004, 8). Durability was important in the manufacturing sector because products often needed to be sold over long distances. If

---

[55] Richardson continues: 'If some slacked off, all would suffer. Guilds that wished to lower the costs of labor had to get all masters to reduced wages. Guilds that wished to raise the prices of products had to get all members to restrict output. Guilds that wished to develop respected reputations had to get all members to sell superior merchandise. The need for coordination was a common denominator'.

The Dilemma of the Commoners

the product proved to be of lower quality, this could seriously affect the reputation of the guild (Richardson 2005, 143–4).

To prevent members from free riding, social control played an important role in these institutions. There is evidence that members of commons or their appointed officials would be fined if they did not report when they saw others cheating (e.g., illegally harvesting resources from the common).[56] Guilds often required members to set up their shops in the same area to encourage social control (Richardson 2005, 160).[57] In both guilds and commons, punishment could entail permanent expulsion from the organization (Richardson 2005, 161).[58]

1.4.4 Local

An important characteristic was the local character of the institutions that emerged during the silent revolution. The members of these institutions concentrated on solving local problems that were part of their everyday lives; they had no supra-local intentions, and in many cases they were not even communicating with others in a similar situation a few villages away. There are examples of commons that had to communicate with neighboring villages because their land was so extensive several villages had part of it within their boundaries. Such inter-commons had resources in common that could be used by the members of several different villages (see, e.g., the Flemish example of the Aard van de Zes Dorpen, a common that was situated in the middle of six villages and could be used by all the inhabitants

---

[56] For example, the regulation of Marke Exel of 15 May 1679 states that the cattle pounders will have to report any offence they encounter; in case they fail to do so, they will be held to pay (the costs of) half a barrel of beer: '... en wort die schutters belast bij een peene van een halve tonne bier sulckx te moeten aenbrengen ...' (Beuzel 1988, 27).

[57] See Richardson (2005) for examples on England.

[58] Guilds, however, also had other trump cards to prevent free riding. Richardson explains that craft guilds combined spiritual and occupational endeavours because 'the former facilitated the success of the later and vice versa. The reciprocal nature of this relationship linked the ability of guilds to attain spiritual and occupational goals. By combining piety and profit the guilds could overcome free-rider problems and achieve common goals' (Richardson 2005, 141–64). This kind of bundling of endeavours 'increased the pain of expulsion. People expelled from guilds with both craft and Christian features lost both business and religious benefits. They lost not only their colleagues but also their church, not only their partners but also their preachers, not only their means of prospering in this life but also their hope of passing through purgatory' (Richardson 2005, 141–64). The advantage of combining religious and economic goals lay – according to Richardson – in the fact that the religious consequences of defection could not be easily calculated as they might have become obvious only in the afterlife. The religious goals of the guild added an extra enforcement tool. Although he gives no evidence for this, Richardson concludes that complex guilds – those that combined endeavors – deterred shirking better than simple, secular associations and that the complex variants would be more profitable than the simple ones.

The emergence of commons

of those six vilages).[59] At their meetings, representatives of all villages had to be present. However, there is no proof of initiatives whereby commoners of different commons joined forces to obtain benefits. In the urban centers, guilds of different crafts sometimes joined forces to put local governments under pressure, but on the whole they minded their own business. Both commoners and guild members invested a lot in internal communication and derived benefits from their collaboration by creating an economy of scale and creating enough critical mass to demand certain benefits from local lords and governments for their own group, but they did not attempt to join forces with similar initiatives elsewhere to gain even more power. Considering the fact that guilds and commons were a ubiquitous and 'normal' phenomenon in early modern times, their members may have considered it unnecessary to use their collective power over the ruling class; in the case of the commons the distance between commons may in some cases also have been an obstacle. In the cities, the competition between guilds – even if they did not practice the same craft – may have prevented guild members from working together as organizations. Overall, one can conclude that these institutions were focused on their own func-tioning, that they were inward looking, and were not very interested in other similar initiatives elsewhere. This is also reflected in the uniqueness of the regulatory documents: there is – to my knowledge – no commons regulations in the whole of Europe that are exactly the same, as there is no common with exactly the same resources and users with the same needs and wants. Many rules designed by commoners or guild members, how-ever, do show similarities in the way they limited resource use, punished infractions, and organized participation.[60] These structural similarities suggest that groups of stakeholders who chose a cooperative strategy to manage and use their resources all refered to some basic set of rules humans believe should be followed to be successful in cooperation. The recurrent demand – regardless of the time, context (rural/urban), or location – that stakeholders must attend meetings shows that early modern villagers and town dwellers realized that being present during the decision-making process contributed to internalization of new or adjusted rules, and that this could enhance success of the organization. It also shows the limits of the cooperative model in its early modern form: the organization had to be

---

[59] See Paepen (2005).

[60] Identifying the similarities in these rules and factors that influence regulation in them is the objective of the Common Rules–project, for which the regulation of cases from the Netherlands (9) Spain (8), and England (8) have been analyzed and compared system-atically throughout time. For more information, see http://www.collective-action.info/_PRO_NWO_CommonRules_Main.

local as physical presence was only possible if people lived nearby, and became difficult to enforce if those entitled to use the common moved away. The implications of emigration to places even as close as neighboring villages made communication increasingly difficult and costly, and put a heavy burden on the active participation of entitled users. Guilds, which often connected membership to citizenship of the city where the guild was located, often suffered less from the effects of emigration.

The local character of these institutions was, on the one hand, a positive element. It focused on what was necessary for the local users and offered the possibility of reacting quickly to immediate dangers, such as a cattle disease that demanded immediate separation of the sick animals from the healthy to avoid further spread of the disease. On the other hand, the local character could also be a potential threat if the organization could not keep pace with rapid emigration of its users. In principle, rules could be adjusted easily by requiring that users be local. But in a situation in which all users have a say, they might have voted against such a proposal. And there was another threat that grew larger over time: as commoners of different commons did not really communicate with one another (as already noted), they also lacked the power to protest against national attempts to privatize their property. As will be explained later, during the eighteenth century common management of land came increasingly under attack by central governments. As local institutions, commons had little power to demonstrate their local use and meaning to the political leaders. They were thus unprepared for the privatization/enclosure movement that would sweep through Europe and would eventually lead to the disappearance of the commons in northwestern Europe. Such lack of visibility due to their local character and limited cooperation with other similar initiatives is also one of the main weaknesses of institutions for collective action today, as will be explained in the Epilogue.

1.4.5 *Features of the governance model versus features of successful institutions*

The already mentioned features of institutions for collective action are given in order to delineate the type of institution that fits into a governance model that is distinctively different from the state or the market as governance models. One could claim that the various types of institutions for collective action fit in between these two extremes: state governance, which is all-inclusive (from the premise that in principle all those belonging to a state are entitled to use the goods and services provided by that state), versus private governance, whereby use can be restricted to its extremes. It is vital to note, however, that all of these governance models, including those of guilds and commons, somehow draw a line between those entitled to use and those who are not entitled to use the goods and services provided. Not considered here is open access as a governance regime because there is essentially no 'governing party' involved and no lines are drawn between those with and without use rights.

Demonstrating the mentioned features of an institution for collective action, however, is no guarantee for success: although the historical records of such cases are limited, some commons and guilds suffered from bad governance and either lingered on as inert institutions, were taken over by a fellow organization, or disappeared in due time. Conversely, as Elinor Ostrom repeatedly mentioned, common-pool institutions should not be considered as a panacea, as a blueprint for solving all types of resource problems (although she mainly pointed towards natural resource management) (Ostrom, Janssen, and Anderies 2007). In summary: things can go wrong, and an institution for collective action can also be a bad choice for a certain types of resources to act as a governance model. This implies two issues: a need to understand under which (external) conditions an institution for collective action is the best choice and which 'internal' features well-functioning institutions for collective action demonstrate. The latter has already been done brilliantly by Ostrom in her 1990 *Governing the Commons* book, leading to a – by now famous – list of eight design principles (Ostrom, 1990, 90). However, being based on present-day examples that are – at least from the perspective of the average historian – not particularly long-lived, the list of design principles is a useful but insufficient instrument to understand why some commons were more robust than others. Elsewhere, I have, along with other colleagues, already compared the regulation of early modern commons in Belgium, the Netherlands, Germany, England, France, and Scandinavia with Ostrom's design list, coming to the conclusion that the eight principles could be easily applied to the historical situation and as such explain why many of these commons were so long-lived (see T. De Moor, Shaw-Taylor, and Warde 2002). However, as Ostrom's list constitutes 'only' principles, and institutions usually demonstrate a variety of organizational structures, it is hard to add benchmark values or other methods that would allow us to put our finger on what works and what doesn't and how this works over very long periods of time. Frameworks, such as the institutional analysis and design (IAD)-framework, to some extent have solved this methodological problem, but in order to grasp the real mechanisms that keep a group of commoners going over very lengthy periods of time, we need another approach that connects commoners' decisions and their impact and which brings to the surface the key drivers in long-term management of institutions for collective action. This book offers an alternative approach to this, supported by extensive case study material (see Chapters 3 and 4), but before diving into such detailed material we first need to deal with a few more aspects of the long-term history of institutions for collective action in early modern Europe.

Another issue, implied by the search for the right governance model, is that of the more external conditions that are required for an institution for collective action to function properly and successfully. In some of the eight design principles, there is already an implicit reference to some necessary conditions for successful functioning, such as the reference to good working relations with and recognition by local and national governments in the principles of self-determination (principle 7) and nested enterprises (principle 8). In the next part (1.5) I try to divide the more general conditions from the factors that may have created a stimulating environment (motors) as well as the incentives or motives that individuals may have had to form and participate in a collectivity, given the necessary conditions are fulfilled and there are a number of motors that stimulate them to do so. One could say that given the situation that in the European past the necessary elements on these three levels were available, it is understandable that institutions for collective action became such an important governance model in those times. This, however, does not imply that these factors are always – in all times and all places – a prerequisite for such institutions to emerge. Moreover, they are no guarantee for success, interpreted in the form of robustness, longevity, or any other way to define institutional success.

1.5 Explaining the origins of institutions for collective action in western Europe

The preceding brief description of the similarities in the institutional design of commons and guilds suggests that their more or less simultaneous emergence in northwestern Europe must have common causes, or that there should at least have been similarities in the circumstances in which they originated. Some factors that may have led to a chain reaction and in the end to the widespread phenomenon of guilds as ways to organize (part of) the urban production system may have similarities to the process that resulted in commons in the countryside as ways to organize (part of) the agricultural production. In the medieval context, there are several reasons why these forms of collective action were often more advantageous than purely private and public solutions. To analyze this, I distinguish between motives, motors, and conditions. Motives are the reasons that lead individuals to choose a cooperative strategy rather than a private one, or to rely on external parties such as the state. Motivating individuals to participate in a collectivity such as a guild or a common requires that individuals have good – rational or other – reasons to do so. They need to see potential advantages over other solutions and be able to weigh them against the disadvantages of their choice. Encouragement for either choice may come from what I will refer to as the 'motors', which are exogenous elements of change that can lead to collective action, such as population growth or market development. Although people may see the advantages of cooperation, they may not see a need to change their behavior. Changed circumstances may shift the odds and lead to changed individual and household strategies. A change in a governance model, however, always implies costs; thus, though individuals might be motivated to cooperate, they need to be sure that their efforts and money are well spent. Even if people see the advantages and wish to benefit from them by changing their strategies, the circumstances through which they can pursue such a change must be sufficiently attractive. Whereas the motives and motors mainly relate to the willingness of individuals to cooperate, the third factor of conditions relates to the ability to make a choice, which might be linked to factors beyond their power. These conditions can be political (the power of the state), societal (the degree of openness in human relationships), and legal (the legal recognition of corporate bodies) circumstances. In the following paragraphs, I will expand on the motives, motors, and conditions of the late medieval and early modern situations in northwestern Europe. I believe these led to a particular outcome in a particular setting, but this doesn't mean that in different times, regions, and circumstances, other factors may not have been at play, leading to a similar outcome.

1.5.1 Motives for collective action: potential advantages of cooperation

What are the motives of a group of people with a common, though basically not-yet-collective, objective to unite and act together in response to a social dilemma? If there is potential for collective action, if the 'right' circumstances develop, what would convince them to invest in a joint effort? I explicitly use the term 'motives' rather than 'causes' in relation to collective action because I am starting from the premise that in theory there might have been other options to individuals to solve social dilemmas. I will discuss here the two most important and relevant motives for choosing collective action: risk sharing and advantages of scale.

The Dilemma of the Commoners

Choosing a cooperative solution has the advantage of possibly sharing the costs that arise from uncertain or risky situations. In the case of commons, and for some types of guilds, such as guilds that dealt with construction works or food processing, for example, the risks depended on nature. When the flow of natural resources is uncertain, for example, due to seasonal variations (flooding, excessive rainfall, etc.), the availability of resources could be seriously hampered, but often it could not be foreseen when this would occur. Pooling resources and costs made the use of such resources less risky. Each participant could be certain of part of the available resources, year after year, but this share was probably lower than the short-term profit that could have been obtained using a system of private property. The average harvest in a collective system might have been more attractive than the seriously fluctuating harvest in a private system. Guilds also provided members with services they might have been unable to afford as individuals (Westlake 1919, 32).

Artisans in medieval times faced similar risks, which they may have tried to limit through collective action. The main objective of a guild was to provide a minimal but secure income for its members. The capital 'good' they pooled to prevent great risks was their skill in combination with specific knowledge about their craft: by joining and exchanging their knowledge and training among members, and taking advantage of the scale of organization (see the following section), they could offer a uniform, high-quality good that would be sold at a fair price, above a collectively set minimum price. The selling channels and commercial knowledge the guild had built up and passed on over the years could prove helpful in this, for example, by reducing transaction costs. Those who were relatively highly skilled might have been able to attain higher incomes than what they obtained through the guild, but it was probably unlikely they would have done so over a long period, as they too were dependent on the fluctuations of the market. This collectivization of human capital could also be setting limits to the exchange of knowledge, as has been described, for example, in connection with the glass makers of Venice:

The skills to make quality glass constituted a form of intellectual property. Knowledge was ... a valuable commodity. In the community of Murano, where practically everyone's livelihood depended on glassmaking to some degree, the knowledge associated with the glass craft was 'communal property'. Failing to protect or maintain this property was to the detriment of the community, the guild and the Venetian state.

(McCray 1999, 150)

The emergence of commons

Larry Epstein clearly described the advantages of the guild as an institution for transferring this specific property. He identified the craft guild as the most direct source of premodern technological innovation. The guild system

> enforced the rules of apprenticeship against free-riding and exploitation ... offered institutional and practical support to the migrant apprentices, journeymen, and masters who transferred their knowledge from town and region of Europe to another ... [and] it [supplied] incentives to invention that the patent system did not by enforcing temporary property rights over members' innovations.
>
> (Epstein 2004, fn. 386)

The resources guilds and commons pooled, albeit of a very different type, were valuable goods, and by joining forces, goods, and knowledge, a variety of important risks could be avoided. Apart from this, Persson (1988, 54) also points to the advantages of guilds as insurance against the risk of declining demand for guild products or limited supply of necessary raw materials. Guild regulation ensured that the consequences of a decrease in demand were evenly spread across the guild members to avoid the temptation of competitive price offers. Rules forbidding members to hoard raw materials limited the consequences of temporary periods of supply restraints, and in this sense, risks to both the supply and demand could be avoided, or at least minimized.

Sticking together also offered advantages of scale, which increased possibilities over individual action. If resources were of low value, as was the case with many commons, the possible, but uncertain benefits would not have covered the cost of fencing the land in the form of individual plots. In those cases where a minimum area of land was necessary to achieve maximal efficiency, forming a collective clearly offered advantages of scale. The same goes for guilds: they could achieve advantages of scale in buying raw materials as a group. Prak (1994) gives the example of guilds in 's-Hertogenbosch, a town in the Northern Netherlands, which would let a representative buy goods in bulk on distant markets for a common account. In medieval Venice, butchers allowed a member of the guild to jointly buy pigs, smiths bought their charcoal in common, and ceramists bought their white lead in bulk.[61] Furthermore, combining the limited individual financial resources allowed guilds to mobilize expensive legal aid. Examples are the many petitions filed by guilds, aimed at obtaining specific privileges from local authorities (Prak 2004, 186).[62]

---

[61] MacKenney (1987), taken from Prak (1994, 18). Prak has the impression that this practice of buying goods in large amounts became less important during the early modern period.

[62] Epstein also refers to advantages of scale for the use of knowledge: 'Much premodern craft and engineering knowledge appears to have been shared or "distributed" within industrial

The Dilemma of the Commoners

Collectively their bargaining power became much larger.[63] In a similar way, the users of a common benefited from collective investments in their common; by joining their forces, investments such as drainage or fencing of pasture land could be achieved at a lower price. Moreover, internal enforcement of social control avoided illegal trespassing and use of resources (T. De Moor 2009).

1.5.2   Motors of institutions for collective action: stimulating factors to form collectivities

Commons and guilds can both be considered as institutions founded with the objective of dealing with problems of collective action to profit from the advantages cooperation could offer (such as economies of scale and risk sharing). They dealt with similar problems (at least abstractly) because the goods they tried to protect were similar. Both types of goods – large-scale vulnerable natural resources in the case of the commons and a common pool of knowledge and skills in the case of the guilds – were similar in that it was difficult to exclude others from using a good that was shared. The natural resources of commons were mostly too large to be physically enclosed; the knowledge and skills of guild members were 'goods' that could easily be copied and thus were difficult to exclude others from: once a guild member had shared his knowledge, it is very plausible that another person could share it with an outsider. Guild members possessed a form of expert knowledge about the production process, which is quite different 'common knowledge', and they also shared within their network knowledge about the functioning of the market (where to obtain the best raw or the cheapest materials, which customers were reliable and which were not, etc.). Protection of their knowledge was – at least in the eyes of the guild members – necessary, not primarily because the knowledge itself could be overexploited, as in the case of natural resources, but because a more intensive use of that knowledge outside of the group of guild members would make this knowledge less valuable. In this sense, what commoners and guild members tried to protect via their collective action may be considered as 'goods' with similar problems and thus with similar needs for specific actions. In both cases a higher consumption of the goods would

---

districts ... sharing was more likely in ship- and edifice-building, mining and metalworking, and in the production of clocks and scientific instruments, which displayed strong division of labor and advanced levels of coordination and where cooperation provided clear economies of scale and scope – sectors that are also notable for having played the most technologically innovative role in the Industrial Revolution' (Epstein 2004, 383).

[63] For an interesting example of the usage of collective bargaining power by the guilds, and a comparison with the unions that were formed later on, see Mastboom (1994).

The emergence of commons

have negative effects on the members of the institution: the natural resources of the common could eventually disappear because of excessive exploitation, and thus threaten the future of the common as an institution. For the guilds, increasing production outside of the guilds, using the knowledge the guild members shared, would lead to lower prices for the goods, too much competition (at least, in the eyes of guild members), and eventually the collapse of the guild structure.

The cause of this growing scarcity was linked to population growth, a growing rate of urbanization, and the accompanying commercialization of land, labor, and capital in the late Middle Ages.[64] For guilds, as with the commons, it only became necessary to exclude others when there actually were others. For many commons, it was possible at first for the resources to be used by all the inhabitants of the village, but over time some people from the village had to be excluded. Lourens, Lucassen, and De Munck (2005) write that a certain population size was necessary for guilds to develop, because there had to be a sufficient number of possible guild members. In cities of less than 500 inhabitants, craft guilds normally would not develop. Considering the real drive behind the guilds, it must also have been true that the larger the population, the greater the possibility that others, who were not members of the guilds, would have taken part in the production for the consumer market.[65] Around 1400 there was a strong correlation between urbanization and the presence of guilds in the Low Countries. In the largest cities there was a limit to this correlation; however, according to Lourens, Lucassen, and De Munck (2005), this was a consequence of the guilds' political involvement in those cities: where some guilds gained political power, they were no longer inclined to allow new organizations, certainly not by splitting up existing guilds.[66]

But besides population growth, the timing of the growth of guilds also suggests that we should look elsewhere for a comprehensive explanation of the movement. After the Black Death, when the population had dropped significantly, there was a very clear rise of the number of guilds in, for example, the Netherlands. In the half century following the first outbreak of the Black Death, the number of functioning guilds rapidly increased (Westlake 1919, 28). The increased demand for labor led to an increase in

---

[64] On urbanization see the article by Bosker, Buringh, and Van Zanden (2013); on the commercialization of factor markets, see Van Bavel (2006) for labor markets and Van Bavel (2008a, 2008b, 2011) for land markets.

[65] However, over time guilds did also subcontract in the countryside (Lis and Soly 1994).

[66] Ghent, for example, had many more citizens than Bruges and Ypres, but hardly any more craft guilds (Lourens, Lucassen, and De Munck 2005).

The Dilemma of the Commoners

income for unskilled and semi-skilled laborers, meaning that for the first time many people could afford to pay the membership fee and yearly dues for a guild (Bainbridge 1996). Moreover, the uncertainty that accompanied the Black Death may have provided an incentive for people to join. Membership in a guild may have been considered a way to safeguard themselves against future problems.

Institutionalized collective action in the form of commons and guilds was a suitable *modus vivendi* to combine participation in the market with protection from the negative side effects of that market, or 'using the market without being abused by it' in an area that was one of the most commercialized in Europe at the time.[67] Both commoners and guild members tried to avoid the negative side effects of the still weak and incompletely developed market by protecting their capital goods. Commoners tried to protect the valuable and exhaustible resources they had through limiting the potential for commercialization of resources. If these could be sold *ad libitum* on the market, it could threaten the sustainable government of the resources and thus also the income of the commoners. The rules designed to restrict such commercialization varied from place to place, but by and large we can distinguish three categories. On some commons the use of the resource by each individual (household) was restricted to the needs of the household. In this category we can find the 'levancy and couchancy-rules', which stated that no more animals were to be allowed on the common in summer than could be kept in the winter on the produce of the farm (Winchester 2002, 45). A variation of this could be found in rules whereby the number of cattle that could be brought on the common was linked to the surface of arable land held in private property. The idea behind this was that a farmer had to be able to provide the fodder needed for the cattle during wintertime by cultivating this fodder on his own private property. If he could not provide this himself, he would have to purchase it, implying that the cattle grazing on the common in the summer would be sold afterwards. Another way of formulating this was by a restriction on cattle bought just before the grazing period started: commoners may have intended to go to market, let the cattle bought there graze on the thick summer grass of the common, and sell them again in the fall, thus reaping a maximal gain from their grazing rights. Another way of keeping the market out was by restricting commercialization of the produce that came indirectly from the common, such as rules that forbade the sale of milk outside the village produced by cows that had grazed on the common.

---

[67] This process of commercialization and accompanying urbanization in the area around the North Sea has been concisely described by Hoyle (2010, 362–6).

The emergence of commons

The size of the market within the village was likely to be limited, and some cash revenue was needed to buy other produce as well. Anywhere outside of those village boundaries, however, lurked the potential of much larger commercialization, which could in the end lead to excessive exploitation due to commercialization. Another restriction dealt with the limitation put on commoners regarding selling or leasing their own rights to non-entitled villagers. The common was intended for personal, household use, not for sale purposes. The general rules mentioned already are examples of the ways commoners tried to secure self-sufficiency and sustainable resource use and to demonstrate their awareness of the threats of commercialization. It should be stressed, however, that these rules did not always appear in commons regulations, and that many variations, depending on the location and resources, were possible. What is important to bear in mind is that commoners were aware of the threats of the market and that they found institutional ways of dealing with these threats. Elsewhere in this book, I will elaborate on this issue.

The guilds faced similar threats to their income if they failed to limit the commercial benefits that could be reaped from their members' production. The capital goods they needed to protect were their knowledge and learned skills. Making this knowledge available to others who were not members of the guild would also be a threat to the members' income, since they, to a certain extent, would thus lose their income security and experience a drop in earnings. There was a need for this *modus vivendi* because of the situation of the factor markets at that time. Capital was available, but only to a certain extent; the labor market was at an early stage of development, but was not yet a threat to independent craftsmen. In situations with such unreliable markets, in which large fluctuations could be expected in return on investment, collective action institutions offered an attractive alternative.

1.5.3 Conditions for collective action: weak family ties, tolerant states, and legal recognition

One hypothesis for the conditions that allowed the growth of these institutions has been suggested by Michael Mitterauer, who, in his *Warum Europa?: Mittelalterliche Grundlagen eines Sonderwegs* (2003), stresses the importance of the disappearance of family bonds as an explanation for the European *Sonderweg* (literally 'exceptional way').[68] This form of social organization, more open than systems based on kinship or tribal relations, may have played a role in the development of collective action, especially

---

[68] See also J. L. Van Zanden 2009a, in particular pages 17–141.

the institutionalized form of collective action, whereas in societies based on strict family bonds (lineage), tribal structures, or clans, there may not have been any place for the development of collective action. Anthony Black (1984) considers the European guilds 'artificial families', which is probably one of the best descriptions of the role played by guilds.[69]

In addition to an open, relatively non-kin based society, freedom to organize was also necessary. Guilds and commons emerged in western Europe in a situation of relatively weak states, of fragmented sovereignty (Van Zanden 2009, 33–4 and 37–41), in which different social classes and groups (the nobility, the Church, independent cities) competed for power and established statelike institutions (such as independent communes) to defend their interests (Van Zanden and Prak 2006; J. L. van Zanden 2008a). It was typical for western Europe during the Middle Ages that power became negotiable. Cooperation then evolved into a broader form of negotiation, accompanied by an institutionalization of the estates into parliaments and imperial and territorial diets (Blickle 1998, 8). In sum, guilds and commons needed the political institutions to allow them to develop.

A last issue is the legal and political recognition of groups. Legal changes made it possible for a group to act as a single body in the name of many members. Legally, entities such as guilds and commons had sufficient recognition to function properly, to defend their rights, and to deal with external attempts to encroach upon their rights, at least until the end of the eighteenth century. In medieval Europe, this was possible because canon law allowed these collectivities rights of assembly, ownership, and (both internal and external) representation (Huff 2003, 134). These organizations received their legal recognition from the principle of *universitas*, giving the group a juridical personality distinct from that of its particular, individual members. As Tierney explains, 'the word *universitas* meant basically "all" in a collective sense and could be used for any group of people cooperating for a common end' (Tierney and Painter 1983, 404).[70] This concept of *universitas* was a novelty introduced into European law in the late eleventh and twelfth centuries. Although the term was derived from Roman law, the twelfth-century western European interpretation was substantially different from what the term meant previously. In practice, the core of *universitas* held that a

---

[69] A more explicit link between the development of new family relations as within the emergence of the European Marriage Pattern and the emergence of collective action institutions has been made by De Moor and Van Zanden (2010).

[70] As such, it also served the purpose of scholars forming a university, as a sort of 'educational guild', which emerged in the late twelfth century in Europe (Tierney and Painter 1983).

The emergence of commons

debt owed by a group was not owed by the members as individuals; an expression of the will of a group did not require the assent of each individual member, but only of a majority (Tierney 1982, 19; Huff 2003, 133). The principle of *universitas* established the existence of 'fictive' legal persons, which are treated as real entities in courts of law and in assemblies before kings and princes (Berman 1983, 214; Huff 2003, 133). For example, whereas collectivities in the form of a firm are today generally considered as separate legal entities, this was at the time a real novelty, which led to both legal and institutional changes.[71]

In addition to the recognition of the group as a legal entity, the regulation of those entities needed support from local and state powers. Although attribution of the right to be a member can in itself be considered a property right – as it gives the right to appropriate some of the resources – it differs significantly from later modern property rights, devised from the late eighteenth century onwards. These state-backed rights to exclude others were devised towards securing the link between individual effort and individual reward, which is a different logic for solving economic problems than that applied by guild members and commoners. These rights would form the basis of a newly constructed political order, in which individuals rather than groups formed the pillars of society (Posner 2000). Considering these conflicting backgrounds, it should not be surprising that in the era preceding their almost simultaneous dissolution at the end of the eighteenth and during the nineteenth century, both guilds and commons were the subject of fierce debate. The abolition of both organizations was fueled by the same arguments: these remnants of a feudal, medieval past were the enemies of innovation and economic progress. The kind of rhetoric that was used to attack the organizations in the eighteenth and also nineteenth centuries is to a large degree applicable to both guilds and commons (see earlier in this chapter, point 1.1). The struggle for the survival of guilds and commons in that period shows that collective action in such a form could not survive without backing from the state.

Taken together one could say that there needs to be sufficient 'room' for forms of collectivities other than those of the more traditional type – that is, based on family/blood ties, tribe structures, clans, castes, and so on – in order for institutions such as commons and guilds to bind people together on their common needs (as craftsmen or farmers) and that the formation of such alternative forms of collectivities is accepted within society as a viable alternative. Considering that – as I pointed out before – most of these

---

[71] For a comparison with other legal regimes and the effect of the absence of such a concept as *universitas* on societies, see Kuran (2010), chapter 6, and in particular page 101.

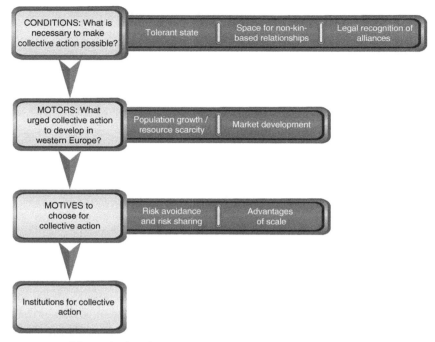

Figure 1 Conditions, motors, and motives for institutions for collective action to emerge[72]

institutions were local, it becomes unavoidable that members also have other commonalities, such as their place of residence, or indeed some family members. At times such additional features of members were also used to limit the total number of users, by further restricting the entry rules, as I will point out when discussing the conditions for membership in the commons in Flanders (see point 2.4.1.1).

1.6 Conclusions

In this chapter, I explained how the emergence of commons in northwestern Europe was part of a much larger development in which many different forms of commons-like institutions emerged. As much as commons in the Western world today are rare forms of resource governance, collective use and management of resources was a normal way to deal with

---

[72] This framework has been elaborated in more detail and applied to the differences in the development of commons in eastern and western Europe in Laborda Pemán and De Moor (2013).

problems of uncertainty, scarcity, population growth, and more. As demonstrated, commons can be compared to, for example, guilds, both in the countryside and the towns. These are much better known in historical literature, in terms of their rise and decline, their relationship to local and national political powers, and their institutional design (Lucassen et al., 2008). We have seen how both institutions constituted ways of dealing with social dilemmas, and how their specific features could lead to enough trust to have highly committed members. The outcome of these comparisons confirms that there are good reasons to claim that the late Middle Ages was a period of innovation in dealing with social dilemmas to such an extent that we can call this development a silent revolution.

Institutions such as commons and guilds spread more rapidly in Europe than elsewhere in the world. In terms of intra-European geographical limitations, however, it remains unclear where exactly the borders of this silent revolution were situated. The rise of other institutions such as beguinages and water boards in the same period as guilds and commons does, however, suggest that the Low Countries in particular were an important center of rapid institutionalization of collective action. Further investigation should help reveal the extent of the correlation between institutionalized collective action and economic development.

On the micro-level, we have found indications that guilds, commons, and other forms of collective action were adequate answers to the economic and social needs of northwestern European society. The economy was developing rapidly but could not provide an answer to the changes on the household level where household members' opportunities to rely on family support had gradually decreased. Markets could not provide the income that could be derived from collective action. Commoners did not sell goods from the common, but they needed the common to provide food for their cattle, indispensable for fertilizing the land. In this way the common indirectly provided products for the market, but at the same time provided a basic income. Investing in goods can be a risky affair; therefore, commoners and craftsmen relied on collective action to minimize costs such risks may entail. As members of a collective, they took advantage of the collective, which promoted unity to provide social welfare for themselves and their families; and as a group with similar interests, they sometimes spoke up in political matters, although there is no evidence that commoners acted likewise. They could do so because the rules of a disintegrated feudalism allowed them to have a voice. Because they lived in relatively small political entities that were always involved in one or another conflict, they may have had no other choice.

The Dilemma of the Commoners

Guilds, more than commons, offered both income security and social security in an insecure society, thus answering two needs. The combination of these two elements was the strength of the system. It was not straightforward, since the social cost engendered by some members affected the economic benefits for others. The social component was necessary, since without it, the (sometimes only temporary) weaker members of the occupational group would work for a lower price, thus affecting the income of the stronger members. Solidarity and compliance to group norms was thus needed to make the system work, because of both economic and societal factors (weaker family bonds). Considering the variations in incomes, this might not have been clear to everyone at all times: hence the necessity of a body of rules, the strict regulation. The collective action organizations discussed in this chapter thrived on what can be called 'bridging social capital', instead of on the old kinship arrangements.[73] Given the right political circumstances (freedom to organize, rulers that can be compromised) and specific economic incentives, pursuing joint welfare within a group by means of collective action should not be seen as unnecessarily burdensome and with little chance for success, but often as a preferred option by those forming the group.

Although it seems clear that villagers in late medieval and early modern Europe understood that there were benefits to be reaped from working together, making – and especially keeping – such collaboration a long-term success remained a challenge. The conditions, motors, and motives shown in Figure 1 can by no means be considered as conditions for good cooperation, nor do they offer a guarantee that the institution initially set up would be long-lived, even if the founders had the intention to establish a resilient institution. Good, resilient self-governance usually entails a robust body of regulations, including mechanisms to prevent and sanction free riding, and the establishment of relationships with other powers. In the next chapter I will explain how commons in Flanders were organized and introduce the case study central to this book. Understanding what is needed for resilient self-governance, capable of dealing with external shocks and internal trouble, requires an in-depth micro-analysis, which will help us discover why rules were changed and which decisions were made.

---

[73] Robert Putnam suggested in a short note in his renowned *Making Democracy Work: Civic Traditions in Modern Italy* that guilds might have made the difference in the construction of civil society in northern Italy (see Putnam, Leonardi, and Nanetti 1992, 229, n. 20).

2. Common land and common rights in Flanders[1]

After the overview given of more general institutional developments in Chapter 1, this chapter gives a more historical explanation of how commons originated in the area in which the case study – central to Chapters 3 and 4 – is located. In this chapter is a discussion of the particularities of the region and the role commons played in agriculture. This is necessary to understand why a change at the individual level of farmers can influence also the participation of commons and in that way also the functioning of the commons as a whole. Apart from the typical names given to commons in this area, the description of the types of commons that could be found in Flanders is not that different from elsewhere in Europe, as has been amply demonstrated by several European scholars (see the chapters in De Moor, Shaw-Taylor, and Warde [2002a]), nor was the 'destiny' of commons during the nineteenth century much different from what commons and their commoners went through elsewhere in Europe around the same time. Although the focus here is on one particular area, the results can also be extrapolated to other areas in Europe.

2.1   Description of the area

In this book, examples and source material are discussed from practically the whole of the Low Countries, which from a present-day perspective would comprise both the Netherlands and Belgium, and which show many similarities in terms of commons' management. Also, the Netherlands and Belgium have a joint political history, although not continuously, until the

---

[1] This chapter has to some extent been based on a previous publication entitled 'Common land and common rights in Flanders' (M. De Moor 2002), published as chapter in *The management of common land in north west Europe, c. 1500–1850* (De Moor, Shaw-Taylor, and Warde 2002a). Substantial changes and additions, however, have been made to the original publication.

61

1830s when Belgium became an independent state. It would lead us too far to explain all the details of the political history of these countries, but some general developments of the later part of the early modern period (1600–1800) and beginning of the modern period (1800–) are needed to frame the terms used in this book in a geographic sense, especially for the reader without a training in history. For a better understanding of the situation of the examples dealt with in this book, it is useful to know that the central case discussed in Chapters 3 and 4 belonged to the Southern Netherlands, an area that comprised roughly the current states of Belgium and Luxembourg. However, in order to sketch the broader geographical and temporal situation, some examples are also given of commons stem from the Northern Netherlands, a territory that was roughly similar to the current Netherlands, with the exception of the province of Limburg (which for a large part belonged to the prince-bishop of Liège). Whereas the economy of the Northern Netherlands during the seventeenth and eighteenth centuries was strong and mainly based on trade, the economy of the Southern Netherlands was relatively weak and for a large part based on agricultural produce. This division was a result of economic sanctions, such as a long-lasting blockade of the river Schelde, imposed by the Protestant Northern Netherlands through the Peace Treaty of Münster (1648) on the – mainly Catholic – towns and cities of the Southern Netherlands due to the latter's support the Catholic Spanish rulers during the second half of the Eighty Years' War (1568–1648) between the Netherlands and Spain. Under French (Napoleon) rule from 1794 to 1815 and the subsequent reign of King William I (1815–1840), the Southern and Northern Netherlands were reunited for some decades. During this period attempts were made to improve the impoverished state of the Southern Netherlands by the construction of long-range canals, among other things. After a revolt in 1830, Belgium, comprising the major part of the former Southern Netherlands, with the exception of the Grand-Duchy of Luxembourg, de jure became an independent state in 1839. Especially during the second half of the nineteenth century, Belgium experienced a process of strong industrialization, also resulting in large-scale cultivation of previously uncultivated land, usually held in common.

The northern part of the Southern Netherlands roughly corresponds to the present district of Flanders, one of the two main parts of present-day Belgium. Bordering the North Sea from France to the Schelde River, the low-lying plain of Flanders has two main sections. Maritime Flanders, extending inland for 5 to 10 miles (8 to 16 kilometers), is a region of

Common land and common rights in Flanders

newly formed and reclaimed land (polder), protected by a line of dunes and dikes and comprised of largely clay soils, whereas the interior part of Flanders has mostly sandy soils. At an elevation of 80 to 300 feet (roughly 24 to 91 meters), it is drained by the Leie, Schelde, and Dender Rivers flowing northeastwards to the Schelde estuary.

The Campine area (or *Kempen* in Dutch, *La Campine* in French, historically *Taxandria*) is a plateau region of northeastern Belgium, occupying most of the province of Antwerp and the northern part of the province of Limburg. It is a dry, mostly infertile region of sandy soil and gravel, with pinewoods interspersed among meadows of thin grass and heather. Poor drainage, especially in the lower, western part, has produced marshes where reeds and alder trees shelter abundant waterfowl. Although market towns and abbeys on the plateau date from the Middle Ages, settlement there was moderate until the nineteenth century.

From the institutional point of view, our main interest goes to the political and administrative units of the County of Flanders and the Duchy of Brabant, which form together the largest part of the northern part of the Southern Netherlands. The County of Flanders encompasses the western part of the selected area, whereas the Duchy of Brabant corresponds with the eastern area, the Campine area. The County of Flanders has been particularly renowned in history for its advanced methods of agriculture, although this goes less for the sandy area of it in which the case study we are considering in this book is situated.[2] During the eighteenth century and even later on, thousands of hectares used and managed as common land could still be found in the Campine area and, to a lesser extent, in the area between Bruges and Ghent (Vandenbroeke 1975, 45). Common land here was rarely woodland, but mostly wasteland (mainly heath) that could be used for pasturing, cutting peat and turf, digging loam, and gathering branches. The soil in this area is sandy and wet, and in some places mixed with loamy soil (see Figure 2). Apart from heath land, meadows were often also governed in the common.

The early disappearance of common arable land in this area must undoubtedly be linked to the advanced agriculture for which the County of Flanders has been so renowned. Several related aspects of Flemish agriculture are likely to have exercised great pressure on common land, both waste and arable. To begin with, there is the early disappearance of the three-field system in most parts of inland Flanders. Agriculture in this

---

[2] This county did indeed contain less common land than the wooded regions on the southern and eastern borders (part of southern Artois, Hainault, southern Brabant, Namur, southern Liège, Limburg, and the province of Luxembourg) of the Southern Netherlands. The macro-study by Hopcroft (1999) obscures regional variations.

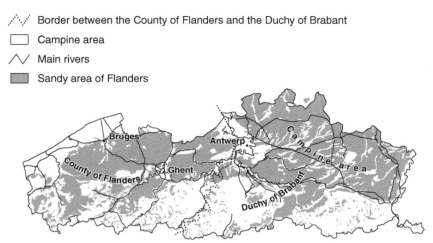

Figure 2 Flanders, with indication of sandy area and indication of case study (gray dot)

region during the (second) reclamation period of the twelfth and thirteenth centuries was fairly extensive for specialized production systems, whereby larger farms dominated.[3] The more intensively cultivated and fertilized areas were tilled according to a three-field system. The arable land of the sandy soils of inner Flanders was often divided into an 'infield' and an 'outfield'. The infields were heavily fertilized and permanently plowed, whereas on the less cultivated outfields, the common practice was 'up-and-down husbandry', or convertible husbandry. After a few years of use as arable land, most likely for oats, the outfield was converted to pasture.

From the second half of the twelfth century, cultivation methods started to intensify. During the thirteenth and fourteenth centuries, the difference between infield and outfield diminished, as many soils became permanently tilled because of increased population. Though agriculture intensified, long periods of fallow and short-term cultivation of land (*dries*) did not disappear completely. In inland Flanders, the switch to four-crop rotations was made in the fourteenth century, but the practice of long fallow periods was not completely abandoned until the seventeenth century. The use of fallow periods would be especially continued by large estates, rather than by the smallholdings. Small peasant farms practicing mixed farming and a rich variety of crops became the trademark of the densely populated and urban regions of the County of Flanders (Dejongh and Thoen 1999, 34–45).

---

[3] Verhulst discerns three periods of reclamations (Verhulst 1957): the first was during the Neolithicum, the second during the Middle Ages (1100–1350), and the third from the middle of the eighteenth until the end of the nineteenth century.

Common land and common rights in Flanders

Although the technical aspects of Flemish agriculture would receive most of the credit, it was primarily the high labor input per land unit enabled by farm fragmentation that was responsible for the higher productivity. The maximization of output these peasants tried to achieve was not primarily oriented to the market, but to self-sufficiency, what Thoen calls the 'commercial survival economy' (Vanhaute and Thoen 1999, 291–2). This was more the case for the area of inner Flanders than in the Campine area. In the latter, wasteland in the form of common land remained important until the nineteenth century. This, however, does not imply that agriculture there remained hopelessly backward compared to the agriculture in the County of Flanders: the availability of sods on the common in combination with stall feeding enabled the farmers in this area to fertilize their plots of land heavily (Van Houtte 1977, 70), as was the general practice until the end of the nineteenth century (Vanhaute and Thoen 1999, 272). Agriculture in this area, however, was certainly less commercially oriented than in inner Flanders, operating within a more closed commercial circuit, indicated by, for example, a rather low share of production dedicated to industrial crops and a better land-pasture ratio (Vanhaute and Thoen 1999, 292).

The second aspect, the introduction of green manuring and especially clover in arable agriculture, is likely to have speeded up expulsion of cattle from the arable commons. It is assumed that clover was already used in Flanders in the sixteenth century, though evidence of its use can only be found in sources from the third decade of the seventeenth century (Dejongh and Thoen 1999, 49). From the second decade of the eighteenth century – in addition to the qualities of clover as pasture – the advantage of green manuring when combined with other crops was discovered. It enriched the soil through its nitrogen-binding capacities, and as with other fodder crops such as turnips, spurry, carrots, and leguminous plants, it contributed to the elimination of fallow and the triple-rotation scheme.

The third factor, the increase in stall feeding in both inner Flanders and the Campine area, is a logical consequence of the increasing use of fodder crops. Both clearly contributed to greater manure production (Dejongh and Thoen 1999, 49–56), possibly leading to a diminished need for pasture land, also in the form of common pastures.[4] The farm techniques that had made Flemish agriculture so progressive were later adopted by other countries, primarily the Northern Netherlands and England.

Considering this progressiveness of Flemish husbandry, it should not be surprising that wasteland in general, and consequently wasteland held in

---

[4] Vanhaute and Thoen (1999, 288) showed in their comparison of two villages – one in the inner Flanders, the other in the Campine area – that fodder crops had to make up for a lesser availability of pasture land in inner Flanders.

common, had largely diminished in some parts of Flanders by the end of the ancien régime. As will be shown later, this process was not entirely natural, but it had been encouraged by the central government. The northern part of the region, especially the sandy areas around Bruges and the Campine area, was where the largest surface of common land had survived (see Figure 2). The declining importance of common land in general is probably also the reason why, except for a few particular cases, the Flemish commons were so poorly documented. The Flemish situation also shows that common land should be approached as part of a regional agrosystem, whereby the different components of the system – field, livestock, and farm household – interacted and influenced one another (Bieleman 1999, 237–47). Change in external factors such as agriculture and how this affected the commoners is clearly important to consider in this study.

It is difficult, if not impossible, to estimate the total surface of common land in this area at any given historical moment. There are several reasons for this. First, in the sources available for the study of agricultural land tenure or productivity, common land was mostly not counted as such (in the tithe lists, for example) because of its minor fiscal importance. Some of the taxes were linked to size of the harvest, of which the lord seized a part, and although pasture land contributed to the productivity of the land via providing the necessary manure, the surface of the common land was in those cases as such not taken into account for taxation. Gradually, the property of land (with variations in taxation level according to the quality of the land) also became a way to set taxes, but overall common land was not included in this.[5] What is more, by the nineteenth century the legal status of commons and their commoners was generally unclear. Common land was sometimes regarded as the private property of a group of people, and then recorded as such (e.g., in the cadastral records). If common land was used and owned by a whole community that was also an administrative unit, it was recorded as community property. It is impossible to distinguish between community property used as common land or held by a private owner. Often the total surface of common land was estimated by calculating the total extent of wasteland.[6] However, although there is a relationship between wasteland and common land, wasteland was not always common land, nor was common land always wasteland (M. De Moor 2003a).

Second, there are few sources left that measured common land, such as specific censuses, and those that exist are completely unreliable. The local variation in common land (and consequently topography) made it impossible

---

[5] On the role of the cadaster in taxation, see Kain (1992, 233–5).

[6] Estimates of the total surface of wasteland reclaimed during the nineteenth century in Belgium can be found in Clicheroux (1957), Goossens (1993), and Dejongh (1996).

for the central or provincial government to calculate the total area. The central government hardly had any understanding of this type of land use. For example, when the Dutch government (1815–1830) asked the local communities to report the names and extent of the *marken* in their community, many communities asked what a *marke* was exactly. As a *marke* was a typical Dutch name for a specific type of common land, mainly to be found in the eastern part of the Northern Netherlands (Hoppenbrouwers 2002), many local governments simply did not know which type of land they were supposed to report on. Moreover, it could very well be that the total area of the local commons was unknown to the local government, as these were often vast plots of land shared by several communities with, as mentioned, vague property titles and with users who for a long time had not been paying taxes.[7]

2.2 The nature of common land

In Chapter 1, several forms of institutions for collective action were taken together and examined from the same perspective. Taking such phenomena together, which have thus far only been considered separately in historiography, demonstrates that what defines a common is not its resources, but the institutionalization of the cooperation to use and manage those resources as a collective, whereas in principle, the same resources could also be governed in private. The way in which the institution was designed, however, also depended on what was available as a resource. As resources differ in the amount of available resource units and how quickly they can regenerate when a unit has been appropriated (Ostrom 1990), rules about appropriation were usually defined separately for the historic commons, depending on the type of resource. But not all resources that were subject to collective use were also subject to collective management, and vice versa. Until the end of the ancien régime, a great diversity of types of common use-rights could be found, but some were limited to a very specific period of the year during which the land was not used for other agricultural activities.

Concerning the management of common lands, the stress in this chapter will be on the common rights resting on uncultivated (waste)land, not on the rights that could be found on arable land that was in private use for most of the year. The latter rights were applicable to land that had been farmed and would be farmed again and could be exercised during certain periods before and after the growing season, and could not be taken advantage of continuously by other villagers. Because these rights are based on a custom permitted

---

[7] See, e.g., the Aard van de Zes Dorpen: a piece of land owned and used in common by six separate villages in the Belgian Campine area. See earlier footnotes.

by the person who owns or rents the land, and the fact that a title has not been conferred to other users, there is little question of common management. The owner or user was only obliged by local custom to allow the locals to use his land during certain periods of the year, without allowing these locals to decide upon the further management of the land.

Several types of common land will be distinguished on the basis of the predominant resource that could be found on the commons. It is, after all, most likely that that type of resource (wood, water, highly nutritious feed, or poor feed) exerted a strong influence on regulation, though ecology can certainly not be regarded as the only influential factor (Hopcroft 1999). Besides, it will be clear that, irrespective of the ecology of a common, regional variations surface.

2.2.1   Common waste

Common waste was uncultivated land, often too poor to be turned into arable land without great effort (especially in the case of heath land). The following parts discuss three types of common waste: common pasture (*aard*), common meadow (*broek*), and woodlands. Each type was especially prevalent in a particular area. However, this does not mean that a particular type could not also be found elsewhere. It is important here to note that it was commons that consisted of common waste, in all its varieties, which survived longest in European history. This in itself makes sense: they were the hardest to cultivate and thus were least threatened by privatization. And as soon as artificial fertilizes were available – in the first half of the nineteenth century – optimistic politicians believed they could increase the productivity of this land. In practice, however, much of these wastes proved to need literally decades of intensive fertilization before they could be used for the cultivation of crops, and hence often turned out to be a waste of investment (see also part 2.3).

2.2.1.1   Common pasture

In the Campine area, nearly every neighborhood (*herdgang, buurtschap*) had its own common (often referred to as *aard*), which could be very extensive, sometimes extending over thousands of hectares. The sandy soil produced poor grazing. The surface was removed to use as stable litter (*aardheide*); subsoil resources such as peat, turf, and loam were cut wherever available. In some cases the villagers were allowed to plant some trees on the *aard* in order to have more firewood. The continuous grazing of sheep and cows prevented the heath from turning into woodland. The word '*aard*' had several meanings: from 'the division of the arable land in the three-field system' to 'manor'. *Aard* is frequently found together with the words *vroente* or *gemeynte*, making it clear

Common land and common rights in Flanders

that a common was meant (De Bo 1873). In the west of Flanders, the heath was normally not called *aarden* but *velden*, literally 'fields', sometimes qualified by the adjective *gemene*, meaning 'common', in order to distinguish it from other noncommunal fields.[8] There is no reason to presume these *gemene velden* were very different from their counterparts in the east, except for terminology. A closer look at their actual management, however, reveals some important differences.

2.2.1.2 Common meadow

Another type of common pasture was the *broek*, which is a kind of marsh. This common land could be found among the low-lying wet and marshy lands, especially along the banks of the many rivers that cross the area of study. This common land was often drained by artificial watercourses and was densely overgrown with highly nutritious grasses. The number and extent of *broeken* was smaller than that of the common fields. Furthermore, they differed in economic value, and, to a certain degree, in organization and management from the previously described types of common land. Unlike the *vroenten*, the *gemene broeken* were (physically) enclosed by fences. In places where hay was taken from the common, a sign (*veken*) was hung at the entrance, usually on a specific day. As soon as this sign was hung, the *broek* could no longer be used by the whole community (Lindemans 1994, 318–20).

Here again, a distinction can be made between *broeken* where a limited number of people had pasture rights, and *broeken* where any inhabitant of the community could pasture their cattle after the hay harvest. In the first case, the authorized persons were very limited in number and were in some cases inheritors of previous benefices or inhabitants of a well-defined hamlet, mostly living around the common arable (*aangelanden*). The landlord had acknowledged their use of the *broek*. They formed an autonomous community that managed the *broek* itself (Lindemans 1994, 321). The Vrijbroek of Mechelen (Malines), for example, was donated by Wouter Bertoud in 1260 to twenty-eight 'good men' (*goede lieden*) whose names were mentioned in the deed of gift. These persons and all their lawful heirs would have the right to use the land, at the price of two *schellingen Lovens* (local currency) a year (Devos 1936 and 1937, 30 and 63). A similar arrangement could be found for the Gemene and Loweiden, a pasture east of Bruges, which is still managed and used as a common to this day.

In the other case, every member of the community had the right to pasture on the leftovers of the meadows. This right was generally based

---

[8] The literal translation of *gemene velden* would be 'common fields'. This would, however, be too confusing with common arable.

69

The Dilemma of the Commoners

on nothing more than tradition; sometimes it was a long-established seigniorial right. Villagers were not supposed to send more cattle than they could feed with their own resources during the period the meadow was closed (i.e., after the harvest).[9] The 'useless' animals were kept out of the *gemene broek*: these were animals that were not useful for the family economy, they did not bring in meat or dairy products, nor were they useful as drag animals. Sheep for fertilizing were allowed on the pasture, but not breeding sheep. Male animals reserved for breeding were not regarded as useful and were thus kept out of the pasture. This rule can be found in other types of common land as well (Lindemans 1994, 334–6).

The bylaw of the Vrijbroek of Mechelen also mentioned that whoever wanted to put cattle on the *broek* had to have bought those cattle before Candlemas, preventing the grazing of cows that had been bought just before the opening of the pasture. It was possible to place a goose on the *broek* with as many goslings as the goose could hatch at a time. If a horse or cow died, the user could buy another one and put the replacement on the *broek* (Lindemans 1994, 334–6). Each year users had a meeting before the second half of March and elected four men who would be responsible for the management of the *broek* (Devos 1936, 31). Similar rules can be found for other *broeken* (see also the case study in this book).

2.2.1.3 Common woodlands

Because of the high value of woodland, local lords were more concerned about use-rights in woods than in non-wooded properties (Godding 1987, 201). After the massive wood clearances of the tenth and eleventh centuries, woodlands had become rare in the area of study, and the lack of woodland caused local lords in Flanders to severely limit local use-rights. In the southern part of the Southern Netherlands (present-day Wallonia), woodland was less scarce and more open to use by villagers. In these areas communal woodlands would remain pivotal to economic life until well into the nineteenth century (Lindemans 1994, 337). Such common woodlands, however, were scarce in Flanders, where most woods were private property.

In the south two broad categories of use-rights for wood could be identified. First, the *prélèvements*[10] which were an amalgam of all kinds of resources on which rested limited collective user rights, such as the right to collect dead wood, to chop wood, to collect humus (*strooisel*), and to mow grass for the cattle in the byre (*faucillage*); but they did include more

---

[9] See for some examples Lindemans (1952, 329, fn. 23).
[10] As common woodlands could mainly be found in the south of the Southern Netherlands, the terms are often only known in their French forms, which will be used here.

important uses, such as the right to collect firewood and construction wood of all kinds (*affouage*).

Second, there was the right to put cattle out to pasture in these woods. The pasturing of cattle was called *pacage* or *champiage* (for horses). In particular the *panage* or *paisson* (for pigs) caused a great deal of damage to the woodland. From the Middle Ages onwards but in particular under the reign of Charles V (1506–1555), these use-rights became increasingly regulated, whereby the central government tried to stop the abuses in the woods with many ordinances. The measures prohibited the pasturing of animals before the end of a specific period – generally a period of five to seven years after clearing the wood – in order to protect the young trees. This period could vary considerably according to the place and type of animal: for example, five years for horses and ten years for cattle. In the eighteenth century, regulation became stricter because of rising timber prices (Godding 1987, 202).

The users could only take wood for themselves and had to make their demands known to the forester, who would indicate the trees that could be cut down (*délivrance*). It was prohibited to cut more wood than necessary for housekeeping, construction works, or repairs. Firewood (*feuille*) was limited to a specific amount per household (not including dead wood). Selling wood, giving it away, or exporting it was prohibited (Lindemans 1994, 315).

2.2.2 Common arable land

In general, four types of common rights on arable land could be found in the area examined in this study. It is important to note that the arable land was not owned in common by a group of people, but by an individual. Arable land in fallow is also to be distinguished from common waste. Moreover, in Flanders the right to use common wasteland was not linked to other possessions (e.g., a farmstead or a plot of land) or rights to pasture cattle on common arable land, as, for example, in England (Winchester 2013).

After the harvest the village poor were allowed to glean the ears (*lezen van de aren, glanage*). The farmers were obliged to grant this right to the village poor, who generally used a scythe to harvest; the after-harvest could also be done using a wooden rake (*naharking*). After all the grain had been removed from the fields, villagers could let their cattle pasture on the stubble of the grains that had been harvested (referred to as *stoppelgang*) for a given period of time. This rule was mentioned in most village bylaws, which proves that *stoppelgang* was a general use. Contrary to the pasture on

The Dilemma of the Commoners

the fallow land, the *stoppelgang* only lasted for a few weeks. The fields that would be sown again had to be enclosed from a certain date onwards, depending on the type of grain (winter or summer). A handful of straw (a so-called *strowis, wiffa,* or *vreewis*) indicated where the cattle could not enter (Lindemans 1994, 352–3). The introduction of certain types of turnips and clover caused the *stoppelgang* to gradually disappear in Brabant and Flanders after the sixteenth century.

In general, the entire village community could pasture cattle on the arable land that lay fallow.[11] Any leftovers on the arable land were considered a common good. This was the case for the fields after the grain harvest, after the hay harvest, and in the woods after woodcutting. This right was called *droit de vaine pâture*, or *vrijgeweide*, and was based on a tacit agreement among farmers and cattle owners: the cattle could pasture from harvest until the land would be sown again, without having to take the limits of private property into account (Ruwet 1943, 189). The pastures along the riverside were often subjected to *vaine pâture* after the first mowing. An area of the grasses could be reserved for animals (horses, cattle) that needed rich feed; in that case, the animals were not allowed in the pastures until August.

Wherever this right existed, a clear distinction was made between the strictly private arable land and other parcels of private arable land where kinds of common pasture were allowed during specific time periods. The most important restriction for pasturing on arable land during its fallow season was the *vreetijd*: that period of the year when the fields were no longer accessible to cattle because they were cropped. It means 'the period during which the land is free [of cattle]'. This period was announced in church and generally began at the beginning or the second half of March and ended after the harvest. During the *vreetijd* the *veken* was hung.

The growing cultivation of fodder crops caused pasture on fallows to be abolished in many villages at the end of the late Middle Ages. In Flanders, this right had already been severely reduced in the Middle Ages, but in Haspengouw, Limburg, the southern parts of Brabant, Hainault, and Namur, this practice would remain important until the nineteenth century. In the eighteenth century, tenants tried to introduce cultivation of clover, but experienced strong opposition from other villagers. The villagers claimed to have the right to pasture their cattle on the clover. A decree of 1730 subsequently allowed tenants to sow two *bunders* (the equivalent of approximately 2.5 hectares) of clover and prohibited pasturing on these

---

[11] The term 'fallow' is used here to indicate that this was land that had been used as arable land before (as distinct from wasteland).

Common land and common rights in Flanders

plots. More decrees would follow restricting pasturing on fallow in order to protect the continuously expanding cultivation of clover. The province of Luxembourg, which had a very large surface of common land, prohibited this type of grazing as late as 1770 on enclosed fields, or fields sown with clover or lucerne (Lindemans 1994, 350–2). *Vaine pâture* did not disappear until the beginning of the twentieth century in the south of the Southern Netherlands (areas such as Entre-Sambre-et-Meuse, Condroz, Haspengouw, Famenne, and Ardennes) (M. De Moor 2003a).

In a few regions the right to pasture on growing grain was exercised. In the winter and until early spring, sheep and pigs could enter the grain fields. This usage was severely limited from the sixteenth century onwards. In 1711, a decree was promulgated by the Prince-Bishop of Liège forbidding pigs from entering fields with growing grain in Haspengouw and the surrounding areas for the period of 1 November to 1 March. Because this decree was ineffective, it had to be repeated in 1725. Only lambs and a few ewes were now allowed. A few years later, in 1734, the government had to concede to the resistance of the villagers and allowed pigs in the grain fields from mid-November until 1 March. Lambs were allowed to pasture on rye until the second half of April; pasturing lambs on wheat and spelt was allowed until 1 May (Lindemans 1994, 354).

This description of the regulation of commons in Flanders and its immediate surroundings shows that the use of land and resources collectively was strictly regulated already from the Middle Ages onwards, and that types of commons and the use-rights that were still in place depended greatly on the regional variety in natural resources but also on the technical progress of agriculture and in particular the relationship and balance between crop farming and husbandry. In some areas where agriculture was for its time highly advanced, collective use rights came much sooner under pressure. This demonstrates that the changes in the agricultural system and their effect on the farmers may be very important to understand – especially when interpreting the historical sources related to the case study – the behavior of the commoners on the common.

2.3 The evolution of the legal basis of common land

Over the past two centuries, (legal) historians have puzzled over the origins of common land. Especially in the context of disputes on property rights of common land at the end of the eighteenth and the nineteenth centuries, the question became particularly relevant as the government tried to privatize and clear all common land to increase national agricultural output and constantly increasing population. At that time so little was known about

The Dilemma of the Commoners

its juridical character that in 1757 the government was obliged to renounce the decision to sell common land in the region of Hainault (a province south of Flanders) because they were not sure whether they had the right to decide on this or not (Recht 1950, 9). Gaining insight into the genesis of common land is not insignificant, since it provides information about the relationship between commoners and external actors. In the first chapter I pointed to the broad societal factors (motors and conditions) that help to explain why institutions for collective action in general developed in north-western Europe. Here I give a more specific treatment of the origin of commons in this specific area.

Theories that claim common land in the Middle Ages descended from the old Germanic joint-ownership tradition are outdated. Such theories associate common land with the Germanic concept of movable (personal) property (e.g., clothing and jewelry); these were regarded as goods that formed personal wealth. Nonmovable goods, however, could not be sub-jected to personal appropriation, but only to collective appropriation, based on the principle that grass, air, water, and woods were free gifts of nature, which should be freely available for use by all men (Engel 1956, nr. 9, 32–55 and 178–205; nr. 10, 72–87; nr. 11, 72–89; Gilissen 1981, 598–9). In pre-feudal times the collective use of the *wastina* (uncultivated land) by members of the rural communities did not pose many problems. The low population density allowed everyone to provide for his needs.

Others believe that common land is related to changes in the domain structure of the early Middle Ages. The Merovingian domain was a terri-torial unit in the hands of a single person and was exploited by *mancipia*, persons without a farmstead, or *servi casati*, persons who owned a *casa* (house). In addition to arable and pasture land, a domain consisted of woodlands and wasteland. In exchange for their services to the lord, the *servi* received the use-right to the woodlands and wastelands: the *commu-nia* (Verhulst 1957, 93; Verhulst and Blok 1981, 169–78; Lindemans 1994, 408). In the early Middle Ages, the area of study where heath was later found, consisted mainly of woodlands. The transition to heath resulted from a degeneration process over several centuries by pasturing cattle in the woods. This process became typical for the Campine area and inner Flanders.

In the early Middle Ages, with the rise of the seigniorial system, the lords claimed the common land of the communities on the principle of 'no land without a lord'. The uncultivated land of the village that the inhabitants used in common were then called *vroengronden*, which means 'land of the lord'. *Vroente* became a widespread toponym for this type of land, especially in the Campine area/Duchy of Brabant where the toponym *gemeynte* could

74

Common land and common rights in Flanders

also frequently be found (Lindemans 1994, 357). *Vroente* refers directly to the *ownership* of the land, not to a specific type of resource; so it could refer to any kind of natural resource such as pasture land, heath, marshes, and meadows. Otherwise, especially in the County of Flanders, common land could be designated by a combination of the type of land (marsh, meadow, etc.) and the commonly used adjective *gemene*, which means 'common'. *Gemene* could be found in combination with words designating the natural state of the good in the Kempen as well: the words *aard*, *heide*, and *wildert* all referred to a type of land that could be used as a common.

From the eleventh and twelfth centuries, much uncultivated land was reclaimed. The reclamations had to provide for the population growth in the tenth and eleventh centuries. In the first stage of reclamation, the villagers dealt with small woods close to their settlements. The landlords did not interfere, as their interests were not yet at stake. From the second half of the twelfth century, cultivation concentrated on the extensive, uninhabited areas where privileged reclamation villages were formed. There, the lords allowed and often encouraged *hospites* willing to cultivate large parts of the *vroente*. Extensive areas were the lord's property either because they had belonged to his Carolingian predecessors, or because they had claimed the property rights (Van Looveren 1983b, 12). In dire need of money, the lords did not hesitate to sell pieces of these *vroentes*, from the beginning of the thirteenth century.

Not surprisingly this created conflicts between the lords and the villagers about rights to the common land, but the latter often gained their suit. The inhabitants of Oostmalle (Campine area/Duchy of Brabant), for example, had to defend themselves against the claims of the lords of the village, Willem van Berchem and Floris de Bie. These lords had used the common land for their own needs without the approval of the villagers. On 14 January 1430, the mayor, aldermen, and the city councilors of Antwerp, where the villagers gave notice of appeal, decided to reprimand the lords. Philip, Duke of Burgundy, confirmed this judgment in 1432 (Moeskop 1985, 3).

In inner Flanders and the Campine area, such conflicts often led to written agreements between the lord and villagers concerning the use of the common (Verhulst 1966, 101; Verhulst 1980, 13). Whereas custom law had thus far regulated the use and management of common land, written law would now become dominant. The villagers would often demand written acknowledgment of their use-rights, even if they had to reduce their claims and pay the lord an annual *cense* or *cijns* as recognition of his sovereignty. Such a written agreement was often the result of the settlement of a conflict. When handing over the letter containing the

The Dilemma of the Commoners

agreement (*vroentebrief*), the villagers had to pay a sum of money (*voorlijf*). Verhulst, Van Houtte, and others regarded such an agreement as confirmation of a situation existing since time immemorial times (Van Houtte 1964, 62; Verhulst 1966, 101).[12] According to Slicher van Bath (1960, 60), population growth led to a stricter and clearer regulation of the use of common land. Commons in Flanders and the Walloon region should not be considered as vestiges of earlier primitive agrarian communism, but as a reflection of the many changes that rural life was undergoing at that time. In addition to preventing and resolving conflicts, new regulations also had to be promulgated because increased numbers of users required some supervision in felling trees, mowing grass, and pasturing (Van Looveren 1983b, 12). A causal and not evolutionary explanation seems to work best to explain the commons' emergence.

It is often difficult to conclude based solely on language used in the bylaws whether these agreements concerned actual transfers of property by sale or donation, or whether they only concerned a transfer of use-rights. Several elements, however, indicate that it should be regarded as a transfer of use-rights. The contribution (whatever its magnitude) must be considered as a repetitive confirmation of the lord's sovereignty. Commoners also had to request that the lord confirm the sale or letting out of parts of the common. The village of Mol (Campine area), for instance, requested the sale of the *vroente* to pay off war debts and taxes. For each section of common land sold, the village had to pay a sum of money to the duke (Moeskop 1985, 18). Many other examples of requests for permission to sell sections of common land demonstrate that the lord had the final say but was limited in his choices by the villagers' demands.

The explicit stipulation in the bylaws that the lord would no longer make free use of the land is another element that set a limit to his power. This promise would be meaningless if a complete property transfer (sale) were the case (Droesen 1927, 26–9). This deal assured the commoners an undisturbed and (more or less) exclusive use of a well-defined area and protection against usurpation by foreigners. Nevertheless, the property rights of the lord to the *vroente* were limited: he could no longer change its use. The lord could not reclaim the land, deforest it, or establish ponds on it. However, he could keep the *altum dominium* of the common and delegate his bailiff (*baljuw* or *schout*) as the representative of his sovereign power. This officer had to make sure disputes among commoners and other

---

[12] Others regarded the abolition of serfdom as the main reason for the confirmation of common land as a common good. From the time the peasants received freedom in exchange for the obligation of paying taxes (levy), there was a clear split in the relationship between farmsteads and wasteland (Droesen 1927, 30).

Common land and common rights in Flanders

parties were resolved and that the lord would receive a part of the imposed fines. The lord and bailiff were also supposed to protect the commoners against the claims of others (Lindemans 1994, 309).

Agreements between lords and commoners could vary. Not all agreements can be regarded as a simple transfer of use-rights. Instead, the lord could lease the land to the community for a specific term (*vrointepacht*) (Godding 1987, 204). The inhabitants of Westmalle and Zoersel (Campine area) rented their *vroente* from 1682 onwards from the abbot of the Saint-Bernard abbey for a term of nine years. The abbot, however, reserved the right to about thirteen *bunders* (a *bunder* was a bit more than one hectare) for the abbey's use. The commoners were also obliged to plant trees in the *vroente*, even though they did not have the right to use the wood. Nor could they use the peat or the loam. Their rights were limited to pasturing their cattle, cutting turf (*schadden steken*), making hay, and using the acorns (Lindemans 1994, 310). In other cases, the lord and the villagers reached an agreement whereby the villagers could use part of the woods, by means of a *cense*, while the lord appropriated the other part (*cantonnement*) (Godding 1987). This indicates that a private property arrangement would also have been an available option, especially with rapid developments on the land market at the time (Van Bavel 2008a and 2008b, Schofield and Van Bavel 2009). This confirms again that behind the origins of the commons lay good reasons to choose a collective solution.

Some examples can be found of actual purchase of the common by the community so that the community received the full property rights (de facto and de jure). Duke John III sold the common land of Turnhout and Arendonk (Campine area) in the fourteenth century. In 1666, the community of Beerse bought the Abtsheide from the Cloister of Saint-Michaels (Moeskop 1985, 19). The removal of the annual *cense* indicates complete independence from the lord from then onwards. Such cases, however, are rare.

Just as historians cannot always clearly interpret the agreements and relationships between lords and commoners in the past, these agreements were also not always clear to contemporaries; ownership of the common land was often a subject of discussion. Agreements could be renewed or adjusted as a consequence of disputes. Renewals were performed from time to time because old documents had become unreadable. These renewals were also occasions for both parties to reassert their rights and to adjust some parts of the agreement that needed to be changed, for example, because of natural circumstances.

Ostrom (1990, 101) stresses that the successful functioning of institutions for collective action requires that the appropriators have the right to devise their own institutions and that external governmental authorities cannot challenge this right. As already pointed out, the relationship between the local lord and the commoners was regulated by the bylaws, in which the lord was assigned some rights and the rights of the commoners were established. The commoners recognized their lord's sovereignty (by means of an annual contribution), while the lord recognized the rights of the commoners. The lord sent his bailiff to keep an eye on the managers. The bailiff would intervene in conflicts and would in many cases claim part of the fines for his lord. Elaborations on the attributes discussed previously have shown that common land did not escape existing power relations. Although local lords challenged the commoners' rights from time to time, minimal recognition was generally guaranteed.

However, the agrarian depression of 1650–1750 in combination with the growth of the population changed the situation. A rise in grain prices and thus potentially higher earnings from arable farming could be expected; rents and land prices rose. It became more profitable to cultivate land of poorer quality (Slicher van Bath 1960, 247). Under the influence of these changes and of the Physiocratic ideas that flourished during the eighteenth century, the Austrian government moved to promote agricultural development and population growth by enacting ordinances for each province on the reclamation of infertile land. Raising the productive capacity of agriculture above subsistence level exploitation became a matter of prime political importance.

With the strengthening of the central government in the early modern period, the common land came increasingly under fire, and such recognition diminished. While before the eighteenth century this challenge was mainly a matter of rivalry on a local level (between lord and community, and in some cases between communities), the centralized government showed a greater interest in converting uncultivated land to arable land from the eighteenth century onwards. Before the second half of the eighteenth century, common land and the rights of commoners had primarily been threatened by local rulers, who acted independently. Thus far the central government had only played a passive role in the history of common land.

From the second half of the eighteenth century especially, the central government exercised great pressure on the provincial administration to promulgate a decree on the privatization and clearing of common land. The Austrian government was not inclined to maintain what they regarded as remnants of feudalism, and common use of land was regarded as an obstacle, no longer appropriate to a modern, rational agricultural policy: the government was convinced that it limited intensification of agriculture and

prevented personal initiative. The central government often acted in cooperation with, or according to the demands of, the provincial authorities,
thereby encouraging reclamation of wasteland. Stimulated by some prema-
turely acclaimed reclamation successes on poor sandy soil by a few private
enterprises, the Estates of Brabant – a sort of provincial government –
became interested in promulgating an ordinance to stimulate the reclamation of wasteland, as had been done before for the region of Hainault
(Willems 1962, 47–90). Though an inquiry among the officials in Brabant
on the desirability of such an ordinance showed that reclamation of common land would lead to great deprivation for many peasants and possible
disputes between lords and peasants, the Estates of Brabant nevertheless
decided to present their request to the central government (Tilborghs
1988, 310–4). The ordinance of Maria-Theresa of 25 June 1772 exempted
uncultivated land from public charges and exonerated their possessors from
paying tithes on the produce of these goods to the Duchy of Brabant.
Infractions committed on reclaimed land would be punished with a dou-
bling of the normal fines. Measures to achieve the forced sale of all uncultivated land, even that belonging to private persons, were taken. Whereas in
other provinces the initiative was taken by provincial institutions, this was
certainly not the case in the County of Flanders. On the contrary, several
members of the Provincial Estates opposed the proposition of the government to promulgate an ordinance similar to that of Brabant, which indicated, the importance common land still had, even in an area with one of
the most progressive agricultural practices of that time (Vandenbroeke
1975, 1; Van Houtte 1977, 201).[13]

The revolutions, wars, and strong resistance of commoners prevented
the ordinance of Brabant from having significant results. In nearly the
whole of the Noorderkempen (the northern part of the Campine area),
the ordinance was ineffective (Willems 1962, 206). Neither communities
nor private persons achieved successful reclamations. Of a total of 25,000
hectares of heath land, only 3,500 to 4,000 were eventually cultivated.
Villagers reacted fiercely to this ordinance because of the economic value
the heath still had for them. On the basis of their use since time immemorial, they claimed property rights on common land. These claims formed the
most important obstacle to cultivation (Willems 1962, 167–74).

During the last years of the Austrian reign (which ended in 1794), a lack
of experience in reclamations, technical problems, means of transport,

---

[13] For a description of similar difficulties and failure of governments to impose enclosures in
continental Europe, see, e.g., the case of the Netherlands in Hoppenbrouwers (2002,
106–7) and in Brusse et al. (2010, 209); a similar process is described for Scandinavia by
Olsson and Morell (2010, 335–7).

The Dilemma of the Commoners

and the war prevented any more attention being paid to reclamation (Van Looveren 1983a, 192). The new revolutionary French regime did not favor the nobility and clergy. The dissolution of convent communities brought an end to some important reclamations under the direction of the clergy (Vliebergh 1908, 149). The nobility lost all feudal claims to common land; the full property of these goods was assigned to the municipalities (Tilborghs 1987, 18). In 1796 the French laws had become legally binding for the former Southern Netherlands, which was now (until 1815) part of France. Consequently, the French law of 10 June 1793 (*Décret concernant le mode de partage des biens communaux*) became applicable to the area in question. This law assigned common land to the municipalities, and from that time it fell under the auspices of the municipality. The law also stimulated municipalities to sell and reclaim their common land. Some municipalities used these facilities to pay off their debts. In the *Code Civil* – introduced in 1804 – the term *communaux* (normally used to refer to common land) was explained as goods that were the property or produce on which the inhabitants of one or several communities had an 'acquired' right ('*à la propriété ou au produit desquels les habitants d'une ou plusieurs communes ont un droit acquis*' [art. 542 of the *Code Civil*]). Common land thus had to be regarded as the collective property of the users, the inhabitants, but as such it became the property of the municipality. The property rights of the inhabitants as formulated in article 542 were thus reduced to a *usufruct* in common (De Page and Dekkers 1975, 677). Based on documents proving centuries-old title, only a few common lands were not absorbed by the municipality. Those few remaining commons often became private property in joint ownership, a legal status that was, and is, characterized by very limited legal security, but which allowed commoners to use and manage the common as during previous centuries.

Under the Dutch reign (1815–1830), apart from the foundation of a few unsuccessful large-scale colonies of reclaimers, reclamation activities would be limited to the local level. In Brecht (Campine area), for example, a large area of the common heath was sold. In 1789 this municipality contained 1,756 hectares of arable land, and by 1835 it had already increased to 2,300 hectares (Vliebergh 1908, 154–5).

The impasse in government interference in reclamations ended a few years after the foundation of the Belgian state in 1830. After a few critical years, the Belgian economy entered on a phase of expansion from 1833 to 1835. Grain prices experienced a boom from 1834 to 1839; land prices rose quickly (Bublot 1957, 42). Thus far only measures such as the exemption of taxes had been used to stimulate privatization and reclamation of

Common land and common rights in Flanders

wasteland, but now new tools were introduced to get this process going. The backward economic and agricultural condition of the Campine area seemed a particular eyesore to the ambitious government. Several laws were enacted to encourage reclamation of the Campine area and to create a favorable investment climate. New initiatives were taken to construct roads, irrigation, canals, and depots to store fertilizers. The crisis in the 1840s and growing liberal dominance would accelerate this process.

The law of 25 June 1847 on the reclamation of uncultivated land (*Loi sur le défrichement des terrains incultes*) was promulgated in a period of deep social and economic crisis and was undoubtedly the most effective of its kind, not least because the government chose another strategy to dissolve the remaining commons.[14] Instead of 'carrots', as was the case with the eighteenth-century laws, 'sticks' were used to force the selling of land held in common. The law stipulated forced privatization of wastelands owned by municipalities or communities (in joint-ownership) and their alienation by the state in order to sell these lands in smaller plots. The state decided on the terms and conditions of sale. By that time most municipalities did not resist the sale of their common land, but in some municipalities (in parts of the Campine area and in some provinces in the south of Belgium) resistance of villagers to the sale of their common land would remain strong until the end of the nineteenth century (Van Looveren 1983b, 121).

In the province of Antwerp (formerly part of the Duchy of Brabant), many communities proceeded to sell their property. The law of 1847, in combination with other laws on irrigation and canalization, promised large subsidies and made the sale of thousands of hectares of wasteland in this province a speculative business, attractive to the bourgeoisie of the city of Antwerp. For instance, in the northeast of Antwerp province, the area of Turnhout, where large parts of common land could still be found at the time of the foundation of the Belgian state, there was a boom in prices for heath after the law of 1847 (Bublot 1957, 43). Consequently, the plots were mainly purchased by non-residents who were not even active in agriculture but belonged to the urban bourgeoisie. These high prices and the fact that heath was sold in large plots prevented local peasants from participating in the sale. In a few municipalities, the urban bourgeoisie remained absent because the local council decided to sell the commons in very small parcels to the advantage of the locals (Tilborghs 1988, 310–12). After these sales, nearly all common land would disappear gradually in the

---

[14] Around the 1840s a linen crisis broke out in Flanders. A few years later, during 1845–1847, several bad harvests threw Belgium into an even deeper crisis (Jacquemyns 1929).

The Dilemma of the Commoners

second half of the nineteenth century. Only a handful of commons survived until the present day owing to the stubbornness of their users and defenders.[15]

The dissolution of the commons in Belgium, which led to the land's privatization and partition in most cases, was not limited to Belgium but was a European-wide process, which in fact hit not only rural collective property but also other forms of collectivities, such as guilds (see also 1.1 in this book). The chronology of the attacks by regional and national governments against the survival of collective property provided by among others Demélas and Vivier (2003) shows the increasing activity of the national governments of France, Spain, Portugal, Italy, England, Germany, Switzerland, and others to design sticks and carrots similar to the ones used by the Belgian government – and its predecessors – from the middle of the eighteenth century. Their efforts met with varying success, but ultimately led to the near to complete extinction of commons by the end of the nineteenth century (Démélas and Vivier 2003; see also Brakensiek 2000 and Congost and Lana Berasain 2007).

Not surprisingly, commons have since disappeared more or less from the 'collective memory' of western Europeans as a whole, although this process of 'memory loss' does not necessarily go to the length or harshness of the process of enclosure of commons that has been witnessed in different varieties throughout Europe. Ironically, in England the enclosures started earlier and have been chronicled as harsh and merciless, but this did not lead to full eradication of the concept of common use and management. Enclosure of commons in England took off in the later fifteenth century, but continued thereafter until modern times.[16] In continental Europe, the population growth of the late fifteenth and sixteenth centuries did have an effect on further restrictions on commoners' use-rights, but the real enclosure process didn't start until much later, around the middle of the eighteenth century. Hoyle (2010) attributes this difference in temporization of the whole process to stronger peasant property rights, higher fragmentation of property rights, and the relatively small number of large farms in

---

[15] At present at least one common in the area of study has survived, namely the Gemene and Loweiden in Assebroek and Oedelem (east of Bruges). It measures about 100 hectares of pasture; more than 1,000 commoners are still entitled to and claim their use-right (by inheritance; see elsewhere in the chapter). Only a few commoners, however, actually use the common. In Limburg another smaller common of the eastern type has survived. In the southern part of Belgium, Wallonia, some woodlands are still governed by the local community as a common, meaning that the revenues of the leasing of the rights to collect or cut specific types of wood are distributed evenly among the inhabitants of the municipality to which the woodland belongs.

[16] For a description of this divergence in the process of enclosure between England and the continent, see Hoyle, 2010, 370–1.

Common land and common rights in Flanders

northwestern (contintental) Europe vis-à-vis the strong English land-holding elite that did not await a government-driven initiative – as was the case in the continental enclosure process – to enclose the land (Hoyle 2012, 370–1).

Although one could claim that the enclosure process in England was a more continuous threat to commoners' use-rights, many British villages today still have their common and today's national legislation actually provides the means to enable common management in the national legal framework (as in the Commons Act of 1965 and its follow-up in 2006[17]), which is rather exceptional within Europe. In comparison, the national laws that ended commons in northwestern Europe, such as in Belgium (1847) and the Netherlands (several laws, e.g., in 1811 and 1886),[18] seem to have been more effective in dissolving the commons, leaving hardly any trace of commons on the landscape or in the minds of their citizens, with the exception of a very small number of cases of commons that have survived until today.[19] The current national legislation does not give much room for collective resource management, nor are there any specific initiatives – such as the Commons Acts in the UK – that offer specific arrangements for the very few remaining historical commons in their original form of governance, or new forms of collective resource governance. One could say that overall there is little use for national legislation such as the UK's Commons Acts to enforce registration and protection of commons and their resources, as on the continent – in particular in the northwestern part of Europe – there has since the end of the nineteenth century simply been little left to register and protect in terms of commons. Since the economic crisis of the early twenty-first century, governments have started to consider collective resource man-agement and service provision as an alternative to market and state gov-ernance of goods and services (see the Epilogue) – but as an austerity measure rather than as a real alternative to governance through the state or market. New forms of institutions for collective action are hereby considered to be part of a new movement, rather than a revival of early modern forms of institutions.

---

[17] See http://www.legislation.gov.uk/ukpga/2006/26/contents for the complete over-view of the Commons Act of 2006. The Commons Act of 2006 was gradually brought into force throughout the UK from 2008 onwards.

[18] See the *Markenwet* of 10 May 1886, 'houdende bepalingen ter bevordering van de verdeeling van markgronden' ['containing measures for the promotion of dividing the marks'].

[19] See, e.g., the case dealt with in this book, and a number of other cases such as Wijkerzand (Hoppenbrouwers [2002], see also the case study at http://www.collec tive-action.info/_CAS_COM_NET_Wijkerzand).

83

The Dilemma of the Commoners

With most of the commons – and similar institutions – being as good as entirely eradicated by the early twentieth century, and with little attention since for the history of commons in continental Europe, new studies dealing with historical commons in both the northwestern and southern parts of Europe have appeared since the early twenty-first century (see, e.g., Demélas and Vivier 2003; Congost and Lana Berasain 2007; Alfani and Rao 2011), partly too as a consequence of the revived interest for commons in disciplines other than history, in particular political science, sociology, and ecology. The lack of interest in the study of common land in Belgium (and before, Southern Netherlands) contrasts with the elaborate research on the area's agricultural system and particularly (and most relevant for this study) the Flemish agro system, which has been underway ever since the 1990s.[20] Flanders was known for its very progressive, advanced agriculture in the late Middle Ages and early modern period, and this may have conveyed the impression that common land was either absent or unimportant in this area. Indeed, in some regions of Flanders – in particular those with intensive crop cultivation and subsequent early disappearance of the triple rotation scheme in crop production – common arable land had completely disappeared by the early modern period. However, in this overview of the literature on common land in Flanders, it has become clear that until the nineteenth century the commons as a governance system for natural resources (e.g., resources to be found on wasteland) still played an important role, especially in the northern part of Flanders.

2.4 Management of common land in Flanders[21]

The history of commons in Flanders clearly demonstrates how important the recognition and support of governments for commons as a valuable form of resource governance was for their survival. But equally important is how the common itself was managed, and whether it was regularly adapted to the changing circumstances, which could, as shown before, significantly affect the role of the common resources in the household economy of its members. Among the European – including the Flemish – commons there

---

[20] One of the main stimuli in this field has been the work by scholars within the so-called CORN-network (Comparative Rural History of the North Sea Area) that started in 1995 and has since produced several volumes on rural and agricultural history of mainly Belgium, the Netherlands, the UK, Ireland, and France (with some excursions into the surrounding areas such as Scandinavia and Germany).

[21] Only the attributes of common waste will be discussed here. The use and management of common woodlands was too different and would hardly be relevant for the area considered in this chapter.

are many good examples of extremely long-lived institutions, with flexible regulations.[22] In the following parts it will be explained what such regulations looked like.

The internal regulation of common land was organized on the basis of local bylaws (*keuren, aardbrieven*, or *vroenbrieven*). These bylaws were drawn up in the presence and with the approval of the villagers. They were announced again annually in the church or attached to the church door (*kerkgebod*) for all to take notice. During the public reading of the bylaws, it was possible to change or add chapters. If the document had become unreadable, it was copied. Apart from the bylaws, other regulations could be added in resolution books (*resolutieboeken*) and in other sources such as court rolls. The following explanations of common land management are essentially theoretical. Implementation of the rules must be derived from other sources such as accounts, and only few have survived the ravages of time; no other (nearly) complete series has been studied elsewhere.

The commons in the western part of Flanders had their own regulations, unlike the *aarden* in the Campine area, where in most cases a general ruling for all the common land in an extensive area was drawn up, applicable to the whole jurisdiction comprised of several villages. The common land of the communities of Mol, Balen, and Dessel (Campine area), for instance, was subject to the same bylaws; the bylaw of Westerlo was valid for several village communities that were part of the *vrijheid*. The specificity of the bylaws depended on the autonomy of the local communities. In Kasterlee (Campine area), for example, each hamlet had its own bylaw for its common (Moeskop 1985, 25–40; Lindemans 1994). This difference in the way in which commons bylaws were drawn up is not the only difference between cases in the eastern and western parts of Flanders. Commons in the western part, where the central case study in this book is situated, were often also substantially smaller and often had much stricter conditions for membership not related to residence in the village (see the overview in Table 1). In other countries, such as the Netherlands, similar differences existed: the *markegenootschap*, predominant in the northeastern part of the country, corresponded best to the associate-like structure of the commons in the western part of Flanders,[23] whereas the *meent* was mainly found in the southern part of the Netherlands, closer to the border with Belgium. The *meent* had similar features to the commons in the area around

---

[22] For an in-depth and detailed study of commons' regulation, in relation to their longevity, see Van Weeren and De Moor (2014).

[23] See, e.g., Marke Het Gooi, where common rights were transferred among a select group of farmers, the *Erfgooiers* (see Kos 2010).

Table 1 Overview of features of commons in the western versus eastern part of Flanders

West	East
• Small commons (100s of hectares) • Not all villages have a common	• Extensive commons (1,000s of hectares), often one large common for one village or even several villages (intercommoning) • Most villages have a common
• Access to the common often based on residence in immediate surroundings, or • Access on other, non-residence–related conditions	• Access on basis of residence in village or neighborhood
• Fenced with hedges or other means to demarcate the physical boundaries of the common • Demarcation often supplemented with references other than only village borders	• Open landscape • Village and neighborhood borders serve as demarcation, indicated with border stones
• Every common has its own regulation • Management by users themselves, though often in cooperation with local government	• Rules often are made for and applicable to several villages, and the regulation of the use and management of the common is part of the village bylaws • Management is often taken care of by local government

Antwerp, just across the Belgian border (see Table 1). Such a dual typology can be distinguished for commons in other European countries as well.[24] Table 1 shows the variety among the commons as an example of an institution for collective action, whereby the governance of the common is to some extent the consequence of the features of the resource: while it was easier to create boundaries around a small common, the common was more prone to overuse and thus required more intensive, direct resource management, and stricter control of access to resources. Larger commons

---

[24] See De Moor, Shaw-Taylor, and Warde (2002a) for an overview per country in western Europe.

Common land and common rights in Flanders

were less at risk of being overused, especially in a sparsely populated area such as the Campine, and could thus enjoy less strict resource management.

Considering the differences in size, scarcity of wasteland in an economy still dependent on mixed agriculture must have played an important role in the differences in management systems. As long as uncultivated land played a role in the village economy, it was equally subject to the laws of supply and demand, and thus to the laws of abundance and scarcity. Apart from being more dependent on common land, the villages in the Campine area had more isolated economies than those in the County of Flanders. Until the government began to invest in canals and road construction, transportation and communication in the Campine area were limited.

The complexity and variation of common land that we find within a relatively small area as in this part of Flanders must, however, temper Ostrom's model (Ostrom 1990). As Ostrom notes, complexity is a fundamental similarity shared by all commons, and variations in natural settings require rules to be tailored accordingly. For Ostrom, the differentiation of regulation is even a necessity for commons to be long enduring because they 'take into account specific attributes of the related physical systems, cultural views of the world, and economic and political relationships that exist in the setting' (Ostrom 1990, 89). Having to obey more general rules that were not adjusted to the setting of the common would have prevented the commoners from taking advantage of the positive and unique features of their common.

A possible explanation for the east/west-differences may perhaps be found in either the differences in local power relations or in the ratio of property holding to lease holding. For the nineteenth century, Vanhaute (1993) found a gradual geographical change, from a large proportion of individual holdings consisting partly, or even completely, of leaseholds in the west, to holdings mainly consisting of owned property in the east. The reflection of this in the strategy of farm management may be related to the greater availability of common land in the east compared to the west (Vanhaute and Thoen 1999, 77). The east-west model outlined here is only a steppingstone to help understand this complexity. Though common lands in the east were clearly more extensive and numerous, this model deserves more research, since it can provide a better understanding of the conditions leading to long-term changes in common land management.

The commons' bylaws that will be discussed in the next few paragraphs allow us to unravel the way common land was organized: the bylaws stated the administrative and geographical borders of the common, they ordered and prohibited what was deemed necessary, and they tried to prevent misbehavior by linking orders and prohibitions to fines. Hereafter, the

The Dilemma of the Commoners

regulation of the non-forested common land (*velden* and *broeken*), especially in the most northern, sandy part of Flanders (the Campine area and the sandy area around Bruges) will be discussed. The common land as just described is in general accords with Ostrom's definition of a Common-Pool Resource and as will become clear also complies with the design principles (Ostrom 1990, 90).

2.4.1 Boundaries of common land

Ostrom stresses that the boundaries of the common, as well as the individuals or households who had rights to withdraw resource units, had to be clearly defined (Ostrom 1990, 91–2). Although overall access to commons in Europe was restricted to specific groups in society, there were regional variations. In the west of Flanders, for example, the boundaries of the common land were very clearly circumscribed in the bylaws, often demanding that several conditions be met before access could be granted. Apart from referring to the border of another village, the bylaws also referred to farmsteads, castles, roads, and other elements to clarify the boundaries of the common. Compared to common land in the east of Flanders, most notably in the Campine area, the area of the commons in the West of Flanders was limited and more clearly demarcated: some hundreds of hectares, often fenced in, compared to several thousands of hectares of heath without any physical boundaries in many villages in the east. While in the east (Campine area) practically every village, or even hamlet, had its own common, in the west commons were not so frequent or widespread. Not only the boundaries of the common, but also the area wherein the products of the common could be consumed, were often clearly defined. Prohibitions on export of milk from a cow that had pastured on the common or on the sale of peat cut on the common restricted commercialization of the common goods. In some cases the sale of products derived from commons use was absolutely forbidden.[25]

---

[25] See, e.g., Vrijgeweid of Donkt (Beveren-Oudenaarde): 'Belovende oec deselve gasten dat, zoo wye van huerlieder beesten voeren sal up deselve meersch om van dien melc te vercoopen sonder oerlof ... deselve sal verbueren de peine van III s., ende dat sal men niemende gedoghen, ten es dat de selve zoe cleine es van werlijcken goede dat behoert van zijne, anghesien de baerlijcke armoede ende necessiteit' [Trans.: 'The same guests [i.e., non-entitled users] also promising that, in case we will lead their animals on to the marshland mentioned earlier in order to sell the milk produced by these animals unauthorized, the same person will be fined three *stuivers*, and no one should allow this [to happen], unless the offender has so little wealth that he is forced to so out of poverty' (Lindemans 1994, 333). And consider Maleveld, 1717: the peat dug at the common could not be sold nor transported out of the jurisdiction. After breaking this rule three times, the commoner would even lose his right (Errera 1891, 215–16).

Common land and common rights in Flanders

Hereafter, the numerous conditions for access to common land mentioned in the bylaws in Flanders will be divided into basic conditions and supplementary conditions. Basic conditions are the minimal conditions that had to be met to be a member, but such variations could be found across the relatively small area included in this analysis. The supplementary conditions were only gradually introduced over the life of a common, in order to restrict access further.

2.4.1.1 Basic conditions of access to the common

Two types of basic conditions relevant to the area discussed can be found, namely, place of residence and (direct or indirect) descent from entitled persons. These basic conditions were absolute: either you were an inhabitant or a descendant, or you were not. But there was a way around these conditions: a person could move to a village and become an inhabitant, but rights to a common could often only be obtained after a few years of residence. In case of descent, it was sometimes also possible to obtain use-rights by marrying a person from an entitled family. As will be demonstrated in the case study, it is not unlikely that common rights were part of the motivation for marrying a female descendant, but often the rights of in-laws were also limited.[26]

Place of residence was the most commonly indicated condition for use of common land. A distinction must be made here between the common land in the east of the area of study (Campine area/Duchy of Brabant) and that in the west (around Bruges/County of Flanders). Whereas being entitled to use the common in the Campine area was mostly limited to the inhabitants of one or several clearly defined hamlets or villages, in the west commoners had to live within a certain area (*vrijdom*) drawn around the – usually relatively small – common. In the Campine area, the common was in most cases so extensive that circumscribing a *vrijdom* would have been meaningless. It should be stressed, however, that in the County of Flanders common land where the inhabitants did not have to belong to a *vrijdom*, but simply to a hamlet of a village, could be found as well. In many cases the inhabitant also had to be a resident for a certain period of time, for instance, three full consecutive years, before being allowed to take up the right. In other cases immigrants had to pay a sum of money before

---

[26] Casari, for example, describes how, in the first half of the seventeenth century, an egalitarian inheritance system for commons membership rights offered the chance to marry a member of a wealthy community, thus promoting access to collective resources of the rich community and the possibility of transmitting this right to descendants (see Casari and Lisciandra 2010; 2011).

The Dilemma of the Commoners

being allowed to claim their rights to the local common (Van Looveren 1983b, 37; Moeskop 1985, 64).

Being a direct descendant of an entitled person was in some cases a condition of being allowed to use the common. For instance, in the case of the common Gemene and Loweiden in Assebroek and Oedelem (east of Bruges), both the sons and daughters of entitled persons could claim the right. The daughters, however, could not take up their right personally; they could only pass it on to their husbands and children. When the wife died, the husband lost his rights; the children, however, remained entitled (see the case study, point 3.1). A similar system could be found in the Vrijbroek in Mechelen (Malines), where the names of the persons to whom the common was originally granted were mentioned in the deed of donation. All their lawful heirs would be entitled to use the common thereafter, on the condition of paying an annual *cense* (De Vos 1937, 30). It is probably not a coincidence that these two cases are examples of *broeken*, pastures where nutritious feed for cattle could be found, whereas such rules were often not found on the eastern, usually poorer wastelands. The strict limitation of the number of users of the common may also indicate that the scarcity of an asset leads to a more restricted access rules.

2.4.1.2 Supplementary conditions for access to common land

Besides these basic conditions we can, however, also discern additional supplementary conditions. Such conditions are relative, as they refer to variables that have to be supplemented with a quantitative specification; for example, a certain amount of money had to be paid before the person became entitled.[27] Socio-economic conditions and financial conditions are the two main types that can be found in this area.

In general, socio-economic conditions can be subdivided into possession of land, possession of cattle/small livestock (Moeskop 1985, 63; Godding 1987, 201), and other socio-economic factors (e.g., paying taxes). Socio-economic conditions could be defined at the advantage of the rich as well as the poor. Both types can be found in the area of study. The poor could merit use on the basis of their poverty; many cases refer to this condition. But what is poverty? Evaluating the degree of poverty or wealth of commoners can only be done in light of the general socio-economic circumstances of the direct surroundings of these commoners. An indicator of the relativity of poverty can be found in the regulation of the Maleveld (east of

---

[27] Whether the payment of a membership fee was needed depended on the local 'access rules'. In some cases being a villager was sufficient to claim rights; elsewhere being a tenant would have given access rights. For a discussion of access rights within northwestern Europe, per country, see the different chapters in De Moor, Shaw-Taylor, and Warde (2002a).

Bruges, County of Flanders): only poor households (*aerme huisgezinnen*) could use the field for pasturing their cattle. The persons we would consider as the real poor (i.e., those without any cattle) were not allowed to use the resources (Errera 1891, 307). This example shows that limits could be set to keep the poorest of the village out of the common. The wealthier among the inhabitants were identified by the fact that they possessed horses. But examples can also be found where those who had horses – by definition the wealthier members of society – could not claim any common rights.[28] Nevertheless, in many cases the poor and the rich could both use the same common, which led to often very heterogeneous groups of users (see also the case study).

Even if a person met all basic conditions and supplementary conditions, he could still be asked to meet several additional financial conditions. Here we can distinguish between the once-only contribution when being accepted as a commoner and the yearly contributions that depended on the number of cattle pasturing on the common. The management of a common did cost money, which could be raised through commoners paying taxes (the yearly *cense*), digging ditches, repairing fencing, and so forth. In several cases new commoners paid a small, once-only sum of money when they claimed their rights. Often a yearly contribution per number of head of cattle (with different sums for each kind of cattle) was also demanded (see the case study).

2.4.2 Regulation of the use of common land

The rules regulating actual use of common land were numerous and consisted of three major elements: the type of resource the rule referred to; an order or a prohibition concerning the use (dos and don'ts) including specifications of the time, place, technology, and quantity of resource units; and finally the fine that would be imposed if the order or prohibition was ignored.

The severity of the restrictions and the accompanying sanctions were often related to the type of resource they were supposed to protect, whether it was a depletable or non-depletable resource. The cutting of peat, which was a resource that can be considered as depletable as it regenerates very slowly and which was used by households as fuel, was strictly regulated. Each household could cut a limited number of pieces in a certain time period. In the Maleveld, for example, a maximum of 8,000 pieces a year was

---

[28] For example, a regulation of 1717 for the Maleveld (east of Bruges) stipulates that those who had a horse would be excluded from the use of the common (Errera 1891, 307–11).

The Dilemma of the Commoners

stipulated for each household, or two households with one fireplace.[29] Before starting to cut the peat, the local manager (*hoofdman*) had to be informed. Peat cut in a common could not be sold to strangers, though the peat cutting itself was sometimes leased out (Moeskop 1985, 33). Turf was another resource intensively used by the locals for roofs or as stable litter.[30] The reclamation of sand (for road construction) and loam (for floors, walls, brick making, etc.) was regulated in a similar way as peat, but given their widespread availability regulations for these resources were not as frequent.

With regard to cattle breeding, the common had a double function. On the one hand, it provided feed for the animals: depending on the type and condition of the common, some animals were allowed and others were excluded (e.g., usually no horses older than one year of age, nor oxen older than two years were allowed). Pigs were generally not welcome on the common because they rooted up the ground; a ring through their nose served to prevent this. Pigs and geese might have to wear a *kennef* too, a kind of harness made of three wooden sticks around the neck of the animal to prevent them from breaking into the surrounding enclosed properties. In the Campine area, heath was predominant. The grasses that grew on heath made especially good feed for sheep, and thus sheep were ubiquitous. In the west, however, sheep were rare and in some cases even forbidden.[31] On the other hand, the cattle produced valuable manure, which was gathered. The cattle spent nights and winters in stables where the manure was absorbed by stable litter and turfs that had been gathered and cut at the common. This phenomenon – typical for the Campine area – was referred to as *potstal* (Lindemans 1994, 349). This valuable compost was introduced to the poor soil, making it more productive. Sheep played the leading part in this process and in the Campine area economy overall, as they provided wool for the proto-industry.

In addition to the more general prohibitions, many supplementary rules were needed to prevent cattle from damaging the common and surroundings. For example, cattle had to keep a certain distance from neighboring lands,[32] animals infected with certain diseases could not pasture on the common (Lindemans 1994, 334), cows that had not calved that year or had become sterile could not enter the common (Berten 1907, CXXXIV), and only animals that could serve a useful purpose (e.g., cows used for dairy production) could be pastured.

---

[29] Maleveld, Resolutieboek, 1710–1726, fol. 68, nr. 1
[30] Turf stands here for the upper layer of the heath land.
[31] On the Maleveld, sheep were forbidden (Maleveld, art. 6. Resolutieboek, 1710–1726, fol. 68, nr. 1).
[32] Maleveld, art. 5. Resolutieboek, 1710–1726, fol. 68, nr. 1.

Common land and common rights in Flanders

Limitations on personal use such as mentioned earlier would have been ineffective if the total use remained unregulated, as strict conditions of access to the common in combination with limitations of personal use could be unsatisfactory under pressure of a fast-growing population. Therefore, not only the rules concerning individuals might have to be changed from time to time, but the total number of resources permitted to the commoners could also be cut back. In Mol (Campine area), for example, in 1631 the total number of sheep was limited to 100 (Knaepen 1982, 265). Such limitations on the number of parts of a resource that could be consumed per individual user were common.

Ever-recurring elements in the regulation of the common land were rules preventing commercialization. On the Maleveld (Flanders) it was forbidden to transport peat dug on the common out of the jurisdiction of the seigniory (Errera 1891, 310). In Donckt (Flanders) it was forbidden to sell the milk of animals pastured on the common without the approval of the priest and the other managers (Errera 1891, 338). Only those animals that had been in the stables of the commoner during wintertime were allowed. If this was not the case, it was assumed that the animals were not the property of the commoners (Errera 1891, 334–5).

Despite these rules that had to limit the potential commercialization of common goods, common land may not be regarded as functioning outside the market system. It is important to understand that in this area common land formed a vital link in the local (both agricultural and proto-industrial) economic system. Arable land depended on the turf and fertilizer from the common; local proto-industry depended on sheep. In fact, the absence of a restriction on the export or sale of wool from sheep pastured on the common suggests that common land did not stand outside the local economy and was more market-related than often suspected. Good management through anticipation of possible excessive exploitation assured a balance between sustainability and economic/market-related use.

2.4.3 Managers and monitors of common land

The commoners realized that management and monitoring was essential to the survival of the common. With the term 'managers', I refer to commoners who took care of the long-term well-being of the common; they were supposed to set strategies, make plans, and ensure these plans were carried out. Monitoring was the day-to-day control of what happened on the common. A monitor was empowered by the managers to interfere

The Dilemma of the Commoners

when the regulations were not met and take measures if needed. Management and monitoring tasks were divided among a great number of commoners. In this complex 'government of the commons', loyalty had to be shown to the lord and his representatives. The actual users, the commoners, played a complementary role in this government. They could suggest changes, turn in miscreants, and, by simply using the common, exercise social control. The division of tasks and the possibilities for the commoners to interfere probably created the internal enforcement and assured quasi-voluntary compliance that Levi (1988, 52–3) referred to as the 'contingent strategy' (see also Ostrom 1990, 95). The division of tasks suggests that this contingency not only existed mutually among commoners but also among those who had a specific task. It is not clear whether this division of tasks made management and monitoring costs higher than the exploitation costs of private property.

In both east and west Flanders, several persons and groups of people could act as managers. As in the surroundings of Bruges, management was implemented by a group of people elected from among the commoners (Godding 1987, 200; see also the case study). Managers were elected by the commoners themselves and in consultation with local rulers. They were called *hoofdmannen, regeerders, donkmeesters, heirnismeester*, and so on, and could vary widely in number: whereas the management of the Beverhoutsveld (east of Bruges) was performed by thirteen people (each of the three involved villages had the right to send a number of men, proportionate to their share in the common), the nearby, smaller Maleveld did this with three men.[33] The number of managers needed depended on the extent of the common. Their term of service varied from one to three years; they were either compensated in kind for their efforts, or were paid a yearly fee.[34] The managers of the Maleveld (east of Bruges), for example, received 2,000 peat cuts more than the other users.[35]

The managers in the Campine area were referred to as the *gezworenen* (sworn members), and were delegates from each hamlet that belonged to the community. They were chosen by the aldermen of the community and had to take an oath before the bailiff. As elsewhere, they had the right to change regulations at their own discretion (Moeskop 1985, 45).

---

[33] Ibid.

[34] By the end of the eighteenth century, payment in kind is often substituted by a sum of money (De Moor and Debbaut 2003).

[35] Ibid.

Common land and common rights in Flanders

The managers in both east and west had to swear an oath to the lord and had to report problems to the bailiff (e.g., Van Speybrouck 1884, 177). They swore:

1. to keep the common in good state of repair and defend the rights, privileges, and liberties of the users on all occasions;
2. to observe the laws, customs, and usages of the domain;
3. to do justice and pass equitable judgment on all infringements and misdeeds, to fine delinquents, and to do everything supposed to be the duty of good and loyal administrators.

They kept an eye on the carrying capacity of the common: if the common was in danger of being used too intensively, they set a limit to the total number of resource units (cattle, peat, etc.) that could be used that year.

The bailiff would come around for an annual inspection (*schouwdag*) with the managers to check whether the agreement with the lord was observed. The managers were also obliged to organize an annual meeting of the commoners. General meetings were on the one hand meant to register and tally the cattle each commoner would pasture on the common the forthcoming year. On the other hand, it was also an opportunity (as was the annual inspection in some cases) to propose changes in the regulation (Moeskop 1985, 58; Lindemans 1994, 320) and discuss these with all the stakeholders. This meeting was not just a formality to the commoners: it could be explicitly mentioned in the bylaw that the annual meeting was meant to assure good maintenance of the common.[36] Commoners could clearly influence operational rules, although the managers, who had a mandate from the commoners and the agreement of the lord, probably introduced most of the changes.

Other persons (such as the *rendant* or *zavelmeester*), selected among the commoners, dealt with the administration. They oversaw the accounts of the common land, which had to be submitted to the commoners and the delegate of the lord for inspection, and they could summon the commoners for compulsory labor.

As Ostrom wrote: 'The presence of good rules ... does not ensure that appropriators will follow them, nor does the initial agreement explain the continued commitment' (Ostrom 1990, 93), commoners and lords

---

[36] In the *keure* of the Gemene and Loweiden of Assebroek and Oedelem one could read ' ... ende dat ghemeene dinghen niet goedelickx en moghen onderhouden syn ende bewaert, sonder daerinne te stellen ordine en policie, hebben van alle tyden hier voortytd ghewoont hemlieden te vergaderen eens t'siaers ... ' [Trans.: 'and [since] common resources may not be maintained and kept properly, if no order and policy would be established, it has always been customary to have an assembly once a year.'] (Andries 1879, 151).

The Dilemma of the Commoners

realized that a system of rules was only the basis of a properly functioning common, complemented by a system of sanctions. The policing of the common land was undertaken by a *schutter* or *veldwachter*, who had the right to lock up (*schutten*) any animal that was illegal on the common land. They were appointed by the managers (*hoofdmannen, gezworenen*) and received a salary (Moeskop 1985, 47–8) and/or part of the fine. They could be fined if they were found to neglect their duties, but could also count on the protection of the lord as well. Anyone trying to hinder the monitor in his work, or offend or threaten him, could be fined (Moeskop 1985, 51). In some cases the *schutter* was accompanied by a *vorster* or *sargant*: a law officer who was responsible for setting the fine, though in small communities the *schutter* and *vorster* were the same person and sometimes these *vorsters* fulfilled the function of bailiff as well.

Depending on the form of the rule, offenders had to pay a sum of money, but could also lose their rights on the common or be brought before court. Sanctions were at times graduated, depending on the type and number of infringements. For example, those commoners of the Maleveld who exported peat out of the jurisdiction of Male would receive a fine of four pounds on the first infringement, six pounds on the second, and would lose their rights on the third. Bringing in illegal animals or too many animals would result in a fine that had to be paid each time the infringement took place, the amount of the fine varying for each kind of animal. The monitors locked the animals in a cage (*schutte, bocht*, or *schutkooi*) until the guilty party paid the fine plus the cost of locking up the animal and payment for the damage caused. These costs varied, depending on the animal involved and sometimes on the time of the year. Examples can be found of common land where a higher fine had to be paid depending on the hour of the day (nightly infractions were punished more severely). If the culprit refused to pay the fine, his animals would be kept in the cage until an arrangement was made, either by mutual agreement or in court. If the animals were released earlier, the monitor had to pay the damages himself. To prevent the animals being left for too long in the cage, fines were systematically raised. If the owner did not show up at all, the animals could be publicly auctioned (Moeskop 1985, 49–52).

The commoners were also involved in monitoring, as they were supposed to make sure no infringements took place to the disadvantage of the community. The commoners were allowed to make accusations (*calengieringen*) (Moeskop 1985, 59; see also the discussion of liability clauses in point 1.4.2). Indeed, they were probably the best qualified to make sure that no strangers from other villages used the common, but of course abuse of this system was also possible.

2.5 Conclusions

On the basis of the analysis of common land in the sandy area of (present) Flanders, some general conclusions can be drawn about the regulation of commons. First, in setting out the attributes of common land in Flanders, I have repeatedly drawn attention to differences between two types of common land (see Table 2). Drawing on the bylaws, the common land in the area of research was allocated to these two types on the basis of several criteria. The first criterion was the noticeable difference in the physical nature of the land: limited plots, often fenced in, versus large plots without clear physical boundaries. A second criterion was the difference in access to the land: limited access versus access for all inhabitants of the village. Another criterion was the variety in management that was undertaken by people with different positions in the village: managers elected mainly out of the group of users versus managers mainly chosen from among members of the local government. These differences were regionally concentrated: common land in the west showed the characteristics of a more closed common as opposed to the eastern open type. The fact that the managers of the common land in the east were part of the local government supports the impression that common land was more central to the village economy and political structure in the east than in the west. In the east, the entire community of a hamlet or village was usually closely associated with the common land, while in the west a commoner had a more exclusive status. On the whole it should be stressed that, although within Flanders there seems to be an east-west pattern – with more closed

Table 2 Features of closed versus open types of commons

Features	Variables	Type of Common	
		Closed Type	Open Type
Physical and technical features	Surface	Limited	Extensive
	Divisibility of the area	High	Low
	Demarcation and fencing of the area	Strong	Weak
Limitations on access		Strong	Weak
Limitations on sue		Weak	Strong
Organization management and monitoring	Division of labor	Weak	Strong
	Degree of autonomy of decision process	Strong	Weak

The Dilemma of the Commoners

types in the west, and more open types in the east – this is also a European-wide pattern. There were concentrations of open and closed types of commons elsewhere too.[37] In the northeastern part of the Netherlands, for example, the commons (*markegenootschappen*) can also be categorized as closed types, whereas in the south, the commons (*gemeynten*) would be of the open type and decidedly resemble the *meenten* on the other side of the border, in the Flemish Campine area. It also shows that the specific physical and technical features of a common – surface, divisibility, demarcation, and fencing – go together with other features of the governance system. It demonstrates how important balance is among all elements of a common, a subject that will also be dealt with further in this book. In cases of physically open commons, it becomes difficult to limit access, but it becomes even more important to restrict use and closely monitor this, with a clear division of labor among all the stakeholders. In turn, this can negatively affect the level of autonomy of the decision-making process, with more interference of local powers and fewer decision-making powers for users who had no political influence. In the case of closed commons, which are often of relatively small size, it is easier to keep the monitoring within the group, although as we will see with the case study even closed types of commons do resort to external monitoring if they are no longer able to take care of this themselves.

It is tempting to claim that commons 'naturally' evolve from an open to a closed system, over time, under the pressure of population growth. One could logically assume that open systems 'close' their boundaries in order to counter the effects of an increasing population. But although overall population growth does play a major role in explaining the emergence of institutions for collective action both in towns and countryside, it does not seem to have had a decisive influence on the variation between open or closed commons across, for example, the Low Countries. We can easily categorize both the Dutch *markegenootschappen* and the commons around Bruges as closed commons, but the former are situated in a much less densely populated area than the latter. Moreover, a change in one domain

---

[37] Errera already described the first 'closed' type in 1891 in his work *Les masuïrs*, assuming these *masuïrs* were somehow related to the Dutch *marken*, without however mentioning that other kinds of common land could be found elsewhere in Belgium/Flanders. According to Droesen (Droesen 1927, 31–5), the open type could especially be found in the Campine area and Ardennes (which is rather strange since Errera described the common land in the south as *masuïrs*, which belonged to the group of closed common land), but he did not mention any regional concentration of the other type.

Common land and common rights in Flanders

of the common's functioning does not necessarily require that the whole system change. This suggests that other factors are at play as well, and that the actual functioning of a common and how factors such as changes in the population pressure are dependent on how such changes can be 'internalized' within the system, how the commoners and the chosen managers deal with such threats, and whether they were able to adjust the behavior of their members to these changes so that the internal balance was kept. In order to understand the mechanisms behind the management and use of a common, and how commoners applied it in such a way that commons survived literally for several centuries – that they were sufficiently robust to survive crises, wars, and conflict – I will analyze one specific case study in depth, and apply a framework that should enable us to capture the key drivers that explain the robustness of commons.[38]

---

[38] Most of the Dutch *markegenootschappen* date back to the early modern period, or even to the late Middle Ages and had a life span of several centuries, sometimes even up to half a millennium (see J. Van Zanden 2005, T. De Moor 2013, Van Weeren and De Moor 2014). Some of those, such as the Wijkerzand, still exist today (see Hoppenbrouwers 1993; 2007; see also, e.g., the case study on http://www.collec tive-action.info/_CAS_COM_NET_Wijkerzand).

3. From rules to practice: case description, sources, and methodology

In the previous chapters it was repeatedly stressed that commoners closely watched the changes in their environment and integrated such changes in their regulation. The change in commons' use and management was described on the level of the common as an institution. Considering that solutions to social dilemmas always need to deal with short-term investments versus long-term outcomes, the solution itself must have a long lifespan so that investments can be won back. Resilience thus not only becomes a result but also a goal in itself, driven by the desire of those involved to be able to reap their investments over the long term. What drives these commoners in their management, which values are essential to understanding the decisions they took, is key to understanding commons. An insight into these individual incentives will demonstrate this. The first part of this chapter will be devoted to describing the case, giving the necessary historical background on its origins and its functioning, and providing a description of the types of historical sources that are available for the case study. Thereafter, on the basis of the existing literature on commons, a number of factors that can help us to unravel the dynamics of the commons, and changes driven by evolutions in the composition of the group of commoners and their behavior, will be presented.

3.1 Case study: the common of the Gemene and Loweiden in the villages of Assebroek and Oedelem, Flanders

The common of the Gemene and Loweiden was a collection of several pastures used and governed by one group of commoners, the so-called *aanborgers*. Its form and organization show it is a typical closed common (see also Table 2 in Chapter 2), in which membership was restricted to a group other than that of the villagers; this group was also in charge of managing and monitoring use, with – at least until the second half of

Figure 3 The Gemene and Loweiden as presented on the detailed maps of Count Ferraris, 1777

Source: Fragments of pages 14 (*Bruges*) and 24 (*Damme*) of the Kabinetskaart van de Oostenrijkse Nederlanden [Cabinet card of the Austrian Netherlands] (combination of fragments by the author), produced by Joseph-Johann-Franz, count of Ferraris, 1770–1776 (original scale 1:11,520). Royal Library of Belgium, Brussels, Maps and plans, Ms. IV.5.567.

the nineteenth century – little involvement of the local government. It was a relatively small common, approximately 80 hectares, and its natural resources did not differ significantly from others in the sandy area around Bruges (in Dutch: *De Brugse Veldzone*), which were largely woodland and pasture land, much of which was used in common. Most of these commons were referred to as *veld* (to name just a few: Beverhoutsveld, Bulskampveld), because of the (poor) pasture land, often overgrown with heath and bracken. The case study dealt with in this chapter is different in the sense that it was for the most part a meadow with excellent grass for the commoners' cattle and horses.

The origins of this institution lie in 'time immemorial' ('*immemoriale tijden*'), but the oldest set of extant regulations regarding the Gemene and Loweiden dates from 23 June 1514 and is referred to as the '*Costumen ende Ordonnantien vande Ghemeene weede van Assebrouck*' [Trans.: 'The customary rights and ordinances concerning the common of Assebroek'], making it clear that the common originally consisted of just the Gemene Weide, and that, in time, other parts, such as the Loweiden, were added.

According to the same charter the Gemene Weide of Assebroek was situated 'near Bruges within the parish of Assebroek, adjacent to [the land of] Fernane Couteberch at one side, at the other side bordered by the Brugse Leie, running between the church of Assebroek and the abbey of Saint Trudo, all belonging to the seigniory of Sijsele' (De Moor and

Debbaut 2003, 11; translation by author). As Figure 3 demonstrates, the largest section of pasture land (commonly referred to as Gemene Weide) was in the south, bordered by a small river called Sint-Trudoledeken, named after the nearby abbey and which in wintertime often flooded the pasture land. The alluvial sediments left on the pasture land enhanced the quality of the grass, but during most of the winter periods the pasture was not fit for grazing. In years with serious flooding, the opening of the pasture period had to be postponed for a few weeks.[1] These regular floodings made the land periodically too wet and hence unfit for continuous use as arable land and made this land a good candidate for collective use and management, which would allow the users to spread the risks among all members of the group. The risks of losing the investments in crop cultivation were too high; pasture land was a less-labor– and less-capital–intensive way of using the land. In the case of this common, the pasture land was also particularly good, due to the floods that left behind alluvial land on which grass would grow abundantly. At the same time, use of such good grassland would also benefit the arable land via the manure produced by the cattle. By joining forces, the commoners could thus avoid high and unpredictable individual costs while receiving individual benefit from their collective efforts. Moreover, thanks to the combination of several plots of pasture land, which were not all at risk of flooding, the risk itself was not only spread over time but also in space: cattle that temporarily could not pasture close to the river would have the opportunity to graze elsewhere, although the total amount of resources available at that time would have been less. By combining these risks and opportunities, the common land offered a relatively secure additional income for each individual commoner who used the common.

Although the preceding explanation would be the most logical in economic terms, the most commonly told story to explain the origins of the common is quite different and altogether 'juicier'. The legend that nowadays is told about the origins of the Gemene and Loweiden goes back to the thirteenth century, when a young unmarried girl of noble descent by the name of Isabella van Beveren was rumored to have donated the pastures to the villagers living around the common as an act of revenge. The story is that after she had lost both her parents, she was raised by family members who had their eyes on her property. They had the girl sterilized – we do not have any details on how this might have been done in those times – in order to prevent her property from being inherited by another family upon marriage. The young lady found out about this and took revenge by giving away all her property. Those living

---

[1] See a complete description in De Moor and Debbaut (2003, 7).

From rules to practice

around the pasture in Assebroek received the perpetual use-rights on what they then called the Gemene Weide. As an act of gratitude the commoners still commemorate the young Miss van Beveren every year – to the present day(!) – with a special church Mass.[2]

3.1.1 *The rights and duties of the* aanborgers

Apart from the vast stretches of heath in the Campine area, north of Antwerp, and in the province of Limburg, this area around Bruges was the last area of Flanders where large plots of common land were still found until the middle of the nineteenth century. Access in the west of Flanders was, however, often more strictly regulated. In the area around Bruges, access was usually based on a number of conditions, of which descent from a number of 'original' families could be one.[3] The way commons were organized in this area was not fundamentally different from elsewhere in Flanders or for that matter Europe, notwithstanding the usual local variety.[4]

Membership in the Gemene and Loweiden was strictly regulated and limited by inheritance.[5] Only those able to prove that their ancestors or their wives had been registered as commoners in the past – even if that had been a long time ago – could claim membership. The oldest charter with rules of the common (1514)[6] indicates that initially women were not excluded from membership, and indeed, until the middle of the seventeenth century, a few female names can be found in the membership

---

[2] The same story is also being told about the origins of the close-by Beverhoutsveld.

[3] For a further explanation of the specificities of commons in Flanders, see M. De Moor (2002, 113–42).

[4] For a comparison, see De Moor, Shaw-Taylor, and Warde (2002c, 247–60).

[5] Although this is not the most regular way to restrict access to a common, restriction via inheritable rights is often found elsewhere in the neighborhood of this common (Beverhoutsveld) and elsewhere in Europe (De Moor, Shaw-Taylor, and Warde 2002c, 261). An interesting comparative case is the one described by Marco Casari for the mountain communities in the Italian Alps, which used originally an egalitarian inheritance system and later on a patrilineal inheritance system in order to restrict the increase of members under the influence of immigration and mixed marriages (see Casari and Lisciandra 2014).

[6] The archive of the Gemene and Loweiden contains a number of original *hoofdboeken* or copies and a number of separate lists of *aanborgers*. Important for this chapter are the following sources: Bouck van de geslachten van de Gemeene weede. Register van inschrijvingen als *aanborger* van 1515 to 1703, Aanwinsten 1984, 68, State Archive at Bruges (Rijksarchief Brugge; hereafter RAB); from the Archives of Gemene and Loweiden (hereafter AGL) at the City Archives of Bruges (Stadsarchief Brugge; hereafter SAB): 12, Hoofdboek. Boek van de geslachten van de Gemene en Loweede, 1622–1703; 13, Hoofdboek. Boek van de geslachten van de Gemene en Loweede, 1718–1767 (copy); 14 Hoofdboek. Boek van de geslachten van de Gemene- en Loweede 1769–1889; 15, Hoofdboek van de *aanborgers* 1889–1981. The *hoofdboeken* were not systematically foliated. Source references to these books hence do not refer to a specific place in the books.

The Dilemma of the Commoners

registers (the *hoofdboeken*).[7] Although there is no official rule excluding women from membership thereafter, from the middle of the seventeenth century women were no longer registered in the *hoofdboeken*. It is thus quite likely that during the sixteenth century women were gradually pushed out of the common as official members, restricting it further to men only. This is a process that is also noted for other commons elsewhere, and is also in line with restrictions to female participation than can be found for other forms of institutions for collective action, such as guilds, and other domains in society and which can most likely be explained by the earlier mentioned economic crises of the time.[8]

Those males who obtained the right of membership via their wife (*'by causen van huwelike alleenlick'* [Trans.: 'solely because of marriage']) could only use this right as long as the wife lived. In a few cases, a widower was able to reclaim his use-rights by marrying another woman from another entitled family. Although the partner could thereafter no longer claim use-rights, each of the children born from this marriage would be entitled to claim use-rights.[9] While in principle, in the period we study here, women could only exercise their right through a man, there are several cases of widows who were allowed to use the common, at least temporarily, after their husband's death.

Members were referred to as *aanborgers* (or *amburger, amborchteghe, ambuerdeghe*), which can be explained as a corruption of the words *aenboordig, aenbortig*, or *aenborchtig*, meaning 'being in the possession of a good or a right' (De Bo 1873).[10] The procedure to obtain that right

---

[7] In the first book several women are mentioned. In the act of 1514 it was stated that both women and men could become members ('zoo wat vrauwen ofte mannen die aen dese vrye geprivilegierde weede ende meersch van Assenbrouc amborchtich worden . . . .' [Trans.: 'regarding those women or men who will become *aanborgers* of the privileged pasture and marshland of Assenbroek']). See chapter 8 of the archival document no. 2 (late seventeenth century) of the AGL. In July 1622, for example, the unwedded daughter Mayken van Ghistele, daughter of Absoloen, from the neighboring village of Male became a member of the common (Hoofdboek. Boek van de geslachten van de Gemene en Loweede, 1622–1703, CAB, AGL, 12). For a complete overview of all the archival documents that can be found in the archive of the Gemene and Loweiden, see M. De Moor (2005).

[8] For an example of restrictions on female access to commons in the sixteenth century, see Casari and Lisciandra (2014); for restrictions to guilds, see, e.g., Wiesner (1991); for restrictions in other domains of society, see De Moor and Van Zanden (2012).

[9] The regulation says: 'vrauwe ofte man, dan weduwe ofte weduwenare zynde, vervremt ende onbekent gherekent van zyn ambordtichede' [Trans.: 'woman or man, either widow or widower, will be regarded as alienated and unknown of his membership']. If they had children from a marriage with a rightful commoner, however ('kinderen commende vande voorseide ambortichede'), then these would remain commoners based on their birthplace and customary law ('daer innen gherecht als amborteghe by generatie ende recht van hoirie van geboorten naer oude costumen') (CAB, AGL 2, art. 8).

[10] The name *aanborger* (or a variation) can also be found elsewhere. Gilliodts, for example, refers to an account of the seigniory (*heerlijkheid*) of Zotschore (of 1547) in which was

From rules to practice

consisted of a visit to the parish priest in the companionship of two witnesses who were able to confirm the applicant's descent from the entitled ancestors. After payment of a sum of one Flemish pound, the priest noted the name of the new *aanborger* in his impressive membership register, which he also consulted to assure himself of the rights of the claimant's ancestors. If the descent of a future *aanborger* was in doubt, he had to show proof of his descent by testimony (within forty days) of at least three registered *aanborgers*, who could state under oath to the *hoofdman* that the man concerned really was the descendant of an already registered – dead or alive – *aanborger*.

The admission fee was a sum equal to a day's wage, and in the case of the Gemene and Loweiden, it served as the only way to restrict the total number of entitled members. Elsewhere, only village inhabitants were allowed, or the poor of the village would have specific advantages, but here no such restrictions can be found.[11] This means that, in principle, inhabitants from far-away villages could claim use-rights too. Before the end of the nineteenth century – when the managers of the common tried to increase the number of registered members to prevent the government from claiming the land (see further on in this paragraph) – this was however hardly ever the case.[12] The commoners also developed other ways to limit the total number of cattle on the common in their attempts to prevent excessive exploitation of the pastures.

The number of members was registered systematically from 1622 onwards. The oldest *hoofdboek* also mentions the names of members for 1515 (37) and 1525 (250). Because these were actually written down in 1622 (as a transcription of the older sources), it remains uncertain whether these figures include all the members of the common in the respective years or only refer to the number of members newly entered in the *hoofdboek*. From 1622 onwards, there has been systematic registration of new *aanborgers* (see Table 3). The tripling of the numbers in the second half of the nineteenth century was a direct consequence of the efforts done by the commoners to save their common from the local authorities. They set up an intensified registration campaign to demonstrate the importance

---

mentioned: 'Ontfaen ter causen van der herfvelicke rente van Zotschoore in veltschattinghe die diversce persoonen en de ambochten jaerlicx ghelden telcken S. Jans avende mits somers' [Trans.: 'Received because of the rent charge of Zotschoore based on land tax various persons and the *aanborgers* have to pay annually on Saint-John's eve at midsummer'] (Gilliodts-Van Severen 1880).

[11] For an overview of access regulation on Flemish commons, see M. De Moor (2002, 113–42).

[12] Today the common even has members from overseas. Every three years they meet to elect a new board, but the use of the common can in no way still be compared to its original use in the eighteenth century and before.

The Dilemma of the Commoners

Table 3 Total number of persons registered as members of the Gemene and Loweiden, in absolute numbers and as average per year (with registrations)

Period	Total number of registrations	Average number of registrations for the years in which registrations were recorded
1623–1699	753	14.48
1700–1749	112	4.15
1750–1799	271	5.89
1800–1849	278	5.56
1850–1899	486	17.36
1900–1965	1,519	47.47

of their institution before the court, when reclaiming their rights on the common. In the course of the twentieth century, we see an even greater number of commoners registering. Obviously, the commoners learned from their previous experience and tried to prevent another 'attack' on their common property by creating a larger critical mass of commoners. Of course, it should not be assumed that all commoners registered from the mid-nineteenth century also used their right in practice. Quite to the contrary: some even lived abroad during the course of their membership. As I will show, the average participation level of the commoners had already declined quite dramatically in the course of the eighteenth century (see Chapter 4).

Although the land was formally owned by the Lord of Sijsele, who had 'final ownership' (*altum dominium*), the commoners held the use-rights on the resources of the common (*dominium directum*), and an assembly of men (*hoofdmannen*) was elected. The assembly of *hoofdmannen* took care of the everyday management and perform most of the executive tasks. Any legal disputes were to be brought before the local bailiff, who also acted as the direct representative of the lord in any other matter. Until the end of the eighteenth century, the person in charge of receiving the fines and taxes from the Gemene Weide also had to present a triennial account to the Lord of Sijsele, who, according to the earliest regulation, had the right to (dis)approve of changes to regulations and the triennial bookkeeping. As for the rest of the activities on the common, the lord or his bailiff were hardly ever involved or allowed to interfere. We can therefore assume that the common to a large extent functioned autonomously and that the commoners' actions were hardly ever hindered by local or other governments until the

From rules to practice

end of the ancien régime. Thereafter, as we will see, the common went through a process of reorganization that would eventually allow the local authorities to encroach on the common's resources and assets, although only temporarily.

3.1.2 Historial sources on the case of the Gemene and Loweiden

Although the material left behind by commoners is in general much more limited than the archives of, for example, the urban guilds, for some commons there is sufficient archival material to reconstruct the day-to-day activities on the common. For the common meadow of the Gemene and Loweiden, a large body of sources has been exceptionally well preserved, and although only a few meters in length, it is very rich in detail about the activities of the commoners, in particular for the period of the ancien régime. Four types of documents form the largest part of the archive: the customary arrangements (*keuren*) made between the lords and the commoners since the fifteenth century, documents regarding the regulation of the commons (*resolutieboeken*) for most of the seventeenth and eighteenth centuries, the lists of commoners from 1515 (*hoofdboeken*, Figure 4) until today,[13] and the detailed bookkeeping from the seventeenth century onwards (which is nearly complete for the whole eighteenth century).[14]

All the names of commoners mentioned in this book from the end of the seventeenth century were linked wherever possible to other sources (such as population registers, parish registers, population censuses, occupational censuses, agricultural censuses, etc.) that provided more information on their social and economic background. The combination of the complete financial records (accounts) for the eighteenth and nineteenth centuries with the preserved lists of legitimate commoners – including their dates of first membership of the common and information about relatives who served as proof for their claims – and biographical information retrieved from other archival sources[15] provided sufficient data to see how commoners behaved as individuals (e.g., when in their lifetime they

---

[13] All the names of the persons who received the use-right between 1515 and 1965 were published in De Moor and Debbaut (2003).

[14] See the records numbered 59 to 124 of the archives of the Gemene and Loweiden preserved in the City Archives of Bruges. An extensive description and an inventory of the sources preserved for this particular common can be found in M. De Moor (2005).

[15] I used both parish registers for the seventeenth and eighteenth centuries that listed data on birth, marriage, and burial, and nineteenth-century population registers, in particular those on marriage, for the villages of Assebroek, Oedelem, and a number of surrounding villages.

107

The Dilemma of the Commoners

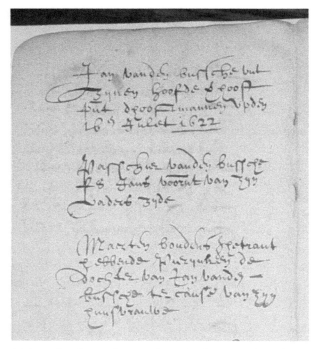

Figure 4 Example of part of a page from the first *hoofdboek* of the Gemene and Loweiden (1515–1622), showing how several members were registered in July 1622
(Source: State Archives in Bruges, Collection Aanwinsten, no. 720, page 28 verso)

Transcription of the text
Jan Van den Bussche uut zijnen hoofde v[er]hooft p[resen]t d' hooftmannen op den 16en julet 1622

Passchier Van den Bussche f[iliu]s Jans voorn[oem]t van zijn vaders zijde

Maerten Boudens ghetraut hebbende Pierijncken de dochter van Jan Van den Bussche ter causen van zijn huusvrauwe

Translation
Jan Van den Bussche, entitled user because of himself, the *hoofdmannen* being present on 16 July 1622

Passchier Van den Bussche, son of the aforementioned Jan, entitled user because of his father

Maerten Boudens, having married Pierijncken, daughter of Jan Van den Bussche, entitled user because of his wife

From rules to practice

possessed animals and how many heads of cattle they had on the common, and whether they participated in general meetings). In particular, parish and population registers on birth/baptism, marriage, and death/burial, and the remaining individual files of population and economic censuses and tax registers contained large amounts of data that could be linked to the names of commoners.

In many cases, linking names was not straightforward, but it nevertheless added up to a sample of 589 *aanborgers* for whom we have found sufficient biographical information. This does not, however, mean we have all significant biographical information (about birth, marriage, and death) for all of these people. A selection was made from these 589 persons that contained information for the variables needed, depending on the kind of analysis required for specific research questions. This data set, combined with the more general data derived from censuses and population registers, gives us information about the way the common was run, as well as more general socio-economic data, such as changes in the number of potential users, the prices of cattle, changes in the type of agriculture, and so on. It provides a wealth of information on the effects of the commoners' behavior. For many individual commoners it was possible to identify the period in their life when they actively used the facilities of the common, and for a significant number, details about their professional life and whether they had any cattle that may have been put on the common could also be retrieved. In my analysis, the commoner's cattle and horses mentioned in the bookkeeping as grazing on the common were compared to the overall number of cattle and horses mentioned in, for example, agricultural censuses. Usually these corresponded, or the number of cattle on the common was less than mentioned in the censuses, thus meaning that the commoner put only some of his animals on the common. All this information provides a clearer picture of the economic importance of the common. It can be expected that the economic importance of the services and resources the common had to offer tells us more about the participation behavior of commoners, as the main advantage offered by membership in the common was the right to pasture cattle.[16] This combination will also allow us to reconstruct how their behavior influenced use and management. In particular I examined the effect of socio-economic heterogeneity, measured

---

[16] Because not all the data on the lives (date of birth, death, marriage, etc.), work (occupation), and property (especially ownership of cattle) could be retrieved for all commoners, I have used a number of samples for the analysis. The sample that was used to retrieve the occupations of the *aanborgers* does to a certain extent include periods other than the sample used to analyze the average age at which the *aanborgers* became commoners.

The Dilemma of the Commoners

mainly by individual occupations (whether the commoner was an independent farmer or wage earner) and the possession of cattle, which could be retrieved from various eighteenth- and nineteenth-century agricultural censuses.

Once a profile of all of the commoners in the eighteenth and nineteenth centuries had been made, it also became possible to study group heterogeneity in depth by comparing the involvement of individuals in the activities of the common, on the basis of the type of activity they were involved in and the frequency of involvement. The evolution of the group heterogeneity could thereafter be linked to, on the one hand, management decisions taken (which were recorded in the resolution books) and, on the other hand, more general demographic and socio-economic changes, which were retrieved from a variety of sources available for this period. Besides the micro-analysis on the level of the individual commoner and his household, the census material also allowed us to reconstruct the broader picture about the evolution of agriculture and the economy as a whole in the region.

Of course, it cannot be denied that historical documents are never complete, and that there are sometimes no ways to fill in the gaps, but as will be shown in the processing of the data, our understanding of the functioning of the common can be enhanced by approaching sources using different perspectives. The account books provide more than simply the usual income and expenditure; they tell us much more about the importance of the resources for the individual commoners and about the size of the group of commoners that was actively using them. In the rest of the book, therefore, I will make a distinction between different types of commoners on the basis of their involvement in the common. Such a categorization, although artificial, will help us to distinguish certain trends in participation, which is necessary for our analyses in Chapter 4. In general, I will distinguish members from nonmembers: those with rightful claims on the common, and those without. Among those registered as members, I will make an additional distinction between active and passive members. Not all members of the common used it regularly, which is a rather simple fact that is however often overlooked in commons studies, whereby the focus is usually more on overexploitation of the group as a whole rather than on the lack of exploitation by some. There are cases when users only registered for membership, but left no further trace in the historical documents we have analyzed. These commoners may have died before they ever got the chance to put their rights to use, they may have moved away, or they simply may not have needed the common, either because they had sufficient land and resources of their own or because they were too impoverished to have cattle they could graze on the common. Though each commoner's situation was different, there are some general trends to the commoners' behavior, mirroring general socio-economic trends that in the end also affected the common's use and management.

To analyze the effect of commoners' behavior on the common, all their actions have been identified and categorized. This allows us to measure the level of participation by the commoners and its evolution over time. Besides the division between active and passive members, I have also made a functional distinction on the basis of the types of activities commoners were involved in. As such, active members can again be split up in two groups. The first group is formed by those who remained simple users, by putting cattle on the common, harvesting wood, and receiving payments from the common for doing small jobs such as repairing fencing. These commoners obtained economic benefits from the common and were thus categorized as 'economic participants'. A second group consists of active members who chose to move up the social hierarchy of the common to become managers and monitors. The common's officials were elected from the regular members and would remain in power for several years; this will be considered as functional participation. I have chosen to distinguish between both groups, as it seems clear from the reports on the common that something was going on in the power delegation and balance, from the middle of the eighteenth century. What exactly, and how it can be explained, will be explored in the following chapter.

A last analysis method that will shed light on changes in the individual's relationship with the common is the measuring of the participation intensity, whereby the number of individual appearances in the common's sources was related to their period of active membership. This indicator is then used to understand how important the common resources were for an individual through his lifetime.

If we consider this case study in the wider framework that was presented in Chapter 2, we find that this case fits very well with the features as described for the commons of the closed type, to which most of the cases in the area around Bruges belonged. In this area, the access rules were often limited to groups living directly around and/or descending from an original group of commoners, and the physical boundaries – due to their more restricted surface – were often more clearly set than in the case of the 'open type'. In terms of the total surface that the commons in Flanders comprised at the time, commons of the open type were in the minority, but as each of these commons was also in itself smaller in surface, the closed type itself was not particularly less represented overall. As such, this case study is definitely representative.

One could potentially argue that the selection of this case study is biased as it is one of the few cases that managed to survive the nineteenth-century attacks by local, regional, and national governments, thus proving that the common in itself was more-than-average successful in the management of its common-pool resources. The fact that this case still exists, although in a somewhat different legal form and with a far less prominent role in the local agriculture, only adds to this suspicion. However, there are two good reasons to discard this supposed bias.

First of all, the argument that examples of failures are less prominently present in the archives is only correct when it concerns the period before the middle of the eighteenth century, or even the start of it. By the middle of the eighteenth century, this type of resource governance model was receiving so much attention that a case of failure would definitely have been spotted by those looking for arguments against common-pool institutions. Moreover, both the governments and legal scholars of the time – such as Errera – inventoried and described cases at length, and among those, we found – in particular, those situated in the same region such as the Maleveld and Beverhoutsveld – similar forms of rules regarding use, access, and management of the common, as mentioned in one of the previous paragraphs.

That most of the commons in the area eventually did disappear was due to top-down dissolution. Although a possible lack of opposition to this may also be considered as a lack of 'strength' of the institution, the cause of their dissolution was not primarily internal, but external. This brings us to our second point. The Gemene and Loweiden did survive these attacks, thanks to a large extent to one person: Canon Andries, who spent considerable time studying the archival documents to prepare the court case that the commoners had brought against the local governments that were attempting to seize their property. In this sense, one could claim that the common's position – and its luck in having a guardian angel to deal with the legal issues – was rather exceptional indeed. But, as mentioned, this was likely the most important factor why this common managed to overcome the threat of privatization that was hanging like a sword of Damocles over the commoners (whereas most other commons did not). But even if one considers the path this common followed after 1882 (when the court case was won by the commoners) as rather exceptional, this in no way influences this case study, which focusses primarily on the eighteenth and first half of the nineteenth centuries. To summarize: the exceptionality of this case lays in its survival until the twenty-first century, but this in itself does not affect the features and functioning of this common, which form the core of this book.

The survival of the Gemene and Loweiden until today is undoubtedly also one of the reasons why it has been possible to find so many rich archival documents on this common; this is hardly ever the case for commons of the closed type in particular. The reason is quite straightforward: the management of commons of the closed type was, as explained, usually in the hands of local managers, not the village boards, as in the open type cases. Information about commons of the open type can often (but not always) be found in the village's historical records, and these were usually in due time transferred to archival institutions where archives were kept in relatively good circumstances, although it must be stressed that here too the documentation is often rather scarce. In the case of the closed commons, the common's archive was passed on from secretary to secretary over the centuries, who then kept it in a box somewhere at home. Although this gave all those with an interest in the common easy access to important documents, it also made the common's archive particularly vulnerable as documents could be easily lost or damaged when transferred from one secretary to another.[17] As part of this study, the complete archive was inventoried and is now being preserved in the City Archives of Bruges, where it can also be consulted by anyone interested in this case's history.[18]

3.2 Methodological framework: the functioning of a common captured in a three-dimensional approach

Although the preceding description suggests that there is much more source material about some historical commons than would be generally expected of a phenomenon that has been largely ignored in continental European historiography, we still need a framework that allows us to link the conclusions drawn on the basis of this common to our present-day knowledge on the functioning of commons delivered by an extremely interdisciplinary debate. Before embarking on a less abstract, more tangible level of analysis, the challenge at this point is to link our knowledge on

---

[17] In comparison: in the case of guilds, the official documents were often held in the guild's house or at the home of one of the leading men (*hoofdmannen*) of the guild and thus didn't have to move from one place to another (see, e.g., Roodenburg 1993, 55, and Slokker 2010, 252).

[18] The full inventory of this archive is added to the list of archival references in this book; a discussion of the archive can be found in M. De Moor (2005).

the commons in the historical context to the larger debates, especially those on the management of the collective resources and the impact of common use and management on its users and available resources. It is essential here to understand that each of these aspects – use, management, and impact – are interrelated: a management decision can influence use and as such also lead to a change in the impact on resources, but changes in resource availability can also impact management and use. Understanding the balance among all aspects will thus be essential to understanding the longevity of this institution.

How such interactions took place, generally between only two of the three aspects, has already been the subject of many studies, although usually not historiographical ones. Though seldom explicitly stated by the authors, there are links to be found between the views of researchers on the origins of commons and their role in agricultural productivity, poverty alleviation, and sustainable resource governance.[19] In this part I will bring various opinions expressed by researchers of various disciplines together in one single conceptual framework. This very general overview should help readers to structure a complex debate into some clearly defined, perhaps too simplistic, lines of reasoning. This overview will then be used to develop our methodological framework that allows us to capture all aspects of the commons and focus on their role in building a resilient institution.

Let us start by considering the perspectives found in the entire body of historical literature on commons, which started to develop during the nineteenth century when the dissolution of the commons received a great deal more attention than their origins or their long-term evolution. As already explained, since the middle of the nineteenth century, common land has disappeared almost completely from the European landscape and from the collective memory of most (continental) Europeans. This process has been accelerated by the questioning of common customs and management of goods since the mid-eighteenth century, in particular by the politically influential Physiocrats. Most historians working on commons focused on Great Britain, especially England, and then primarily on the social consequences of the Enclosure movement, on its possible negative effects (proletarianization) on commoners. Social scientists working on commons, in particular from the 1970s, mainly as a consequence of the tragedy-of-the-commons-debate, were often not aware of the long-standing tradition of historians working on this particular topic. Since the

---

[19] Considering the size of the literature on commons – in general, not just historical – by itself, it would be impossible to do the same exercise for the guilds here as well.

From rules to practice

start of the International Association for the Study of Common Property (IASCP) in 1984, a considerable number of studies have pointed out the capacities of common management regimes for sustainably managing natural resources, but this was done on the basis of studies dealing with contemporary situations, without much attention to the long previous history many cases had.[20] The studies examined in the first place the management of the common-pool resources (CPRs), with less interest in the surroundings, the context, or the structural factors (influence of the authorities' measures, changes in the social structure, and the agricultural system). In general, the focus has been on the internal functioning of these institutions. Historians, on the other hand, have hardly considered internal conflict as a possible cause of dissolution. But my case study will demonstrate that the degree and manner of participation of the commoners could influence the management of the common greatly and could also endanger its future.

If we try to divide the literature as a whole (without regard to the discipline) in the categories shown in Figure 5, a clear pattern starts to emerge. First, on the level of the emergence of commons, a distinction can be made between those who support a causal explanation and those who believe in an evolutionary perspective of institutions. In the second explanation, there is only one possible direction common property can move towards, namely private property. This goes with the conviction that common property stems from ancient forms of 'Germanic' tribal communism and evolves via clan holdings to individual property in several ways.[21] Although this view on the origins of common land is now considered outmoded (see the earlier discussion on the origins of commons in point 1.5), it does implicitly continue to live on in the literature and debates on other aspects of common land, as is illustrated in Figure 5. More in line with the causal explanation, it has in previous chapters already been demonstrated that there are a number of clear causes (explained in terms of motives, motors, and conditions) that together led to a change in governance regime in some cases (see 1.5.1 and further). Not all land was held in common from the late Middle Ages onwards, but in many cases a combination of private land with other

---

[20] The IASCP has since dropped the 'P' and is now known as the International Association for the Study of the Commons. See http://www.iasc-commons.org/about/history.

[21] When the transition of collective to individual property happened is still not clear. Those who support this view consider common land as an archaic and inadequate system for the management of natural resources. See earlier in this book for an explanation about the view of Emile De Laveleye, who in his substantial work *De la propriété collective et de ses formes primitives* (1894) made an international comparison of collective property and discerned a similar evolution in different parts of the world: common 'primitive' systems always had to clear the field for private property, a view that is typical for the late nineteenth century.

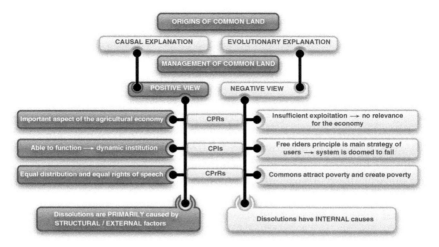

Figure 5 Overview of the debates on the resource, institution, and users of commons[22]

resources held in common was chosen. We have thus already demonstrated that a more causal approach to the origins of commons and other forms of institutions for collective action is rather obvious.

On a second level, that of the management of commons, I see a need to distinguish a negative versus a positive line of interpretation of several aspects of commons: it is the negative or positive causal relation between the type of resource governance model, in this case a common-pool institution (CPI) and the state of the resource, in this case common-pool resources (CPRs) and/or its users, in this case the holders of rights as defined in the common-property regime (CPrR). We start halfway down the figure to explain the framework. A first distinction between negative and positive approaches to commons management can be made on the level of the CPI. The negative view assumes that common use and management led to a deteriorated state of the CPR. The positive view (on the left-hand side) assumes that the property regime is a necessary consequence of the resource: it is the property regime that is adjusted to the particular type, amount, and value of the available resources, not the other way around. In this view a common-property regime can be useful or even necessary to govern resources successfully. The positive view also

---

[22] For more examples and for an in-depth explanation of the ideas presented in this part, see T. De Moor (2007); see also T. De Moor (2012).

From rules to practice

allows other property regimes to co-exist and does not consider the management and use in common as infallible. The negative view claims the opposite: resource governance in the form of commons is precisely the cause of, and can lead to, an inferior outcome; it deteriorates the state of the resource. The most obvious advocates of the positive and negative views are of course Elinor Ostrom and Garett Hardin, respectively (see the Introduction to this book).

This overview gives a very general and little nuanced structure of by now a massive amount of literature from various disciplines on the commons, but it helps to distinguish which elements make or break a common-pool institution, which aspects of an institution deserve attention when trying to avoid a tragedy and to achieve resilience. Three main dimensions of a common should thus be considered: the natural resource (the CPR), its users (the CPrR), and the institution (the CPI) they created. In this combination of dimensions, the property regime refers primarily to those who hold the property and the institutional side covers the rules and norms that are developed in order to facilitate the collective management and use of the resources, which then again, is captured in the dimension of the common-pool resource. In this model, the users, the resources, and the rules and norms that connect users and resources are thus separated, but as the figure demonstrates, they are also closely intertwined and all three dimensions are needed.

Each of these dimensions plays an important role in the complexity that forms the daily context in which commoners dealt with problems related to their common. The real complexity, however, lies in the interaction among all these dimensions and how a change in one domain influences the other two domains. In addition, it is essential to see how all these factors are influenced by factors such as slow and sudden changes in climate, in the economic and social welfare of the region, and new methods in agriculture. The biggest challenge to the commons was to keep the institution alive, taking into account the internal balance and the external changes. This challenge, however difficult, might in fact also be the strength of the model: if the system is sufficiently robust, it becomes possible to live up to all of the expectations and needs of those involved and also deal with extreme changes in the environment.

Besides summarizing the literature, the flow chart in Figure 5 also suggests that the three dimensions of the resource, the users, and the institution are interconnected, and that a change in one dimension may have an effect on another dimension. In order to make this overview useful for new research on commons, we need to go one step further. As shown in Figure 6, the interaction between each of these dimensions is also connected to specific evaluation criteria. The criteria of utility, efficiency, and equity help us to understand how to achieve a resilient system. Utility refers to the degree to which the use of the resources is adequate for the users. Efficiency refers to the effects of this use upon the availability of the resource, in the sense of an ecological optimum. Equity is used to indicate the degree of involvement and participation of the commoners in the economic use and management of the common. Analyzing the interaction (as indicated by the arrows in Figure 6) between the components (CPI, CPrR, CPR) helps us identify the potential dangers that can bring the whole system out of balance, and thus lead to tragedy. One of the main differences from many other studies is that this study does not look for optima in each of these domains, but rather for a balanced system as a way to explain resilience. The model in Figure 6 acknowledges that, although efficiency is the objective of the interaction

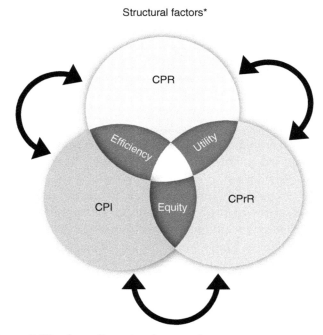

Figure 6 The three-dimensional approach to commons: commons as common-pool resources, common-pool institutions, and common-property regimes
*External factors can include: population growth, economic change, political processes, etc.

between the resource and the institution, at some point the temporary need for more resources demanded by the commoners – and thus the interaction between the users and the resource – may affect efficiency through a change in the resource. At the same time this approach acknowledges that each of these domains that interact among each other are simultaneously influenced by a number of contextual factors, such as population growth, economic change, and climate. A change in one of the contextual factors can enforce a change in, for example, the use of the common, and this in its turn can affect the internal balance between, for example, users and the institution. In the discussion on the case study results, this search for balance and in some cases the near failure to find such a balance will be linked to this framework. As I will demonstrate, the commoners decided to decrease the size of their resources by leasing out part of their land, also to non-commoners, in order to deal with the changed utility at the users' side. Due to the changes in the occupational background of the commoners, they were using the common land less intensively, and this could in due time lead to under-exploitation, which in itself could be a threat for the future of the common (see more in point 4.3 in Chapter 4).

Placing changes within the commons within the following framework is useful because it demonstrates that a decision taken by the commoners can have important consequences for all dimensions of the commons, but (even if it affects the resource negatively) it might be taken because of a need to find a new balance between other dimensions. Similarly, new measures may have to be taken to ensure ecological stability, which in the end also affects the utility for the commoners. Although the framework appears static, in a well-functioning common there would be constant interaction among all dimensions of the common in order to achieve a balance sufficiently optimal to ensure the resilience of the common as a resource for its users, as an institution, and as an ecological system in itself.

As mentioned before in this book, the monumental work of Elinor Ostrom *Governing the Commons* (1990) provided us with an excellent tool to make a general check-up of an institution, to evaluate whether it features the basic elements to develop into a robust institution, but it remains a momentary description of the features and not of the functioning of the institution, and how changes within the system react to and interact with other internal and external changes. This is to a large extent possible with frameworks that have been developed with the Ostrom-school such as the IAD-framework, but there is still something missing that is needed to understand long-term robustness and the driving forces

The Dilemma of the Commoners

behind some decisions by commoners, whether made collectively or by their delegated managers. For historians the available frameworks as yet do not offer the necessary instruments to capture the interplay among the resources, the people using the resources, and those designing the rules on how to do and not to do so, in particular when studying the very long-term survival of commons. Without a tool to describe and capture these dynamics, it is hard to understand why changes within the system were made, how these interacted, and whether the incentives to do so were internal or external. Moreover, the approach in this book does not focus on the individual motives of commoners to cooperate or defect, but zooms in on the group dynamics, whereby a shift in power balance between, for example, those with and those without cattle, may lead to a change in the management system. I would like to argue that the balance between the dimensions – in different kinds of constellations – within the system is vital for the resilience of an institution for collective action, possibly even more so than having all the design principles right. Without a tool that allows us to describe such dynamics between resources, users, and use whereby they focus both on the individual and on the changes of types of commoners, we cannot explain how so many commons in western Europe managed to survive such long periods of time.

In the rest of the book, I will try to operationalize this framework, on the basis of the historical sources available for our case study. The case study will serve as an illustration of how the continuous search for the balance between the mentioned dimensions, also in interaction with external change, worked in the historical context. Although the sources will also be analyzed in a quantitative way, the framework itself will not be translated into a model that can be tested quantitatively, as this would require more input from various other disciplines, ranging from ecology (for the efficiency part) to, among others, economics (for the utility part). One of the goals of this book is to demonstrate how factors such as efficiency and utility or utility and equity can affect each other and how institutions adapt over time to changing circumstances. Application on other – historical or present-day – examples could contribute to further the framework and create the necessary tools for testing it.

4. The choices of the commoners: understanding utility, efficiency, and equity on the commons through the behavior of commoners

Comparative historical research on common land has increased our understanding of how common-property regimes regulated access to and management of their resources, showing throughout Europe that there are clear similarities in the way commoners tried to restrict access to and use of those resources. Historians in the meanwhile have found plenty of evidence that regulating mechanisms were sufficiently dynamic to cope with severe external stresses (McC. Netting 1981; Neeson 1993; De Moor, Shaw-Taylor, and Warde 2002c; Demélas and Vivier 2003). We also know that commoners were usually very involved in setting up and changing the regulations as well as keeping an eye on their implementation (see, e.g., Rodgers et al. 2011). One of the issues that has been overlooked so far in terms of understanding why the rules of such bottom-up organizations were changed, is the internal composition of the group of commoners. Although historical researchers have generally assumed that commoners were a homogeneous group, with a similar effect of enclosures on each of the group members, evidence from nonhistorical research suggests that the size of these groups, and their internal heterogeneity, influenced their functioning as well, and potentially also their vulnerability to external attempts to dissolve their common.[1] Given that enclosures were

---

[1] I have not found any historical studies on commons that actually considered the effect of group size and heterogeneity on the behavior of commoners or on the functioning of commons. If we consider other than purely historical literature, then Mancur Olson was the first to refer to the effect of group size (Olson 1965; see also De Moor and Debbaut 2003); he claims that collective action becomes less effective when groups become larger. His work has been challenged by authors such as Oliver and Marwell (Oliver's paradox; see Oliver and Marwell 1988), who claim that Olson incorrectly believed that larger groups were less likely to support collective action than smaller ones. They assert that the effect of group size depends on cost. If the cost of collective goods increases with the number who share in them, larger groups will act less frequently than smaller ones. If the cost varies little with group size, larger groups should exhibit more collective action than smaller ones because larger groups have more resources and are more likely to have a critical mass of highly interested and resourceful actors. The positive effects of group size increase with

The Dilemma of the Commoners

a mainly government-orchestrated procedure, whereby there was little concern for the effect it would have on the powerless individual farmers who lost their rights, this emphasis in historiography is quite understandable and also explains why not enough attention has gone to the motives and backgrounds of the individual commoner.[2] Very likely each individual commoner's interests in the use of the resources must have varied. Experimental research has shown that studying this behavior is absolutely necessary to understand the processes involved in environmental degradation, processes that may have been going on even before the privatization of the commons was ordered from above (Jager et al. 2000, 357–79). The way commoners experienced the potential value of the common in their daily lives and the changes herein may well have affected their willingness to defend their rights and thus may have influenced the speed of the privatization process or at least the willingness to resist enclosure measures enforced upon the commoners. This may in turn explain the vulnerability of the commoners as in the specific case study we are examining in the first half of the nineteenth century, when the commoners were under great pressure from local, regional, and national governments to sell off their land.

To link changes in behavior to the consequences they may have had for the resources used, we need to focus on the types of interaction found, and determine ways to distinguish among different kinds of behavior, both in the types of use and intensity the common resources were used.[3] Commoners could have a variety of profiles, from active users and managers to members who hardly ever showed up at meetings, from users whose main interest was grazing cattle on the common or performing jobs for the common, to those who saw the common as a way to increase their prestige in the village by fulfilling functions on the common's board.

Strangely enough, in commons literature the possibility that members were not actively involved in using or managing their common land is not even considered. It seems to be regarded as a given that those who has pasture rights would graze cattle on it, or at least try to obtain benefits in

---

group heterogeneity and social ties. Other scholars, such as Brewer and Kramer (1986, 543–9), have focused on the psychological effect of group size.

[2] Whereas some eighteenth-century rulers (such as Maria Theresia) had proposed – though unsuccessfully – social ways of subdividing the commons, the mid-nineteenth-century legislation of many continental European governments that aimed to dissolve the commons was just as ruthless. Most of the commons in western Europe had disappeared by the end of the nineteenth century. Elsewhere in continental Europe they were considerably reduced. The most comprehensive overviews in this regard are given by the edited volumes of Demélas and Vivier (2003) and Congost and Lana Berasain (2007).

[3] For most European commons, grazing was probably the most frequently offered facility. Despite the fact that many commoners would have had some animals, grazing was often restricted to cows and horses, excluding those commoners who had only smaller animals, such as pigs, geese, and goats (see earlier, point 2.4.2).

The choices of the commoners

another way, for example, by becoming a member of the common's board, and thus gaining social status. These conjectures derive from two frequently expressed assumptions that are part of the enclosure debate. First, much of the literature assumes that commoners were poor by definition, and that they would seize any opportunity for extra sources of income. Yet, if the main advantage of a common was obtained from having cattle, many poor commoners would be automatically excluded from its benefits, and even those with cattle may have had reasons not to become active users of the common. Distinguishing participants on the basis of their occupation, as has been done by, for example, Leigh Shaw-Taylor (2001a), is a first step towards understanding differences in their participation, but indicators such as the use of the common at various stages of the commoner's life cycle might tell us even more about the motives on to use the common or not.

Second, central to a different debate on the use of the common and its effect on natural resources is the idea that common land could be easily excessively exploited because individual commoners tried to maximize their incomes. Many scholars involved in this debate are defeatist and consider this maximization as having eventually led to a tragedy for the commons.[4] In many examples of collective use of resources today and in the past, however, commoners devise rules, sanctions, and instruments to restrict their own behavior to a level that allows long-term use without significant overuse.[5] The possibility that some commoners may not use the common at all, even though they have the right to do so, seems to run counter to the idea that a *homo economicus* – interpreted in its strictest way – would act rationally and try to maximize his welfare by using more than would be necessary for himself and thereby make a profit from the surplus harvest. But even within literature that belongs to the more positive side (see 3.2), the possibility that common resources were not used is hardly ever considered, whereas the lack of usage of the common would have had a similar detrimental effect on the available resources. The influence of those who do not participate can be of significant importance for the group as a whole.

---

[4] Elsewhere I have made an overview of the literature on commons according to the authors' view on commons, and I have explained how their views on the economic, ecologic, and social meaning of the commons is mostly intertwined (see T. De Moor 2007).

[5] The main advocate of the claim that commoners are indeed able to make their common work and avoid overexploitation is 2009 Nobel Prize winner Elinor Ostrom (see her book *Governing the Commons* [1990]). Among historians, Susan Cox (1985) was long the only scholar who offered historical counterevidence to Hardin's theory (Hardin 1968). In the meantime this group of historians has now grown, and various projects on the theme of commons and their exploitation are currently running. There is even an association – the International Association for the Study of the Commons – that is entirely devoted to bringing together scholars from all over the world who study the functioning of the commons.

The Dilemma of the Commoners

Taken together, this chapter starts from the assumption that commoners formed a far more heterogeneous group than is usually supposed, and that individuals' motivations and decision power within the group may have changed the overall management significantly. Because a large part of the decision making on the commons was conducted in a democratic way, through general and ad hoc meetings, it can be assumed that the changes in individual profiles may have affected not only commoners' own use of the resources, but also their decisions about access to the commons and the use and management of resources in general. The board of the common, which was usually elected, was responsible for daily management, but the commoners were usually the ones deciding the long-term management strategy. Rather than analyzing how regulation affected commoners, both as a group and as individuals, I will concentrate on different questions: How did (changes in) the commoners' daily lives affect regulation and functioning of the common? And can we explain why certain decisions were taken?

In this chapter, I demonstrate how, on the basis of very detailed nominative analyses, the behavior of a large group of commoners over nearly two centuries can be evaluated in terms of participation type and intensity. To some extent I will need to reinvent the wheel to make this possible, but logical thinking goes a long way. Because no similar analysis of group behavior for commoners has been done, it is difficult to compare it to other case studies.[6] In the conclusion of this chapter I provide some suggestions for further comparative research on this topic.

4.1 The commoners' changing participation in use and management of the common

For this case study a comparison of the names of members with the names that appear in the bookkeeping and resolution books yields a striking number and unexpected results. First of all, there is among the members of the common a clear trend towards fewer and fewer users that were actively using the common. While it seems reasonable to suppose that members were also those who actually used the common, this was not necessarily the case. It was not at all unusual to become a member and then never again appear in the written documents of the common: some

---

[6] In experimental sociology the effect of micro-level processes (such as individual behavior) on macro-level outcomes is studied, but in an entirely different way. See, e.g., Jager et al. (2000, 357–79) on how a *homo economicus* and *homo psychologicus* act in an experimental commons-dilemma situation. They conclude that the incorporation of a micro-level perspective on human behavior within integrated models of the environment yields a better understanding and eventual management of the processes involved in environmental degradation.

The choices of the commoners

commoners simply never used their right to pasture cattle or to participate in any other way. Given the large number and the high quality of the sources the data are based on, we can assume that the absence of some members in the sources is no coincidence. In most cases, commoners' names could be found year after year as having a cow to graze, or they were mentioned as being one of the commons' officials who reported regularly on their activities. But, as mentioned previously, there were a number of registered commoners for whom there is no evidence they ever participated – not in the bookkeeping, nor in the resolution books, nor in any other sources. There was also a clear evolution in the number of new members who never again appeared in the sources after their first registration. Of the commoners registered in the period 1680–1790, about 65 percent were actually involved in the common (on the basis of activities in the period 1700–1790). From the last decade of the eighteenth century, however, this percentage started to decline considerably: by the middle of the nineteenth century, less than half of the new members were actually involved in the common, in one way or another.[7] The absence of so many commoners from the records can only to a very limited extent result from gaps in the series of sources. Clearly, something was happening on the common: the proportion of active participants among the total number of members became smaller and smaller.[8] It also meant, logically, that the proportion of passive members (those who gained no concrete benefits from the common) was becoming a greater burden over time on the more active participants.

Some individual examples can illustrate the passive behavior of some members. Bernardus Mulle became an *aanborger* in 1804 through his wife Rosa De Schepper, and is a typical example of a passive member.[9] In the population censuses of 1796 and 1814, he was registered as a wage laborer. From other censuses that registered the number of cattle during the 1820s, we

---

[7] For the analysis of the participation level and intensity of the commoners, the names of the *aanborgers* were linked to bookkeeping. As most entries in the bookkeeping were nominative, this could be done fairly easily. For both the lists of names of *aanborgers* (*hoofdboeken*) and the bookkeeping, see the three *hoofdboeken* from 1622 to 1889 (AGL, CAB, nrs. 12–6) and the records of the triennial bookkeeping between 1693 and 1841 (AGL, CAB, nrs. 55–117). For a few short periods of time, the most significant one stretching from 1789 until 1811, no bookkeeping was preserved.

[8] Considering that we could not retrieve data on the death of all *aanborgers*, it is not possible to put this proportion of active participants among those who once registered, in relation to the total number of *aanborgers* at any given moment in time. It can be assumed, however, that the total number of commoners was growing over time, as the number of newly registered commoners increased as well.

[9] Bernardus Dermulle, commoner from 1804, see Hoofdboek. Boek van de geslachten van de Gemene– en Loweede 1769–1889 (CAB, AGL, 14).

The Dilemma of the Commoners

know that he owned at least two cows.[10] Nonetheless, we cannot find any traces of Bernardus Mulle being active on the common. Distance can hardly have been an argument in his decision, since during the entire period he lived in the village Assebroek, and the largest part of the pastures was located in that village. The same was true of Franciscus Van den Berghe:[11] according to the censuses of 1794 and 1814, he was a wage laborer. The marriage acts mention that he was a servant. Both sources contain the same essential information: he worked for wages. He never appeared in the censuses as a cattle owner. In the case of Franciscus, this may have been the main reason he was never mentioned as an active member of the Gemene and Loweiden.

According to our information, another passive commoner, Laurentius Van Belleghem, was also a wage laborer in 1811 and in 1835.[12] The records show that he was born in 1778 and was a commoner from 1802. When he was 34, in 1812, he did use the common. In the book-keeping record of July of that year, we find that he had (a leased) right to collect turf.[13] But after that, he simply disappears from the bookkeeping records. Nor does he appear in the village's cattle censuses, which means it was not likely he used the common, unless he was not telling the truth to the census taker about the number of cattle in his possession. It is not a coincidence that the three early nineteenth-century examples we chose were all *aanborgers* who lived primarily from wages, as the increasing wage dependency of commoners and other villagers influenced their participation in important ways. Considering that the main use of this common was for pasturing, having no cattle would more or less exclude a commoner from active (economic) participation in the common, unless via working for wages on the common.

The possibility that commoners entitled to use the common's resources chose not to do so, whether deliberately or because they did not have the means, may have threatened the smooth functioning and even the future of the institution in several different ways. Apart from the potential threat that insufficient cattle would be grazed on the common (discussed earlier), a lack of active participation could have led to less involvement of the commoners, hence weakening social control. This was especially true for an institution like that of the case study in this book, which was entirely

[10] This becomes clear on the basis of the censuses to be found in Numerieke staten van het belastbaar vee (hoornvee, schapen en paarden), 1823 (Provinciearchief West-Vlaanderen, Modern Archief (2de reeks, TBO7), nrs. 701–8).

[11] Franciscus Van den Berghe, became *aanborger* in 1832, see ibid.

[12] Laurentius Van Belleghem, became *aanborger* in 1802, see ibid.

[13] In 1815 he paid his debts (lease) of 1812; see Rekening 1811–1813, beëindigd in 1815 (CAB, AGL, 108).

self-governed and where most decisions were taken by the members themselves. The effect of a large group of passive members cannot be underestimated: it can be assumed that those who did not receive substantial benefits from the common would not care about the common either, and thus might refrain from reporting abuse or problems on the common as well.

To identify the motives for the changes in the commoners' participation level and the growing number of passive members, it is necessary to add another, more qualitative dimension to the analysis. Those commoners who did participate could do so in many different ways. A more detailed analysis of the bookkeeping allows for distinguishing between various types of economic and functional participation. The former refers to any activity noted in the books that involved some sort of economic exchange: from grazing cattle on the common, buying wood or peat at members-only prices, and using the small river along the common for retting flax, to performing jobs such as digging or making fences on the common. Such activities one way or another contributed to the commoners' welfare: they could benefit from using the inexpensive pasture or they could receive wages from the commons' treasurer. The discrepancy between the price commoners paid for grazing their cattle on the common and the price nonmembers were asked (and willing!) to pay for the same benefit gives us a clear indication of the benefits of being a member. It shows that the benefits must have been substantial, at least if a person had cattle to graze on the common.

Commoners who did not graze cattle on the common probably missed out on a substantial benefit. By analyzing the commoners' ways of economic participation, it becomes possible to determine what their main interests were. A variety of official functions for the commons was included as functional participation, and some of these were remunerated. Several members of the board were entrusted with daily management of the common for a term of three years. Those elected to one of the offices not only received wages, but also moved up the social ladder, an extra incentive for being actively involved. The *hoofdmannen* were assisted by a treasurer, the lowest paid function. In addition to the official appointment, simple attendance at the annual meetings was also included in the analysis as a form of functional participation. Although commoners were in principle obligated to be present, the accounts show that in most instances some members abstained. Increasingly, the commoners lived further away from the common and found it difficult to appear at the annual meetings. At first the *hoofdmannen* tried to invite distant

The Dilemma of the Commoners

commoners by announcing the meetings after Mass in most of the surrounding villages (see De Moor and Debbaut 2003). In the nineteenth century, however, only churchgoers from neighboring villages were informed about the meetings and decisions. This change in communication strategy probably also influenced commoners' attendance at meetings and their participation level in general (Figure 7).

Joannes De Schepper, whose family was involved in the common from the second half of the seventeenth century,[14] is a good example of the diversity of participation among the commoners. Of all the *aanborgers* in his family (and these were numerous), he was the most active: even before he officially became a member of the common in 1752, he had been involved as a laborer to help with drainage works on the common. He must have had a good reputation in the village, since he became the treasurer of the common soon after he became a member, and he fulfilled this function almost continuously until 1782. No doubt Joannes' main job contributed to his election: in the population census of 1748, he was registered as an innkeeper (and carpenter), probably one of the best occupations to build a wide network in the village. The fact that he managed to obtain the job of treasurer year after year by demanding the lowest remuneration for it was probably also a consequence of the benefits he could obtain by providing food and drink at the meetings of the commoners. Combining the job of innkeeper with being the local common's treasurer was clearly a smart way of using your membership. Joannes saw his participation as a source of income, either through his inn or his work for the common, and did not see a need to take advantage of the other facilities the common offered him: in all the time he was involved with the common, he never had any cattle to graze on it.

In 1831 another Johannes, of the Claeys family, became *aanborger*, and he became treasurer of the common in 1842. After that we lose track of him in the sources. His father Ignatius had followed a very different strategy:[15] for ten years he grazed cattle on the common but never held any office. Another example was Frans Tanghe, also from a family with a long tradition in the Gemene and Loweiden, both via his father Jan and his mother Isabelle Van Laethem. He became a member in 1843, and thereafter combined various forms of functional and economic participation. One-quarter of his

---

[14] Joannes De Schepper: Joannes De Scheppere, commoner from 1752, see Hoofdboek. Boek van de geslachten van de Gemene en Loweede, 1718–1767 (copy) (CAB, AGL, 13). The first registration of the family De Schepper(e) was Lieven De Scheppere, commoner from 1679 onwards (see Hoofdboek. Boek van de geslachten van de Gemene en Loweede, 1622–1703, CAB, AGL, 12).

[15] Joannes Claeys, became *aanborger* in 1831, and Ignatius Claeys, became *aanborger* in 1821; see ibid.

The choices of the commoners

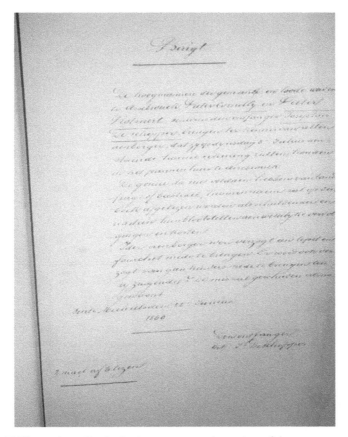

Figure 7 Illustration of an invitation to a general meeting of the commoners to be held on 22 June 1860

Transcription	Translation
Berigt	Notification
De hoogmannen der Gemeene en Loode weiden te Assebrouck, Pieter Cournilly en Pieter Rotsaert, benevens den ontfanger Josephus Deschepper, brengen ter kennis van allen aenborger, dat zij op dynsdag 3 n julius aen- staende hunnen rekening zullen houden in het pannenhuis te Assebrouck.	The *hoogmannen*[a] of the Gemene and Loweiden at Assebroek, Pieter Cournilly and Pieter Rotsaert, together with the collector Josephus Deschepper, notify all *aanborgers* that they will present their accounts on Tuesday July 3rd forthcoming at the *pannenhuis*[b] te Assebrouck.

The Dilemma of the Commoners

Degonne die niet voldaen hebben van land-pagt of beestiael, hunnen naem zal op den boek afgelezen worden als schuldenaer en nadien hun blootstellen aen wettelijke vervolgingen en kosten.	Those who have not yet paid their due land lease or did not pay their livestock taxes, will be proclaimed as being debtors and will be subjected to legal prosecution and payment of costs.
Ider aenborger word verzogt een lepel en fourcket mede te brengen. Er word ook ver-zogt van geen kinders mede te brengen ten-zij zuigendel [inge]n. De mis zal geschieden als na gewoont.	Every *aanborger* is asked to bring along a spoon and fork. Everyone is also asked not to bring along any children, with the exception of breast-fed children. Mass will be celebrated as usual.
Sinte Michiels den 22en junius 1860.	Sinte Michiels, 22 June 1860.
Den ontfanger	The collector
Get. Jh. Deschepper	Signed. Jh. Deschepper
2 mael af te lezen	To be proclaimed twice

Source: City Archives of Bruges, Archive of the Gemene and Loweiden, entry nr. X, inv. no. 197.

[a] The *hoogmannen* (better known as *hooftmannen* or *hoofdmannen*) were those members of the assembly of commoners who were elected at the annual general meeting of the assembly to supervise the day-to-day management of the commons. Since this function required adequate literacy and quite some time, this function was usually occupied by the more educated dignitaries of the assembly of commoners (see also De Moor and Debbaut 2003, 14).

[b] 'In het Pannenhuis' was the name of a local inn at Assebroek, which was the common meeting place of the *aanborgers*. From the seventeenth century until 1964, when the inn had fallen into decay and was torn down, the three-yearly election of the *hoofdmannen* (see note a) and the payment of annual taxes took place at this location.

registered activities related to leasing out land for cattle rearing and crops (which became possible from the 1820s onwards, see further). His other activities involved performing jobs on the common.[16] From 1868 to 1879, he worked as overseer for the common and as treasurer. In total, his name was mentioned in the records for thirty-six years, and he was one of the most active commoners of the entire period.[17]

---

[16] Frans Tanghe did not have any cattle on the common because by the time of his first participation, the system of '*schatgelden*' had already been abolished. This was a system in which a given sum of money was paid per head of cattle grazed on the common. The land he leased from the common could, however, have been used for pasturing.

[17] Frans Tanghe participated on average 3.78 times a year (during his membership), which included 2.59 economic participations between 1836 and 1879.

The choices of the commoners

Table 4 Subdivision of ways (economically or functionally) in which *aanborgers* were active, 1700–1900

Last year of activity	Share of *aanborgers* who were only active *economically* (%)	Share of *aanborgers* who were both *economically* and *function-ally* active (%)	Share of *aanborgers* who were only active *functionally* (%)	Total N
1700–1724	58.00	34.00	8.00	50
1725–1749	44.44	53.97	1.59	63
1750–1774	51.81	43.37	4.82	83
1775–1799	68.70	28.70	2.61	115
1800–1824	44.83	31.03	24.14	58
1825–1849	60.00	37.89	2.11	95
1850–1874	85.71	11.43	2.86	70
1875–1900	81.25	17.50	1.25	80
Total	**63.11**	**31.72**	**5.18**	**614**

This way of 'categorizing' the commoners can help to point out changes in the participatory behavior of commoners, which in itself may be an indicator of the utility of the common resources for its users, and brings us to the second major conclusion on the commoners' behavior. One of the most interesting trends is that, starting from the middle of the eighteenth century, there was growing polarization between economic participants and functional participants. At first, nearly half the active commoners combined economic participation with some sort of functional involvement; a century later this was only true for one out of every ten commoners. By the middle of the nineteenth century, most commoners (eight out of ten) had become economic participants only and were no longer involved in the management of the common (De Moor and Debbaut 2003, 273–4).

Although these figures tell us that the majority of the commoners did use the common in one way or another, and that a large number of them were also actively involved in keeping the management going; the degree to which they were active may also tell us something more about their behavior. Were they active now and then, or did they constantly invest time and money in being part of the common? It can be assumed that enforcement through social control required a high intensity of participation, with many commoners keeping an eye on the use of the resources, preferably on a continuous basis. A system in which different individuals use the common

The Dilemma of the Commoners

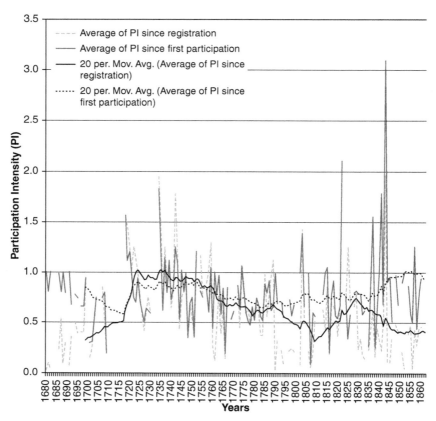

Figure 8 Evolution of the average participation intensity per 20 years, 1680–1860

only every now and then may not be a system with a high degree of social control. An analysis of the number of times commoners used the common per annum from their subscription to the common until their last participation, shows that from the middle of the eighteenth century commoners' participation intensity dropped dramatically. During a period of approximately twenty-five years, between the early nineteenth century and the 1930s, participation increased, but then it went down again (Figure 8).[18]

The evolution in types of commoners' participation described earlier and the declining active participation can be combined with another indicator to

---

[18] This participation does not only including the act of putting cattle on the common but could also involve working for the common or taking part in meetings. All possible activities commoners and others could take part in were calculated as 'participations'.

The choices of the commoners

show the importance commoners attached to their membership. Combining the participation data with the marriage registers for the villages of Assebroek, Oedelem, and surrounding villages, enables us to estimate the age at subscription of new members. New members were listed in the *hoofdboeken* by the local parish (see point 3.1). This age is an indicator of the importance a new member (or if he was very young, his parents) attributed to belonging to the common and the community of commoners. It can be assumed that joining the group when a person was very young (early childhood to early teens) indicates the parents' high expectations: becoming a member could offer a son the guarantee of more social security, or at least a source of income and a network that could be called upon in times of need. Late subscriptions were more likely when a man became a member via his wife, but it could also imply lower expectations for professional life. The reference point used here is the moment at which a son began to live his life independent of his parents. In a rural society, such a marker would be marriage, which in areas with neo-locality such as West Flanders was the same as setting up an independent business (usually a farm).[19]

Since it was not possible to retrieve both the age at subscription and the age at marriage for all commoners, I used a sample of nearly 600 commoners to calculate the average age at subscription, and compared this with the average age at marriage for the region in this period. The sample was selected on the basis of availability of data: for some commoners there was more information available than for others, and for some the date of birth could not be found.[20]

On the basis of this age analysis at subscription, I detect another major trend in the members' behavior, next to the decreased activity level and the growing divergence between economic and functional participants (Figure 9). This sample of *aanborgers* shows that the average age at which commoners were registered gradually increased in the course of the nineteenth century. Around the end of the eighteenth century, the new commoner was on average twenty years old; by the first decade of the nineteenth century the average age at subscription was nearly thirty. The average age remained under thirty until the middle of the nineteenth century, but thereafter it rose again, and around 1880 the average age at the time of becoming a member was forty. In the course of time, potential *aanborgers* thus postponed their subscription to later in life. This may to some extent be a consequence of more members registering who obtained

---

[19] Although it should also be mentioned that it was quite likely youngsters left the parental home to work as servants before marriage, which was quite typical for this part of Europe (see Smith [1979, 74–112]; De Moor and van Zanden [2010]).

[20] We do not have sufficiently reliable data for the rest of the eighteenth century.

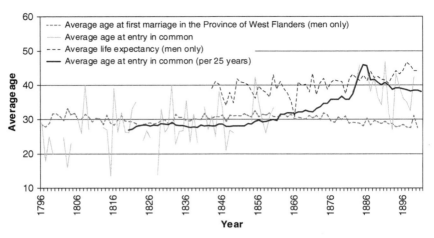

Figure 9 Average age at subscription compared to average marriage age in the region, 1796–1900

the right via their in-laws. The percentage of those who became members via their in-laws increased over time, from 21 percent of all new members in the period 1775 to 1799, to 38 percent in the period 1875–1900. But still, even these members needed to see the utility of their – possibly later than average – registration. From the middle of the nineteenth century, young men usually joined the commons after their marriage, the average age at first marriage (for men) at that time being around thirty. By the end of the nineteenth century, the average marriage age had decreased by a few years, but the age at subscription remained as high as before. This evolution indicates that commoners started to become members of the common at a different point in their life course: if commoners did not find it necessary to claim their right before they were forty, we can assume that they did not consider the commons' resources and facilities essential for their professional activities, or they did not have the means to participate, perhaps because they did not have cattle to graze.

Figure 9 demonstrates that not only did the age of commoners at registration go up over time, but the time they took to become active commoners went up as well. It can be assumed that the common lost some of its utility, since the number of farmers who used the common as a surplus pasture in times of insufficient grass and fodder production on private land was reduced. Laborers may not have had the opportunity to graze livestock during winter when the common was not accessible. Since they probably had fewer cattle to feed, they would eventually also benefit less from the common as an extra source of

The choices of the commoners

income. It should be no surprise then that the number of subscribed commoners who made active use of the common would diminish considerably over time.

I have now provided several indications that something was happening on the common that deeply influenced the commoners' behavioral strategy: an increasing number of commoners did not use their rights actively, there was a growing gap between users and rulers, a serious decrease in their intensity of participation, and more and more members were registering at an increasingly older age. The relative decrease in the active participation was visible first, the rest followed. By linking the available information in the sources on the Gemene and Loweiden to other information, such as the population and economic censuses, it can be concluded that the changes identified may have been related to the changing occupational background of commoners. A very important explanation is the extent to which commoners were bound to agriculture as a source of income. Independent, self-sustaining small farmers benefited most from the common: they would have primarily focused on mixed farming and thus needed the grazing facilities offered by the common. Maintaining cattle was an essential part of the mixed-farming chain, as it provided the manure necessary to fertilize the arable land (see earlier in this book). It was not until the mid-nineteenth century that fertilizers such as guano would be imported in large quantities and that chalk deposits would be developed, solving part of the fertilization bottleneck of mixed farming. Thus, in seeking to explain the changes in the commoners' behavioral strategy, we should concentrate on the farmers among the commoners.

The analysis shows that just over 50 percent of the commoners who became members in the first half of the eighteenth century were registered as farmers, nearly 19 percent as agricultural wage laborers, and about 14 percent worked as wage laborers outside agriculture.[21] Thereafter, the

---

[21] These results are entirely based on a dataset comprised of sixty-four *aanborgers*, who became commoners in the first half of the eighteenth century and who appeared in the population census of 1748. No other census material was used. Of these sixty-four, sixty were known as active on the common, which is not surprising considering the high participation level around that time, as mentioned earlier in the chapter. The other percentages for the periods thereafter are based on a large number of diverse sources, ranging from registers of birth/baptism (for occupations of parents who were *aanborgers*), marriage and death/burial, composed by the parish priest in the ancien régime and by the local government thereafter. In combination with the data on the registration of the commoners retrieved from the *hoofdboeken*, we obtained a sample of 710 *aanborgers* for the whole period 1700–1900, of whom 418 can be considered as active.

The Dilemma of the Commoners

number of commoners registered as farmers dropped significantly. In the second half of the eighteenth century, this group accounted for only 24 percent; among the commoners registered in the first half of the nineteenth century, only one out of five was a farmer, but nearly four out of ten were registered as agricultural laborers. Together with the other wage-laboring commoners, they accounted for two-thirds of all commoners. In the second half of the nineteenth century, those engaged in wage labor (including agricultural laborers) dropped to 44 percent, but the proportion of farmers did not increase to more than one-quarter of the group. Although sometimes confusing statements in the sources made categorizing the commoners' occupational status difficult, there was a clear evolution in the socio-economic background of the commoners: wage-dependent commoners increasingly replaced farmers among commoners.[22] For 1748, when comparing the occupational structure of the commoners to the overall occupational structure of the villages of Assebroek and Oedelem, I found that 65 percent of the inhabitants of these villages were active in agriculture either as farmers (23 percent of the total) or as wage laborers (41 percent of the total), which is only slightly less than the 69 percent of the *aanborgers* active in agriculture in 1748.[23] For the other periods, such a comparison would not be reliable, as data on the commoners' backgrounds came from various sources. This evolution is no different from the general trend towards more wage dependency in this period elsewhere in Flanders, and it demonstrates how important changes in the external factors were for the behavior of individuals on the commons.

The example of Andreas De Rijcker, born in 1763 and registered as a commoner in 1786, illustrates the evolution from farmer to wage laborer that many commoners experienced in this period.[24] Andreas came from a family that included four ancestors registered as commoners in the sixteenth century.[25] In the nineteenth century, after Andreas, there were Bruno, Henri, Louis, Bernard, Félix, and others of the same lineage.[26]

---

[22] These data were collected on the basis of a variety of sources: resolution books, bookkeeping records, *hoofdboeken*, parish registers, population registers, and demographic and economic censuses.

[23] We can do this because all occupational information on the commoners for the period 1700–1750 is based on the 1748 census. See the preceding footnotes.

[24] Andreas De Rijckere, a commoner from 1757, see Hoofdboek. Boek van de geslachten van de Gemene en Loweede, 1718–1767 (copy) (CAB, AGL, 13).

[25] Jan De Rijckere, commoner from 1698, see Hoofdboek. Boek van de geslachten van de Gemene en Loweede, 1622–1703 (CAB, AGL, 12) and Pieter De Rijcker, commoner from 1779, see CAB, AGL, 14.

[26] Bruno De Rijcker, commoner from 1787 (CAB, AGL, 14), Henricus De Rycker, commoner from in 1820 (CAB, AGL, 14), Ludovicus De Rycker, commoner from 1825 (ibid.), Bernardus De Rijckere, commoner from 1833 onwards (ibid.), Félix De Rijckere, who became commoner in 1839 (ibid.).

Table 5 Evolution per half century of the percentage of farmers, farm laborers (including servants and day laborers), and laborers among the *aanborgers*, 1700–1900

Period	A. Farmers (%)	B. Farm laborers (servants, day laborers) (%)	C. Laborers (%)	D = C + B (%)	Other occupations	N
1700–1749	51.56	18.75	14.06	32.81	15.63	64
1750–1799	24.14	13.79	37.93	51.72	24.14	58
1800–1849	20.99	39.51	27.16	66.67	12.35	243
1850–1900	25.51	7.25	37.39	44.64	29.86	345
Total	**26.2**	**19.86**	**31.83**	**51.69**	**22.11**	**710**

The Dilemma of the Commoners

The De Rijcker family was among the most active groups on the common, which makes them a good 'barometer' for revealing how the changes came about. The family had a clear interest in the economic advantages of the common, but was less concerned about being elected to an office (except for Adriaen De Rijckere,[27] who in 1843 became one of the *hoofdmannen*). Three years after his registration, Andreas began to use his rights on the common:[28] between 1789 and 1827 he usually grazed one cow on the common, sometimes also a swine. In 1813 and 1814, he had two cows and one horse on the common. According to the censuses, he already had a horse at the end of the eighteenth century, but by the 1820s he was back to one single cow, which he placed on the common. And after that he lost even more: in 1827, when he was sixty-four years old, the last mention of Andreas in the bookkeeping record qualified him as a debtor. His worsening situation can also be shown from the occupational category attributed to him in the censuses. While he was still listed as a farmer in 1796, in 1814 and 1826 he was registered as a laborer. The other members of the family for whom we could retrieve occupations were nearly all registered as working for wages.[29]

This is just one example of the dramatic changes in the social and economic backgrounds of commoners from the late eighteenth century onwards. This process may have set in a few decades earlier, but the necessary sources to make the analysis before that time are not available. The decrease in the number of farmers – among both active and passive commoners – was part of a more general proletarianization of the Flemish countryside during this period. This process influenced commoners' participation and the way they participated. Yet, when considering the commoners' behavior and the possible reasons why that behavior changed over time, it's important to ask why they still registered as members and paid the one pound for subscription if their individual advantages had become so limited. The total number of new members increased from 31 new members in the earlier period to 217 in the later one, which indicates that within the village communities the need for the common was still very great, although it may have been less directly linked to the family farm, which was nevertheless still very important. Many, it seems, became members to secure use-rights for their retirement and possibly also for future generations.

---

[27] Adriaen De Rijcker, who became *aanborger* in 1728 (CAB, AGL, nr. 13), was also the grandfather of Andreas De Rijcker, who became *aanborger* in 1786 (CAB, AGL, nr. 14).

[28] This part refers to Andreas De Rijcker, *aanborger* from 1786 onwards (CAB, AGL, nr. 14).

[29] We do not know the occupation of Adriaen De Rijcker, who became *aanborger* in 1728 (CAB, AGL, nr. 13).

4.2 The effect of changing power balances on the management of the common

This analysis so far has shown that commoners followed different strategies, that their choices were influenced by social and economic changes; and that their individual strategies represented a considerable shift in the role of the common in agriculture. Another consequence of the shift in participant profiles was a growing polarization among the group of active participants, between the 'simple' users and the managers. The internal power balances changed over time, from a fairly democratic regime to a system in which decisions were increasingly taken by the administrative elite, without much interference from those who actually used the common, the small- and medium-scale farmers.

The data available for the Gemene and Loweiden show that imbalances in power relations may have had serious consequences on the use of the commons' natural resources. Commoners could use the meadows for grazing their cattle by paying per head. Through this system it became possible for the managers of the common to control the total number of cattle units on the common, which was very useful in preventing over-exploitation of resources: if use of the common became too great, the prices per head of cattle were raised. Conversely, if commoners did not have sufficient cattle to graze on the common, prices were reduced. Moreover, in periods when there was a serious lack of cattle to maintain the necessary level of grazing, villagers who were not commoners were sometimes allowed to graze cattle on the common. In the 1840s, however, this highly efficient system was threatened. On the one hand, there was increasing pressure from passive members, many of whom were too poor to make good use of their membership. It is quite likely that they used their precarious economic position as an argument to move the other com-moners towards freeing more pasture land for other means, such as crop production. On the other hand, a small number of commoners had the power to change the system entirely. As a result the system that had long been used to regulate the number of cattle on the common was replaced by a lease system. Commoners could apply to lease a plot of land, and use it according to their needs, also for crop production. In the 1820s, part of the land had also been turned into arable land, which should have made it more attractive for non-cattle owners as well. Restrictions on how the land was used became less strict from the 1840s onwards, and the former restrictions on the number of cattle permitted on the common were no longer applied.

The fact that from the 1820s decisions about how to use the resources of the common were increasingly made by individual leaseholders – who

The Dilemma of the Commoners

might have been commoners – must have led to reduced social control by the commoners themselves. In general, it can be assumed that a low participation level can have serious consequences for the functioning of an institution such as a common. When less active participants reduce already suboptimal social control, it can mean that undesired outcomes are less easily spotted by others. The commoners were aware of this potential risk; nevertheless, it was not unusual to find systems that sanctioned those who saw an infraction of the regulation but did not report it to the management of the common.[30] To make the control system watertight, young cow herders were often recruited to keep an eye on the common and its users while working, as a form of extra control.

If the intensity of participation diminished, it may have been necessary to resort to methods other than social control to govern the behavior of the users. For many years, *koewachters*, boys in their early teens, had been recruited to guard the livestock and report problems or infringements of rules. The commoners tried to solve this problem by calling in external controllers. From the late eighteenth century onwards, they paid the local constable to inspect the common.[31] In the account book of 1791 we can read that control of use of the common was in the hands of an external official.[32] From then onwards, the local constable received an annual payment to ensure enforcement of common's rules. In addition to decreased involvement of commoners in the commons, the increased meddling of local government in their affairs suggests escalating involvement of external control. Local government meddling was a process that would accumulate in the later claims that the municipality of Assebroek would try to take of the Gemene and Loweiden (see elsewhere in this chapter).[33]

Increased involvement of external controllers may have also reflected the increasing attempts of local government to interfere in the management of the common.[34]

---

[30] For many references to the regulation, see M. De Moor (2002; 2005) for Flanders. For examples of other western European countries, see the other chapters in De Moor, Shaw-Taylor, and Warde (2002a).

[31] Experimental research claims that inspection and sanctioning of behavior does not necessarily encourage people to behave better. In this sense it can be questioned whether external monitoring/inspection can be considered a valuable alternative for social control (Ostmann 1998).

[32] Rekening 1787–1789, closed in 1791, CAB, AGL, nr. 106.

[33] For a more extensive description of the sequester period, see M. De Moor (2005).

[34] It is unclear – in the absence of accounts for the period 1843–1868 – whether the committee in charge of the management of the common recorded this expense every year. But in the period when the common was put under supervision of a sequester (1862–1882), the extra expenditure to control the common was considered completely superfluous.

The choices of the commoners

In the 1840s and 1850s, the common also came under increasing pressure from the local and national governments, leading to the forced abdication of the management board in 1862. The control over the common was taken out of the hands of the commoners until 1882, when the commoners won a court case against the municipalities of Assebroek and Oedelem. In 1847, the government passed a new law, ostensibly to encourage reclamation of the remaining wastelands in Flanders, but it actually provided the local governments with an instrument to dissolve all common property in their territory and sell the land for their own benefit. Long before 1847, laws from the eighteenth and early nineteenth centuries had tried to dissolve the commons in the territory that would later become Belgium (which was then commonly known as the Southern Netherlands), but to little avail (M. De Moor 2003a). This forced dissolution of land held in common became legally possible with the introduction of the new *Code Civil*, which under article 542 held that all common property was communal property. Local governments referred to this chapter and had the support of the national and provincial governments when trying to seize commoners' land. With the crisis of 1846 that drove many Belgians into poverty, the government saw a new opportunity to dissolve the commons, with the excuse that it would be beneficial for agricultural output. Great pressure was placed on local governments to sell all common property in their territory. If no action was taken, the government could even proceed to a forced selling of the common. The Gemene and Loweiden is one of the very few commons in Flanders that survived this period. The only reason for this survival may have been the legal support it received from a local priest, Canon Andries, who was able to trace all the documents (dating back to the sixteenth century) that proved the commoners' rights, even in the new legal system of the nineteenth century.

Ostrom (1990) states that systems in which commoners participate in the decision-making process of the common-pool institution (CPI) are more likely to survive because 'being involved' enhances reciprocal behavior.[35] As described earlier in this chapter, the number of active participants remained relatively high in the eighteenth century: seven out of every ten commoners who subscribed to the common would eventually also use the common. About 42 percent of these participants would not only use the common for economic reasons, but also took part

---

[35] See, e.g., nr. 3 in the 'design principles illustrated by long-enduring CPR institutions': 'Collective-choice arrangements: most individuals affected by the operational rules can participate in modifying the operational rules' (Ostrom 1990, 90).

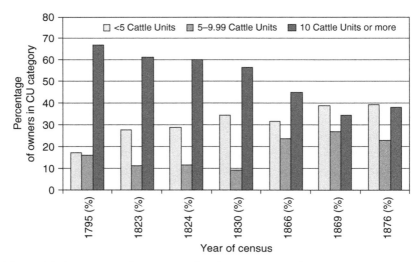

Figure 10 Percentage of categories of cattle owners according to the total number of cattle units in their possession

in the management of the common, albeit at different decision-making levels and not necessarily on a continuous basis.[36]

Apart from this, there were some clear changes in the socio-economic conditions of the commoners and, as mentioned earlier, in their average participation level. Not only was the relative number of commoners who used the common seriously diminishing, the average number of cattle on the common per user dropped too in that period. Figure 10 shows the declining percentage of the group of large cattle owners (more than 10 CUs) among the commoners, to the advantage of the owners of small- and medium-size cattle herds. Moreover, as the number of independent farmers dropped, more wage laborers appeared among the commoners and in the Flemish countryside in general. As prices for dairy products and meat had been rising, more intensive exploitation of the common became more attractive. All these factors indicate that the common was no longer in balance: whereas before, the utility of the land for the users was in harmony with an efficient, sustainable management of resources, later, the managers – possibly under pressure from the commoners – decided to act to the

---

[36] In the calculations, different forms of taking part in the management were taken into account. Participation in management included a wide range of activities, from simply attending a meeting of the common or performing an administrative task to becoming an official representative (*hoofdman*) of the common.

The choices of the commoners

advantage of the commoners (utility) first. In cases of emergency, the commoners did use their rights; by the end of the nineteenth century, the managers of the common started contributing more to the local charity fund, at the request of the local municipality board.

4.3 Dealing with over- and under-exploitation

Descriptions of historical commons in the past often gave a very static picture of their organization. We have already seen that commoners' behavior could change substantially, as a consequence of changes in their social and economic background; this change in utility affected both the equity – how the use was distributed – and the efficiency – how the use was regulated. But could changes in the institution also affect the behavior of the commoners in such a way that their use of the common did not affect the resource's viability? Sources on the regulation of the commons' use show that the managers were willing and able to adjust their management to changes in the local social, economic, legal, and political conditions. Researching the commons from the perspective of the commoner is unusual in historical research on commons, mainly due to the lack of adequate sources. However, for the case study in this book sufficient data on its daily functioning has been preserved.

The sources allow us to link the regulation of commons as it was agreed upon in the charters with the actual effects in practice. Here the background information on the Gemene and Loweiden mentioned earlier is important. The right to use the resources of this common could only be obtained via inheritance – for the period in this study only via the male descendants.[37] The inheritance arrangement that regulated access to the common on the Gemene and Loweiden, however, was not exceptional; it can be found in several other places in Flanders and the rest of Europe.[38] Most likely it is the result of the exclusion process as described earlier in this book: originally all inhabitants of the villages of Assebroek and Oedelem (where the common was situated) could claim rights on the common. Being a legitimate commoner, however, did not necessarily entail usage of the common, as has been demonstrated in the previous chapter.

---

[37] In the earliest *hoofdboeken*, the names of several women were registered as new members (De Moor and Debbaut 2003).

[38] A similar example in Flanders is the 'Vrijbroek' in Mechelen. This was in 1260 donated by Wouter Bertoud to twenty-eight 'good people'. These and all their descendants could enjoy the use of it, after having paid two schillings a year (Devos 1936, 30).

143

Notwithstanding efforts to keep the number of potential new users on the Gemene and Loweiden down, the total number of registered *aanborgers* was too high for the limited amount of space available on the common-pool resource (CPR), even when many of the members were not actively taking part. During the eighteenth century, the total acreage of the common varied between only 80 and 100 hectares. Between 1700 and 1800 on average seven new persons per year subscribed to the common.[39] Although there was a clear threat of population growth and risk of commercialization by these commoners – since the common was in the vicinity of large trading centers (Bruges and the livestock market in Oedelem) – there were on this common no particular rules limiting commercialization of resources from the common. The commoners of the Gemene and Loweiden used an ingenious price mechanism instead. This system – whereby the commoner paid a sum of money per head of livestock put on the common – was set up to achieve a fairly constant level of exploitation of the CPR. The archival sources are not detailed enough to reveal the particular reasons for each of the price adjustments, but Figure 11, based on a detailed analysis of the available bookkeeping for the eighteenth and the first half of the nineteenth century (until 1841), shows that these decisions cannot have been arbitrary: until the end of the eighteenth century, the changes in the number of horses and cows and the changes in the price per head of livestock were clearly related to the grazing pressure on the common (see prices as indicated underneath the x-axis of Figure 11).[40] The meticulous bookkeeping of the common allows us to reconstruct and to demonstrate the effectiveness of the price mechanism. In addition to the number of livestock per type (horses, cows, and pigs) the graph shows the aggregated total of livestock units and the total number of users to whom this livestock belonged.[41]

What the graph does not show, however – simply because of the lack of precise data – is the number of livestock units that were provided by non-entitled users. In general it is assumed that only commoners were allowed to use the resources and that any other person entering and using the common was doing so illegally. The case of the Gemene and Loweiden, however, demonstrates that non-entitled users were not only sometimes officially temporarily accepted as users, but that this

---

[39] The yearly growth of the number of *aanborgers* was calculated on the basis of the analysis of all the *hoofdboeken* (AGL, CAB), see footnote 21 of this chapter.

[40] The bookkeeping on which Figure 12 is based can be found at the City Archives of Bruges, Archief Gemene en Loweiden, numbers 55 to 117.

[41] The following weighing coefficients were used: cows were considered as 1 livestock unit, horses as 1.2 livestock units, and pigs as 0.2 livestock units.

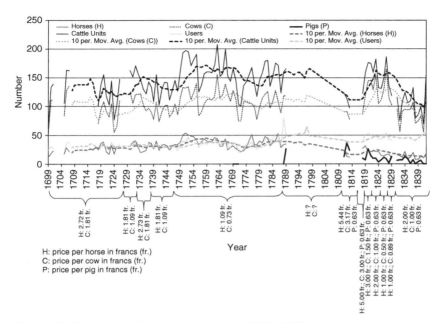

Figure 11 Exploitation level of the common, 1699–1840, in terms of cattle units

practice was also a method to avoid an unstable exploitation level. Until the middle of the eighteenth century, non-commoners could request the management of the common to allow some of their livestock to graze for a given period of time. In some cases this was accepted, as in 1709, when several persons put their livestock on the common because there was an abundance of grass. This practice was introduced because commoners could not provide a sufficient number of livestock to graze on this grass and it provided some additional cash income in those times of heavy war duties. In the first half of the eighteenth century, most of the entitled commoners also used the common, but because of the few newly subscribing commoners,[42] the number of animals was insufficient to achieve an optimal exploitation level. Therefore, other non-entitled users were temporarily granted the right to use the common, though only for a restricted number of cattle and often only for a few weeks. This

---

[42] Whereas in the period 1623–1699, on average twelve new commoners subscribed to the common per year, only four did so during the first half of the eighteenth century. In the century thereafter, there were again about six new members every year (De Moor and Debbaut 2003).

temporary permission and the price mechanism that was used suggest that the managers kept a close eye on the grazing pressure and did take steps when an optimal pressure level was not achieved.

Changes in the methods used to achieve an optimal grazing pressure clearly reflected changes in the socio-economic background of the commoners. Taking into consideration the added number of livestock, the exploitation level of the common would on average have been 150 livestock units (LU). Population growth did not start until the second half of the eighteenth century. From the 1750s onwards, requests from non-commoners were no longer granted, and between 1747 and 1788 the prices per head of cattle remained stable. Adjustments of the prices to put livestock on the common were no longer necessary until the end of that century.[43] The attitude towards outsiders also changed significantly over time. In 1763 the common experienced a serious drop in the number of cows (from 155 to 115), which probably caused temporary under-exploitation.[44] Instead of allowing livestock from non-entitled users in to solve this problem, as had been done before, the managers had a different solution this time: although it was commonly known that it could cause great damage to the common, they decided to accept pigs, but only those of their own commoners.[45] The nonmembers' animals were no longer needed to keep the level of exploitation stable, suggesting that the situation among the commoners themselves might have become more dire and that the managers preferred to take care of their own members first. Though, from an ecological point of view, this decision to accept pigs on the commons might have been a pernicious one, the managers primarily responded to the general impoverishment of the commoners (see earlier in this chapter). As pigs were cheaper to keep, as well as less demanding and less choosy about their food than cows and horses, they became increasingly popular as substitutes for the larger cattle among the villagers, a typical sign that the community was becoming poorer. The managers must have noticed the negative effect of the pigs on the common after a while, as they stopped this practice by 1789, here again putting the common as a resource first instead of the benefit of the commoners.

---

[43] For the period 1790–1811, there are no accounts available. For an overview of the available accounts see M. De Moor (2005, 40–3).

[44] CAB, AGL, nr. 94.

[45] In older documents it was clearly stated that pigs, sheep, goats, and geese were not allowed on the common since these root up the pasture land. See, e.g., the charter of 1514 as published in Gilliodts-van Severen (1880) and the numbers 2 and 3 in AGL, CAB.

The choices of the commoners

For the period 1790–1811, no data are available. Thereafter the number of livestock pasturing on the common dropped significantly. This was partially a consequence of the reclamation of part of the common, reducing the available pasture land and thus the acceptable number of livestock, and partially of the general decrease of the average number of livestock units per person in this period. These changes in management and use can be explained by the relative importance of the common for the active users: although the group of new commoners kept increasing, the number of active users remained more or less the same and thus this group became relatively smaller and smaller. The group of commoners who did not use the common for cattle grazing exercised increasing pressure on those with cattle to make some parts of the land available for crop production.

A detailed analysis of the exploitation level and the resolution books of the Gemene and Loweiden illustrate that the commoners themselves were aware of the potential negative effects of both over- and under-exploitation. In the first half of the eighteenth century, the commoners did not have enough cattle to prevent under-grazing on the common. Eventually, this could lead to under-exploitation and a lack of social control on the use of the common. To achieve a constant grazing level of about 150 cattle units (which was the number that could be held in a sustainable way on this size meadow) the common's managers temporarily allowed others to graze their cattle on the common. For this privilege they asked considerable sums, often amounting to more than twenty times the price entitled commoners had to pay to let their cattle graze on the common (see earlier). Apart from the fact that they simply wanted to seize this opportunity to acquire some extra income, this decision can be seen as part of the overall management strategy of the commoners to avoid a 'tragedy of the commons'.

Apart from the diminution at the end of the period, it can be concluded that the exploitation level obtained by the managers was fairly stable overall. This indicates that the commoners – through their managers – strove for a constant grazing pressure. But was not it too high for the small pasture? At the height of the exploitation (1750–1759), the grazing pressure would have been half a hectare per livestock unit. As the livestock was only on the common in the spring and summer seasons, and as it was likely that they received extra food, it can be assumed that the total number of livestock units did not lead to excessive exploitation of the common's resources.[46]

---

[46] During the summer season a cow (= 1.0 LU) needs around 0.8 hectares. However, the livestock normally received plenty of other feeding, necessitating only 0.4 hectares per LU of extra pasture land per annum (see Slicher van Bath [1960]).

The Dilemma of the Commoners

In this case it can thus be assumed that the continuity of the exploitation level stems from a concern to exploit the pasture in a sustainable way.

4.4 Keeping it in common: the choice between collective and private property

Considering the evolution just described, why not privatize the common in its entirety? Why not simply subdivide the whole area into separate plots, sell them, and divide the money brought in among the commoners?[47] This might indeed have been a beneficial solution from an economic point of view, but here, again, there is more to the story: a close look at the bookkeeping of the commoners shows that the *aanborgers* were not an average *homo economicus*, but rather what can be called a *homo reciprocans* or a *homo cooperans*. I have demonstrated earlier in this book that, on average, the commoners were (with a few exceptions) no longer very active on the common. Moreover, in the course of time the age commoners became active shifted from their early teens to after their marriage. These are all indications that the common had lost much of its value for active economic/agricultural use for individual commoners. But the three-yearly bookkeeping balances suggest that on the group level, getting the most out of the common was not a priority. The balances show that their intention was to keep the common alive, not to make the most profit out of it. This does change during the first decades of the nineteenth century, but overall the commoners were not really making any money out of the common. The graph in Figure 12 is in many ways a peculiar one: it shows the zero – or close to zero – outcome for much of the eighteenth century, a rise in the early nineteenth century, and then a spectacular peak during the years the common was in the hands of representatives of the local government. This temporary board of common managers found a very easy way of making money: they simply cut all the trees on the common and sold the wood, hence the peak in income. Although such resources can only be harvested once – and the temporary board had already done that – the commoners were otherwise not inspired by this commercial attitude once

---

[47] There may have also been other economic reasons. Elaine Tan (2002) gives the interesting example of a 'common bull': common fields reduced the transaction costs for a commoner to maintain a cow by lowering the cost of insemination, provided by that common bull, and thus avoided the need to seek this 'service' via the market. After enclosure, the cost of maintaining a cow increased for small owners who, unlike large-farm owners, could neither jointly own the bull and the cow, nor lease the bull easily. The minimum acreage required to restore cow keepers to their pre-enclosure economic position indicates that many commoners who were given some land in settlement were inadequately compensated for the change in property rights.

The choices of the commoners

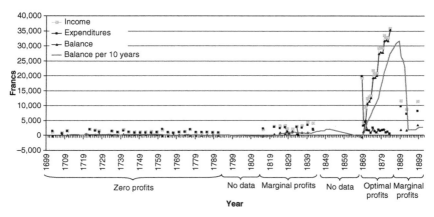

Figure 12 Evolution of the balance of accounts, 1699–1899

they got their common back. The graph shows that they just went back to the way it used to be: without any or hardly any profit. What does this tell us? It shows that it was not impossible to make a profit from the common: the trees could have been cut gradually as well, and the commoners could have also profited from the common in this way, even before the local government took over. Second, it shows that commoners' prime interest was not profit: the commons were considered part of a survival strategy to be invoked in times of scarcity. This strategy, in combination with what we know about the regulation of commons and the mechanisms commoners used to limit the exploitation of the common via grazing (see the previous chapter) reveal – I may even say prove – that it was not the short-term strategy (whereby each individual got the most from the common) that motivated the commoners and their appointed managers and monitors: the long-term perspective was much more important.

4.5 Conclusions

This chapter has demonstrated that a detailed analysis of the behavior of commoners as users can help explain the deeper motivations of commoners in using the commons' facilities and why the use and importance of commons changed over time. For the specific case study of the Gemene and Loweiden in the eighteenth and nineteenth centuries, not far from the eastern city gates of Bruges, we saw a growing number of passive members, who, by the nineteenth century, had a significant influence on the decision-making process on the common. Second, among the users of the common a clear polarization was found between those who were

The Dilemma of the Commoners

involved in the common for economic reasons and those who acted as managers. While originally managers were also usually users, the two groups became increasingly distinct from one another. This process went together with changes in the participation intensity. Moreover, by the middle of the nineteenth century, the age at which commoners registered as members was considerably higher than it had been in the eighteenth century, suggesting that the immediate need to use the common had become less important. These four developments – activity rate, type of participation, intensity of participation, and age of subscription – had a clear influence on the way in which the resources were used (from pasture land to partial conversion into arable), how their use was controlled (from the payment-per-head-of-cattle system to leasing out parts of the land), the internal power balance (with diminished interference from the real users), and the potential social control on use (increasingly done by local village officials instead of the users themselves). As the common became less used by cattle owners, there was little opposition to the abolition of the efficient system of payment per head of cattle and to leasing out a substantial part of the common land. This change in management system may reflect the decreasing utility of the common for many of its users and as such may have weakened the commoners' ability to oppose the local governments' interference: the constable of the local government had already been asked to control use of the common, which is in itself an indication of decreasing self-governance. It is likely that such control was needed to compensate for reduced social control, a result of the less regular use by the commoners, and thus also their reduced physical presence on the common. The main cause identified for the commoners' changing behavior was their proletarianization, which was apparent from the increasing wage dependence of not all, but likely many of the villagers in the surroundings. Commoners were to a lesser extent independent farmers, and the number of cattle per farmer had diminished greatly over time.

This particular case study provides a unique insight into the workings of a pre-industrial common, thanks to the availability of a large set of account books for an impressively long period when major changes took place among commoners and in society as a whole. Although bookkeeping records are available for other commons that were managed more independently, it might not be possible to develop a similar dataset and conduct similar analyses for other commons. To be sure, there are other forms of institutions for collective action, such as guilds, for studying group heterogeneity and size in similar detail. Elsewhere in this book, I have argued that the commons can be considered the rural counterparts of guilds, in view of

The choices of the commoners

their many similar objectives, organization, rise, and decline (see also T. De Moor 2008). An understanding of internal regulation by cooperating individuals, whether living in the countryside or in urban environments, could benefit from similar analyses in the future for other forms of self-governed institutions.

In this chapter, it has been shown that the users of the common were able to manage resource use in a sustainable way, but that under the stress of internal changes and external pressure to privatize, the original institutional set-up was affected. For a limited period of time, the common's management was also taken away from the commoners and ran by representatives of local and provincial authorities. Over a period of twenty years, management was taken over by a committee that acted without regard for the previous regulation or objectives that commoners had set for centuries for their own managers. This contrast in goals and way of dealing with the same resource, but in a different management structure, suggests it would be fruitful to investigate the economic potential of the resources and the degree to which they were important to the commoners. This process shows that when the use of the common-pool resources diminishes for its users, with a relatively large number of commoners no longer interested in using those resources, the resistance to usurpation and eventually also dissolution becomes weak. This common survived this very difficult period during which commoners were deprived of the right to manage their own land. Interestingly, the way in which they managed the institution after they won a court case and regained their rights, shows the deeper motivations of the commoners to cooperate. These were not primarily economic, but social. Whereas they could have made a large profit from the common, they returned to the way they used the common before the period of usurpation by the local government: not for individual profit but for the profit of the community. This shows that commons answered a real social need – by way of serving as an insurance system for its members – and that it mattered to the community as a means to relieve poverty (via charity work).

5. Dealing with dilemmas: conclusions

Since the beginning of the twenty-first century, commons have gained new interest, especially in activist circles. The term 'common' is frequently used to point to the 'shared' nature of goods or services, or collective ownership of goods such as air, water, and the ocean. This book takes the term back to its historic, original meaning and context: land – in many different forms – that is used and managed collectively. Considering the exclusiveness of the historical commons – a feature repeatedly stressed in this book – the historic meaning does not necessarily correspond to the current interpretation. A historical study of this phenomenon shows that delimitation and a clear description of rights and duties are vital elements for protecting what is shared, for achieving that important balance between resources and those who need them. But when digging deeper into the historical documents, more was discovered about the mechanisms needed to achieve an optimal use of the common, and how this was conditioned by the changes in the circumstances of commoners. The livelihood of the households that benefitted from the common was not restricted to what the common had to offer. They also relied on other land – leased or in private property – that produced crops and for doing so efficiently also needed the cattle that had grazed on the common. What happened on the commons was closely connected to what happened off the common, inasmuch as the commoners' welfare was not linked to common resources only. This interconnectivity shows that commons were an integral part of society, and that institutional diversity was also important for the survival of the commons.

Such diversity implies that some goods and services are better off within a common-pool institution, while others might be better off within a system of private or public governance. This also implies – and this is also confirmed with the historical narrative – that the emergence of common-pool

Dealing with dilemmas: conclusions

institutions in European history cannot have been part of an evolutionary process, which would eventually culminate in all goods being private, as some historians seemingly want to suggest. There are a number of general conditions and specific motors that have led to individuals recognizing the value of solving social dilemmas collectively for their own benefit and that of their offspring. In describing the three factors that have played a role in this process – conditions, motors, and motives – I have kept the geographical and institutional perspective very wide, focusing on different types of institutions for collective action, in both towns and countryside, within most of northwestern Europe, where the conditions and motors for new institutions for collective action were widely available from the late Middle Ages onwards.

The willingness of these Europeans to unite in collectivities can be traced – and gains in uniqueness – because they wrote down their agreements in charters that included descriptions of how the collectively used resources were accessed, used, and managed. Thanks to the survival of many such documents, it can be demonstrated that commons were a widely chosen form of resource governance, and we can see how they functioned internally, at least on paper. In this book I have not attempted to systematically include a comparison of the rules found with the design principles of Lin Ostrom (1990, 90), but elsewhere it has been demonstrated that the historical commons in Europe would have had no problem living up to the conditions she set forth. We could suffice with such an analysis and conclude that this also explains why so many historical commons managed to survive, often for centuries. Their regular adaptation of the rules to changes in the agricultural production system, or the economic situation, enabled them to be sufficiently flexible to prevent the effect of or to overcome crises. A study of only the regulation, however, would only give us a theoretical perspective of the functioning of commons and would not disclose the internal dynamics of the commons, nor would it tell us why some decisions were taken by the commoners and how these related to changes in the user profile of the commoners. Individuals' behavior during dilemmas is an important field within experimental studies, but the nature of the method prevents our looking at the interaction between the behavior of an individual commoner and his personal, social, and economic situation, and over a long period of time. How do individual decisions of commoners interact with collective decisions on the level of the institution? And what is most important: Which are the guiding principles, the key drivers so to speak, in making those decisions? What makes commoners choose one decision and not the other?

The Dilemma of the Commoners

As an example of this interactive decision-making process, I used a case in Flanders for which I could reconstruct in detail the behavior of the commoners, the Gemene and Loweiden. The analysis of this case demonstrated that a common was more than just its resources: it was a complex interplay among the resources, users, and rules and norms the users devised, often in reaction to external changes. From this particular case study we can draw some general lessons, without claiming that these could serve as principles to be followed by just any case. Lesson one of the Gemene and Loweiden tells us that it is of great importance to guard the total number of potential users as well as whether these members use the common's resources and how this relates to their needs. Also, it has become clear that the internal balance between users and non-users can lead to a shift in the way in which the resources are managed. Self-monitoring by users is likely to be more effective and cheaper than control by an external party. If the common, in the end, needs to resort to other than its own members to take care of the internal monitoring, this in itself can be interpreted as a sign of diminished interest, which may lead to increased vulnerability. Given these circumstances, the interference of the local government in the case study and their temporary takeover of the management is probably a near-to-logic consequence. However, for the commoners of this case, the utility was – though in a different form – still high enough to mobilize their commoners and win back their use-rights, demonstrating that commoners who stuck together did not have to be entirely powerless vis-à-vis authorities. In some other countries, for example, in southern Europe, commons have also survived to some extent the nineteenth-century attacks on common property. Their capacity to achieve a good balance between utility, efficiency, and equity might be part of the explanation.

Understanding this exercise in achieving balance among utility, equity, and efficiency is essential for capturing the methods to deal with change over long periods of time. Although initially this conclusion and the subsequent method were 'distilled' out of existing literature on commons, these three elements have not surfaced in the literature as the guiding principles for achieving a well-balanced common's use and management, which secures sufficient resilience to become robust, long-living institutions. Over the past decennia, tools were defined to describe the general institutional design of commons (e.g., the design principles of Ostrom) and their functioning (e.g., the IAD-framework). But what drives these commons to repeat this process over and over again, to change, adapt, and even dissolve, if needed?

Dealing with dilemmas: conclusions

Many commons in western Europe managed to bridge centuries of economic, social, and political change without fundamentally altering their objectives as set by their ancestors when reaching an agreement with the local lord about the usage of the common's resources. Adaptation to change was done according to the needs of the resource and the users, by means of new rules or changes to old rules. They tried to create simple, yet adequate bodies of rules that offered sufficient incentives while also including enough punitive threats to prevent free riding and to stimulate reciprocity among the commoners. The examples offered show that commons – and in fact any kind of well-governed institution for collective action – can survive for centuries through adaptation. Such longevity is a feature of resilience, if not quality, in institutional design.

But we have seen that there is more to the story: the detailed analysis of the participatory behavior of the commoners showed that intensity of participation and ways of participation both signal changes in the position of the common as a resource necessary for the household economy. Moreover, the ways in which people took part in the use and management could have been the result of changed power balances within the common – between those who used the common and those who no longer did so or had never done so –, which again may have led to alternative ways of resource management and monitoring. Whereas most attention in literature has been going to potential over-exploitation of resources, insufficient exploitation seems to have been as much on the minds of the contemporary commoners. The data demonstrate that a potential tragedy is not only hidden with too many users, but possible also in a case with too few users or too little interest in the resources the common has to offer overall. They also demonstrate that balance and continuity in resource use were essential in the use of the common resources, as is clearly shown in periods when non-entitled commoners were allowed to step in, at least temporarily. Being a self-governed and self-controlled system also had implications for the monitoring and social control mechanisms: when those entitled to use the common were no longer physically present or even stopped using the resource, alternative ways of 'policing' the use of the common needed to be introduced. This in itself may have made the institution more vulnerable for external force, and may help to explain the ease with which the case study in this book – but likewise most other commons in Flanders – underwent the privatization process set in motion by governments on various levels.

Although commons as institutions clearly had a different place in the household economy by the first decades of the nineteenth century,

155

The Dilemma of the Commoners

their role had not entirely dwindled. The fierce attempts of nearly all national governments in western Europe to dissolve collective property arrangements in the first half of the nineteenth century (although the prologue to this process had already started around the middle of the eighteenth century) put enormous pressure on commoners. In some cases they did manage to survive this threat, or regain their rights later on, as was the case in Gemene and Loweiden. The protest against the dissolution of commons was less fierce than that against the English enclosures; nevertheless, both the altered role of commons within the agricultural system – due to the introduction of new crops and new forms of fertilizers – and the social and economic position of commoners prior to the dissolution led to resistance. Proletarianization left many without cattle to graze on the common, thus affecting the usefulness of the common for grazing rights. As the data show, commoners did attach great value to being a commoner, but their registration increasingly late in their lives suggests that they saw the commons more as an old-age pension than as an active part of their income strategy. These results demonstrate that there is another unit between the individual commoner and the group of commoners that needs to be taken into account: the household. Commoners represent individual households, which have their own needs and wishes (and particular composition). Even if households are to a large extent similar in terms of dependence on wage labor, we still need to take into account the life course not of the individual commoner but of its entire household: what they expected from the common was a consequence of these factors, and their expectations were reflected in management decisions. Commoners should not be treated as a group, nor as individuals, but as units representing households that each followed a different path. The reason to stress this as an essential point to be learned from historical analysis is not simply to understand the transfer of user rights from father to son in the case study, but the omnipresent reference to the relationship between the use of the resource and the needs of the household as a whole. In many commons, commoners were restricted in their use not by number of resource units but by the limits of their own needs, judged by themselves. This demonstrates that the common was explicitly not intended for commercial use. The nineteenth-century change described in land use for the Gemene and Loweiden, whereby land was increasingly leased instead of used by the commoners, should be interpreted in the first place as an answer to decreased household needs for pasture land, instead of a desire to privatize and commercialize the land entirely.

Dealing with dilemmas: conclusions

The strict regulation of access to the commons of the European past shows that the way Hardin (1968) pictured the commons – as open-access pasture areas – and their users is incorrect: there was no absolute freedom on the commons, nor were the commoners solely oriented towards achieving higher personal gains. Commoners and representative managers of the commons were clearly very aware of the factors that could bring ruin to the common, such as a population increase or the commercialization of the common's resources. In practice, they strove towards an optimal balance between use and users, with a strikingly accurate idea of the level of resource exploitation that was ecologically acceptable, thereby trying to avoid overuse but also under-exploitation, a danger largely forgotten in the commons debate but clearly on the minds of the commoners themselves. The regular changes in the use of the common's resources were a direct consequence of the commoners' own need to use the common, and this in turn was affected by general social-economic changes and temporary shocks such as a cattle plague that killed most of the cattle in the village. Adjusting to the many changes in a society where no government compensations for lost cattle or insurance were available was constantly on the radar of the commoners. Self-government required this, as daily management was directed and put into practice by the stakeholders themselves, but it also allowed immediate reaction to threats that could affect more than just the group of commoners if not taken care of immediately. Individual responsible behavior was thus essential to assure an optimal collective outcome, and to achieve this, compulsory social control and participation in the decision-making process were essential to make the common work. How significant a change in the participation level can be for the common as a whole becomes clear in the decisions taken on the common. It also becomes clear that participation was more than simply being a member: if members did not take part in meetings and reap the benefits of being a commoner by daily use of the common, the internal balance between active and passive users could have led to new forms of resource management.

Decisions were carefully balanced, taking into account objectives other than strictly economic ones. All these aspects made the common a flexible institution that could easily adapt to changing circumstances and changing needs. I have shown this for one case study, but this common does not stand alone in its success, nor in its occasional failure. Although I do not claim that this formula worked for all commons, there is now historical evidence that, if the commons' managers did their job and the commoners respected the rules, dilemmas could have been solved and

The Dilemma of the Commoners

tragedies avoided. One of the central elements to be learned from this is that collective use and management can be successful, but it requires intensive, active, and adequate participation.

This book has also attempted to demonstrate that the historical study of commons is more than stories about farmers joyfully working together. And although the case study did manage to survive, it was also shown that working together as commoners is difficult, not just because of individual discord but also major changes in society that require adaptation time and time again. One of the most essential aspects of historical research – which is often insufficiently acknowledged, even by historians – is the process of change it allows us to discover, and in doing so, to determine the factors that have caused the changes, with ample attention to the context in which change takes place. The detection of intended change is in itself proof of the dynamics of commons and a counterproof for the much-proclaimed inertia such institutions would have been expected to demonstrate. Going deeper into the causes of changes in the way commoners used and managed their common demonstrates that changes in regulation were a reaction to changes in the composition of the group of commoners; in the availability of the resources; and/or in the economic, political, or social circumstances of the area where the common was situated. Some regulation proved to be insufficiently efficient and was altered, although there were also cases in which this was not done accordingly, or the effect of the changes was inadequate. What needs to be stressed here is the commoners' capacities to regulate and adjust their own behavior and that of their fellow commoners over time. Historical analysis thus gives us the possibility to study dynamics of commons over the very long term and the role of commoners' behavior therein, which is a clear competitive advantage over the methodologies of other social sciences. As much as this book presents a narrative on the history of commons in western Europe, it is also intended as a step towards developing an interdisciplinary method to study change in institutions for collective action.

The essential ingredient for a well-functioning and resilient common is the balance between internal factors and adaptation to change taking place in the world around the common. The institution is the binding factor in achieving such a balance and the consequent robustness, but the secret is quick detection of problems and adaptation of the rules in such a way that they also influence the behavior of the commoners. That is how this form of self-governance differs from models of state-oriented resource governance: problems are detected more easily and remedied faster without losing other elements. This is not to say that problems were always detected and it is a

Dealing with dilemmas: conclusions

guarantee for success, but it does create a more favorable environment for collective action.

Throughout this book dilemmas have been discussed in different time frames: from the dilemma of the commoners in the late Middle Ages, who had the choice between demanding private use of the increasingly used pastures and the collective use, which was probably the most efficient alternative economically, to the nineteenth-century, when commoners had the choice to either sell off their land (as the government wanted them to) or stick together and go to court. In between these tumultuous times, commoners had to make daily choices: using more resources from the common than allowed or sticking to the rules; going to the general meeting or not; reporting abuses of fellow commoners at the risk of getting into an unpleasant personal situation or looking the other way? Commons' dilemmas were constantly present at all levels of decision making, and as such formed a huge challenge for all members and their managers. In this book I have demonstrated that individual and group choices of commoners could have a long-lasting effect on the common, but that trends which could lead to a sure tragedy within a common-pool institution could be adjusted to maintain or restore the much needed balance between the usefulness of the resource, the survival of the resource, and the accessibility of that resource for its users. In some periods one factor may have prevailed over another, but never to the extent that the institution would better be dissolved.

I have demonstrated that the commons in historical western Europe can be situated in a spectrum that goes from the open – very vast and accessible – type to the more closed – smaller, hard to access – type, and that these were able to come about among others because conditions such as recognition of commoners' rights to governments were fulfilled. This last condition is also included in Ostrom's design principle list (1990, 90) but is not sufficient to guarantee a well-functioning and long-lasting common, nor is staying within that spectrum of features that has been described in this book, which are in broad terms indeed also in line with that same design principle list. The many instruments to be found in commons' regulations to deal with the potential commercialization of common goods, or with the internal division of such goods demonstrate that the commoners themselves were very aware of the many mini-dilemmas they had to deal with on a daily basis, but that combinations of features within the described spectrum were sufficient to deal with them. These instruments, of which some are far more creative than what we as contemporaries have come up with, to regulate each other's behavior can become part of a toolbox from which present-day institutions for collective action can borrow.

The historical complexity of this book demonstrates that the commons in European history were not clubs of simple farmers always trying to get the most of their resources, without consideration for future generations, although commons were in the end part of a system of which the produce was also destined for the market. This task – to actually keep the resource and the group that uses it alive for several generations in a row under the pressure of population growth and commercialization – is really difficult. This should not be a surprise: when the needs and opinions of many are to be taken into account, then compromises will be necessary, but not to such an extent that it affects the willingness of those that feel they have lost the battle. But history also shows that it is doable.

Epilogue: The revenge of history?

The return of homo cooperans in present-day western European countries

Commons are again a hot topic. After their rapid elimination in most parts of (continental) Europe, they disappeared from the collective European memory. But recently the term has again appeared, although in very different contexts. It is now applied to all types of resources and even services that are collective, including water, the Internet, and the air we breathe, which are regularly referred to as 'commons'. This conceptual evolution from commons as small-scale, local resources to large-scale, global resources has taken place over the past half century and is now leading to a new era in commons studies, but also to some additional confusion on what commons really are, and what they could mean for future societies.

Notwithstanding some of the historical misconceptions of what a common stood for in his 'Tragedy of the commons' (1968), Hardin's work has been responsible for broadening the debate on the commons. Given the growing visible and tangible consequences of climate change, the issue of global commons – those resources we share globally – is receiving increased attention. In addition, another more local evolution towards more self-governance is taking place in many places in northwestern Europe: new forms of institutional collective action are emerging to deal with the vacuum created by the retreating state and the failing markets.

Citizens are increasingly uniting in collectivities to provide goods and services that until now have been assumed as public.[1] Over the past few years it has become apparent that numerous social welfare provisions are becoming less accessible, either because they are increasingly becoming unaffordable in the often privatized form or because the government 'retreats' and no longer considers these services its responsibility. In many

---

[1] See the following site to get a – non-exhaustive – list of examples of current institutions for collective action: http://www.collective-action.info/_ICA_Today. For more specific Dutch examples, see http://www.krachtinnl.nl/.

The Dilemma of the Commoners

cases this 'decline of the welfare state' has resulted in a transfer of trust and responsibilities to a private partner, perhaps through a public-private partnership (PPP), but often at a high cost. Privatization of public goods and services limits accessibility for those who are not capable or willing to pay for such goods and services. In response, people are increasingly banding together to provide services that the government has left to the whims of the market economy, as the latter cannot always live up to the expectations to provide goods and services for the promised competitive prices, nor can it do so wherever these goods and services are needed, particularly in less-populated areas where demand is lower than elsewhere.[2]

Examples of the new 'bottom-up' movement in the 'old Europe' are plenty: freelancers who set up joint insurance systems that look much the same as the early-twentieth-century mutual insurance companies, in case of bad times,[3] day-care centers run jointly by parents,[4] cooperatives for neighbors who create and utilize their own energy,[5] and numerous collectives providing care for specific social groups.[6] This development is occurring throughout Europe, especially in countries referred to as the best 'students' in Europe's liberalization class, such as the Netherlands and Germany, but also elsewhere, particularly in those countries where the crisis has hit exceptionally hard, such as Greece, with a paralyzed state and an out-of-control market. These countries share the situation that the market is not functioning optimally, whether this is due to the crisis or not.

However, simultaneously there are countries, such as Belgium, where the movement remains small, mainly because the welfare state has

---

[2] To give an example: in many of the mentioned areas in the Netherlands, where the population is declining and where the inhabitants are predominantly elderly, local supermarkets leave. To overcome this problem, some of the communities have taken over local supermarkets; the shops are now owned and managed by members of the community. See, e.g., http://www.sterksel.nu/ons-dorp/dorpswinkel and http://www.degavesuper.nl/ (both in Dutch).

[3] See, e.g., the Dutch *Broodfondsen*, set up for small entrepreneurs who have no employees (the so-called ZZP-ers), see http://www.broodfonds.nl/wat_is_broodfonds/brood fonds-enqute_de_uitkomsten.

[4] In the Netherlands these are called *Ouderparticipatiecrèches* (parent-participation-child-care-centers); see, for one example, http://www.ouderparticipatiecreche.nl/. But there are also other examples whereby the parents do not provide the care but the capital to run a child-care center in a cooperative format (see, e.g., http://www.crecheparentalelln.be/ in Belgium).

[5] A recent survey showed that 430 new energy cooperatives were formed in Germany from 2006 to 2011, see http://www.dgrv.de/en/cooperatives/newcooperatives/energycoo peratives.html. For an overview of recently developed local Dutch energy initiatives, see http://www.hieropgewekt.nl/initiatieven.

[6] There is a real 'boom' taking place in collective provisions in, for example, the elderly care sector. See for many examples in the Netherlands http://www.kenniscentrumwonenzorg.nl/ actueel/specials/innuvatie. But see also the Belgian example http://www.thinkoutofthe box.be/ which provides care for disabled children.

Epilogue

progressed less in transferring its responsibilities in the direction of the market. But even there we find a growing interest among its citizens to deal with problems – those that are already present or those they believe there is a need to anticipate – to act together and independently from the market or state. The omnipresence of such initiatives all over Europe is an indication that this development is more than just a response to the economic crisis; progressively it is a response to providing services the government is no longer willing or – as in the case of Greece – no longer able to provide.

Although the press often claims otherwise, the crisis is not the cause of this revolution in resource governance and provision we are witnessing, though the crisis has indeed put the spotlight on cracks in the system that have built up over the past decades. In many cases privatization has not yielded the preferred and promised results: the market did not always bring about high-quality, affordable, and diversified offerings, as competition functions only when there is sufficient demand. In many less populated and increasingly aging regions of the Netherlands, for example, the demand for child care is insufficient to make it attractive for a child-care company to set up in a new location. Similarly over the past decades of liberalization, 'the market' has discovered – and the consumers with it – that for many formerly public services there is a limit to commercialization, to the profit that can be reasonably and morally expected on some services. In the care sector in particular, where budget cuts easily lead to a reduction of quality in the service that can be directly felt by the elderly, children, the disabled, and others in need of care and support, the liberalization of public goods and services is an issue. Taken to the extreme, it is possible to claim that any cut made to care provided for the needy is equal to a decline in quality for that care, or at least a missed opportunity to improve it. Moreover, in those domains, which are usually the playground of the private market, such as energy production and consumption, new opportunities arise due to recent developments in technology. Individual energy production becomes feasible for citizens, thanks to the availability of individual solar panels and stand-alone windmills.

The do-it-yourself society that is currently emerging is building institutions that are very much like the former, historic commons and their urban counterparts, the guilds, and as such they face similar challenges to create resilient institutions that serve cooperative members. Though times have changed, the past does provide us with highly valuable lessons; there are new challenges ahead to translate those lessons learned from the past – and as such also from historical studies. Contemporary consumer and producer collectives are aimed at overcoming problems similar to the institutions for collective action in the medieval and early modern period, but there

The Dilemma of the Commoners

are some clear differences in the way they function. An important difference between the two is that institutions for collective action in the past offered solutions to both economic and social – and to some extent, such as with the commons, even ecological – problems, whereas the goals of the contemporary citizens' cooperatives are usually focused on solving a single issue, such as producing renewable energy or providing qualitative care. Early modern guild masters could benefit from economic advantages when joining a guild, but they could equally benefit from funeral insurance, by which their wives and children would be taken care of after their death. As long as they lived up to the expectations that were set, and this is exactly where the benefits of multipurpose institutions are to be reaped, they could benefit from all services and goods offered by the collective. Linking various benefits together is not only efficient in terms of time spent on achieving goals as an individual, it also creates complementary reciprocal behavior: if it is possible to lose multiple benefits by free riding in only one domain of activities – for example, not respecting the quality standards set by the guild – members will be encouraged to 'behave' in all the domains covered by the organization. Abusing the social benefits provided by the guild would equally affect the standing of the guild master among his peers.

In today's society services are subdivided in separate organizations; this has certain advantages, but also disadvantages for collectives. Nowadays, if people misbehave in one domain, it does not necessarily affect other parts of their life directly. As previously described, reciprocity ensures that people are more willing to yield to the collective's norms, and when a system encompasses multiple parts of a person's life, this effect becomes cumulative. In the past, institutions for collective action were able to combine social and economic goals, and have a complementary system of monitoring and sanctioning. Present-day civil cooperatives cannot implement a similar arrangement. Creating an institution that serves multiple purposes can thus benefit from what one could refer to as 'double reciprocity'.

A clear difference between the first wave of the late Middle Ages and early modern times, and organizations that emerged during this second 'revival period' from 1880 to 1920, is that a striking number of smaller organizations from the second wave merged over the course of time, and have sometimes become very large cooperatives indeed. Although there were some mergers of guilds in the early modern period, there was not a distinct shift in size – the number of guild members per guild remained relatively limited during the early modern period. Furthermore, there are no known examples of mergers by *markegenootschappen*, although they did at times cooperate. The institutions of the first wave often had a considerably longer lifespan than their counterparts during the second wave. From the

Epilogue

cooperatives that emerged between 1880 and 1920, only a fifth is still active today, while more than 90 percent of the *markegenootschappen* that we studied in the provinces of Overijssel, Gelderland, and Drenthe survived much longer, and easily passed the 150 years' mark. Regarding the guilds, about 62 percent survived for more than 150 years, which is considerably longer than the cooperatives of the second wave.[7]

Another difference links up to this: the historical examples considered future generations in their own workings. Commoners aimed for a sustainable use of their common resources by restricting them to the member-households' real needs. By doing so they guaranteed that others, possibly their children, would also be able to rely on these resources in the future. But there are also new opportunities – such as modern techniques – that enable parties to cooperate without meeting face to face. Although this can also have a negative effect on the level of social control, digital platforms prove that people are willing to trust others and contribute to the collective interests, as long as there are clear guidelines that all members understand and accept.[8]

A further important difference between past and present is the mutual interaction of contemporary collectives with market and state. This interaction with the market occurs in two forms, first by collective consumption, for instance, by citizens who manage a common good, such as sharing a car with the neighborhood or sharing files via a portal, legally or illegally, such as via *eMule*.[9] These collectives are based on mutual governance by peers. Collectives can enter the market as a single consumer with enough purchasing power to have a good or service produced for them, or to receive discounts. Alternatively, the market can appeal to collectives seeking to gain a large consumer base, a strategy used by, for instance, *Nederlandzoektenergie* and *Groupon*.[10] Second, collectives are active in the market through collective production, for instance, in the nonprofit sector, such as *Linux* where open-source software is freely accessible, and

---

[7] With thanks to Miguel Laborda Pemán for the calculations based on the files created in the framework of the NWO-Middelgroot project 'Data Infrastructure for the Study of Guilds and Other Forms of Collective Action', see https://www.dataverse.nl/dvn/dv/Website ICACommons/faces/study/StudyPage.xhtml?globalId=hdl:10411/10026&studyListing Index=10_e65c3494de2f199a14193eeac8ec (commons) and https://www.dataverse.nl/ dvn/dv/WebsiteICAGuilds/faces/study/StudyPage.xhtml?globalId=hdl:10411/10101& studyListingIndex=4_e65c3494de2f199a14193eeac8ec (guilds).

[8] One example can be found on http://samenkopen.net/, a Dutch online community run by volunteers that wants to generate discounts by buying goods in bulk. To control the organizers of a specific buying action, strict rules are set and the members of the website can monitor the organizers through a rating system.

[9] http://www.emule-project.net/home/perl/general.cgi?l=1

[10] http://www.nederlandzoektenergie.nl; http://www.groupon.com

The Dilemma of the Commoners

tested and improved by its collective users.[11] In some cases civil collectives have entered the market to offer their services in exchange for payment. Collective production can take the form of cooperative businesses, which have received much attention after the United Nations declared 2012 as the International Year of Cooperatives. There are many successful examples of cooperative businesses, for instance, Rabobank and Mondragon.[12]

Interaction also occurs between collectives and the government, because civil initiatives have taken up public services such day care for children and care for the elderly. These collectives were set up to fill a gap that neither the state nor the market was/is willing or able to supply at reasonable cost and acceptable quality. It is this interaction among civil collectives, market, and state that offers many possibilities for all parties. Additionally, this provides the opportunity to reevaluate the predominance of the market and state in providing public goods and services – by considering citizens as a third party, it is possible to increase institutional diversity. Institutional diversity can be a means to arm a society against another crisis: a greater diversity of solutions that is readily available can contribute to the resilience of a society. If one solution fails, there are still many (potential) options to solve the problem. It is important, however, to also consider the limitations of this development; not all forms of collective action are desirable. The mafia and militias may both be extreme examples, but they do fit the same principles as the institutions for collective action discussed. Both the possibilities and the limitations of cooperative solutions must be considered, and experience will show which party – market, state, society, or a combination of these – offers the best solution for a specific problem.

Currently governments are hesitant to relinquish too many responsibilities, in fear of total chaos or loss of control; however, many previously considered 'government duties' have already been taken out of the hands of governmental institutions and taken over by the private sector. In the

---

[11] http://www.linux.org

[12] The Mondragon Corporation (founded in the town of Mondragón in 1956) provides employment for approximately 84,000 people working in 256 companies in finance, industry, retail, and knowledge. See http://www.mondragon-corporation.com/ENG.aspx. The Dutch Rabobank is a cooperative bank, which has its origins in two so-called *Boerenleenbanken*, founded in the second half of the nineteenth century: the Coöperatieve Centrale Raiffeisen-Bank and the Coöperatieve Centrale Boerenleenbank. In 1972, both banks merged to form the Coöperatieve Centrale Raiffeisen-Boerenleenbank, which changed its name to Rabobank in 1980. Currently, the Rabobank has 872 locations, belonging to 139 individual cooperative banks. Each local bank is fairly autonomous and has its own council of members and its own general meetings. Everyone can join as a member, which also includes the right to vote on decisions concerning the strategy and the management of the bank. The Rabobank is not listed on the stock market; it reinvests its profits into the cooperative.

Epilogue

current system the government fully supports the market: even when things go wrong and mistakes are made, failing businesses are rarely held accountable, and the state maintains faith that the market will solve all. It is peculiar that people believe the market can solve all kinds of problems, and that citizens cannot and do not deserve the same level of trust given to market institutions. If consumer initiatives are to be considered a worthy third party, then it is imperative that they have the same right to succeed and fail as the state and the market. As a consequence every alternative – whether it is offered by the market, the state, a collective, or a combination of these – must be evaluated on an equal footing. Only then can it be decided which partner or partners provide the most viable solution to a problem. To increase the institutional diversity it is necessary to get imaginative about organizational forms. The role of the government is vital in this aspect, because the government decides which organizational forms are accepted and has the power to stimulate and facilitate new initiatives.

The government can contribute to developing institutional diversity by breaking the predominance of state and market in fulfilling public services, allowing more organizational forms, and by stimulating institutions, thereby allowing society to become more adaptable. The past teaches us that institutions for collective action have the potential to cushion the effect of crises for its members. These collectives may not have functioned optimally according to current economic measurements, but their goal was not maximizing profit or output; it was facilitating the sustainable use and management of collective goods.

The state and its citizens could and should unite, and to achieve this, civil initiatives have to become more visible. At the moment, such collectivities are merely a small speck on the entire spectrum of public services. It is not strange that the Dutch government has only been able to find a few successful examples. The state's policy is to study these collectives in order to construct a blueprint for other collectives, which is a problem because citizens' collectives are entirely directed towards local circumstances, and their success is completely dependent on context. Therefore, governments have to be aware that copying solutions from one collective would only create problems if they were applied to another collective. To promote the development of collectives, governments must refrain from attempting to find a blueprint. On the one hand, governments need to recognize and accept the potential of solutions offered by citizens' collectives, and on the other hand, the collectives need to demonstrate the success and effectiveness of their governance in order for them to be taken seriously and for state policy to be adjusted to suit their needs. It is not in the nature of civil collectives to focus on PR – much like the institutions for collective action in the past – because they are too busy solving problems. However, when it is the government's task to assess the most successful way of offering public goods, this can only be done when collective institutions reveal their potential.

Once civil collectives are recognized and accepted, further research can help to determine the conditions that help to enhance their visibility. The state can assist collectives in finding the necessary conditions for them to succeed. Many local cooperatives are trying to reinvent the wheel because they rarely communicate with other collectives or the government. This is impractical both from a management as well as a business administration perspective. There are ways, however, that the state can play a decisive role in this process, such as providing advice on what an ideal group size is, at what level an institution is manageable, and whether members would know each other well enough to be able to exert some form of fair social control.

The biggest challenge, and the greatest potential, lies in the dialogue that needs to be developed between government and civil initiatives. This dialogue must also be 'structured': citizens need frameworks that have a clear legal footing and operational guidelines. New types of institutions must be developed to achieve higher levels of institutional diversity without too much effort and taking into account the different goals that might be set, depending on the type of good or service with which citizens are dealing. This in itself will be a challenge for governments, to change the mind set when addressing problems, but addressing this challenge may help to prevent other larger ones from developing.

References

Akkerman, J. B. 1962. 'Het koopmansgilde van Tiel omstreeks het jaar 1000', *Tijdschrift voor Rechtsgeschiedenis* 30: 409–71.

Alfani, G. and Rao, R. (eds.). 2011. *La gestione delle risorse collettive. Italia settentrionale, secoli XII–XVIII.* Milano: Franco Angeli.

Allen, R. C. 1992. *Enclosure and the yeoman: the agricultural development of the South Midlands, 1450–1850.* Oxford: Clarendon Press.

Andries, J. O. 1879. 'Recueil de documents tendant à résourdre la question de propriété des Gemeene et Looweiden situées à Assebrouck et Oedelem les Bruges', *Annales de la Société d'Émulation de Bruges* 5–10: 141–86.

Axelrod, R. 1984. *The evolution of cooperation.* New York: Basic Books.

Bainbridge, V. R. 1996. *Gilds in the medieval countryside: social and religious change in Cambridgeshire, c.1350–1558.* Studies in the history of medieval religion, 10. Woodbridge, Suffolk: Boydell Press.

Berman, H. J. 1983. *Law and revolution: the formation of the western legal tradition.* Cambridge, MA: Harvard University Press.

Berten, D. 1907. *Coutumes de la seigneurie de Saint Bavon.* Coutumes des pays et comté de Flandre. Recueil des anciennes coutumes de la Belgique. Vol. 14, Quartier de Gand. Bruxelles: Goemaere.

Beuzel, G. J. 1988. *Het markeboek van de marke Exel 1616–1837.* S.l.: Oostgelders Tijdschrift voor Genealogie en Boerderij-onderzoek.

Bieleman, J. 1999. 'Farming system research as a guideline in agricultural history', in Van Bavel and Thoen (eds.), 1999, pp. 235–50.

Black, A. 1984. *Guilds and civil society in European political thought from the twelfth century to the present.* London: Methuen.

Blickle, P. 1998. *From the communal reformation to the revolution of the common man.* Studies in Medieval and Reformation Thought, 65. Leiden/Boston: Brill.

Blok, D. P. (ed.). 1982. *Algemene geschiedenis der nederlanden,* Vol. 2. Haarlem: Fibula-Van Dishoeck.

Bosker, E. M., Buringh, E., and van Zanden, J. L. 2013. 'From Baghdad to London: unraveling urban development in Europe, the Middle East,

References

and North Africa, 800–1800', *Review of Economics and Statistics* 95: 1418–37.

Brakensiek, S. 2000. 'Gemeinheitsteilungen in Europa. Neue Forschungsergebnisse und Deutungsangebote der europäischen Geschichtsschreibung', *Jahrbuch für Wirtschaftsgeschichte* 2: 9–16.

Brewer, M. B. and Kramer, R. M. 1986. 'Choice behavior in social dilemmas: effects of social identity, group size, and decision framing', *Journal of Personality and Social Psychology* 50: 543–9.

Brusse, P. G., Schuurman, A., Molle, I., and Vanhaute, E. 2010. 'The Low Countries, 1750–2000', in Van Bavel and Hoyle (eds.), 2010, pp. 199–224.

Bublot, G. 1957. *La production agricole belge. Etude économique séculaire, 1846–1955.* Leuven-Paris: Editions NauwelAerts-Béatrice NauwelAerts.

Bull, I. 2004. 'Professions, absolutism and the role of widows', *Scandinavian Journal of History* 29: 193–208.

Buskens, V. W. and Maas, I. (eds.). 2012. *Samenwerking in sociale dilemma's; voorbeelden van Nederlands onderzoek.* Amsterdam: Amsterdam University Press.

Campbell, B. M. S. 1980. 'Population change and the genesis of common fields on a Norfolk manor', *The Economic History Review* 33: 174–92.

Casari, M. and Lisciandra, M. 2014. 'Gender discrimination in property rights: six centuries of commons governance in the Alps', Working Paper, University of Bologna. Available online at http://www2.dse.unibo.it/casari/research/wp-gender.pdf (Accessed 13 August 2014).

2011. 'L'evoluzione della trasmissione ereditaria delle risorse collettive in Trentino tra i secoli XIII e XIX', in Alfani and Rao (eds.), 2011, pp. 17–31.

2010. 'Gender-biased inheritance systems are evolutionary stable: a case study in northern Italy in the XII–XIX century', Working Paper, University of Bologna.

Clicheroux, E. 1957. 'L'évolution des terrains incultes en Belgique', *Bulletin de l'Institut de recherches économiques et sociales* 23: 497–524.

Congost, R. 2007. *Tierras, leyes, historia: estudios sobre la gran obra de la propriedad.* Barcelona: Critica.

Congost, R. and Lana Berasain, J. M. (eds.) 2007. *Campos cerrados, debates abiertos. Análisis histórico y propriedad de la tierra en Europa (siglos XVI–XIX).* Pamplona: Public University of Navarre.

Cox, S. J. B. 1985. 'No tragedy of the commons', *Environmental Ethics* 7: 49–61.

Dahlman, C. J. 1980. *The open field system and beyond: a property rights analysis of an economic institution.* Cambridge: Cambridge University Press.

Darwin, C. 1859. *On the origin of species by means of natural selection, or the preservation of favoured races in the struggle for life.* London: John Murray.

De Bo, L. L. 1873. *Westvlaamsch idioticon, bewerkt door L. L. de Bo, . . .* Brugge: Boek– en steendrukkerij E. Gailliard.

De Kerf, R. 2010. *De juiste prijs in de laatmiddeleeuwse stad: een onderzoek naar middeleeuwse economische ethiek op de ambachtelijke markt en in moralistische lekenliteratuur.* Studies stadsgeschiedenis, 6. Amsterdam: Aksant.

References

De Laveleye, E. 1891. *De la proriété et de ses formes primitives.* 4th ed. Paris: Félix Alcan.

De Monté Verloren, J. Ph. 2000. *Hoofdlijnen uit de ontwikkeling der rechterlijke organisatie in de Noordelijke Nederlanden tot de Bataafse omwenteling.* 7th ed. Deventer: Kluwer.

De Moor, M. 2005. 'De Gemene en Loweiden in Assebroek als één van de laatste gemene gronden in Vlaanderen. Beknopte geschiedenis van de instelling en inventaris van het archief', *Handelingen van het Genootschap voor Geschiedenis, gesticht onder de benaming 'Sociéte d'Émulation' te Brugge: driemaandelijks tijdschrift voor de studie van geschiedenis en oudheden van Vlaanderen* 142: 3–45.

2003a. 'Les terres communes en Belgique', in Demélas and Vivier (eds.), 2003, pp. 119–38.

2003b. 'Tot proffijt van de ghemeensaemheijt. Gebruik, gebruikers en beheer van gemene gronden in Zandig Vlaanderen, 18de en 19de eeuw', unpublished PhD thesis, Ghent University.

2002. 'Common land and common rights in Flanders', in De Moor, Shaw-Taylor, and Warde (eds.), 2002a, pp. 113–42.

De Moor, M. and Debbaut, R. 2003. *De aanborgers van de Gemene en Loweiden, 1515–1965.* Brugge: Van de Wiele.

De Moor, M., Shaw-Taylor, L, and Warde, P. 2002a. *The management of common land in north west Europe, c.1500–1850.* Turnhout: Brepols.

2002b. 'Comparing the historical commons of north west Europe. An introduction'. In De Moor, Shaw-Taylor, and Warde (eds.), 2002a, pp. 15–32.

2002c. 'Preliminary conclusions. The commons of north west Europe', in De Moor, Shaw-Taylor, and Warde (eds.), 2002a, pp. 247–60.

De Moor, T., 2014. 'Single, safe, and sorry? Explaining the early modern beguine movement in the Low Countries', *Journal of Family History* 39: 3–21.

2013. *Homo cooperans. Institutions for collective action and the compassionate society.* Utrecht: Utrecht University.

2012. 'Inspiratie uit ons institutionele geheugen. Instituties voor collectieve actie als structurele oplossingen voor sociale dilemma's in het Europese verleden', in Buskens and Maas (eds.), 2012, pp. 185–208.

2009. 'Avoiding tragedies: a Flemish common and its commoners under the pressure of social and economic change during the eighteenth century', *The Economic History Review* 62: 1–22.

2008. 'The silent revolution: a new perspective on the emergence of commons, guilds, and other forms of corporate collective action in western Europe', *International Review of Social History* 53: 179–212.

2007. 'La función del común. La trayectoria de un comunal en Flandes durante los siglos XVIII y XIX', in Congost and Lana Berasain (eds.), pp. 111–39.

De Moor, T. and Van Zanden, J. L. 2012. 'Debat. Een reactie van De Moor en Van Zanden op het tseg-artikel van Manon van der Heijden, Elise van Nederveen Meerkerk en Ariadne Schmidt: "Terugkeer van het patriarchaat?

References

Vrije vrouwen in de republiek"', *Tijdschrift voor Sociale en Economische Geschiedenis* 9: 61–8.

2010. 'Girl power: the European marriage pattern and labour markets in the north sea region in the late medieval and early modern period', *The Economic History Review* 63: 1–33.

2006. *Vrouwen en de geboorte van het kapitalisme in West-Europa*. Amsterdam: Boom.

De Munck, B., Lourens, P., and Lucassen, J. 2006. 'The establishment and distribution of craft guilds in the Low Countries, 1000–1800', in Prak et al. (eds.), 2006, pp. 32–73.

De Page, H. and Dekkers, R. 1975. *Traité élémentaire de droit civil Belge*. Tôme V. Les principaux contracts usuels II Les biens I. Bruxelles: Bruylant.

De Vries, B. and Van Tijn, Th. (eds.). 1992. *De kracht der zwakken: studies over arbeid en arbeidersbeweging in het verleden opstellen aangeboden aan Theo van Tijn bij zijn afscheid als hoogleraar economische en sociale geschiedenis aan de Rijksuniversiteit Utrecht*. Amsterdam: Stichting Beheer IISG.

Dejongh, G. 1996. *Krachtlijnen in de ontwikkeling van het agrarische bodemgebruik in België, 1750–1850*. Onderzoeksrapport Centrum voor Economische Studiën. Leuven: Centrum voor Economische Studiën (KUL).

Dejongh, G. and Thoen, E. 1999. 'Arable productivity in Flanders and the former territory of Belgium in a long-term perspective (from the Middle Ages to the end of the Ancien ancien Rgimerégime)', in Van Bavel and Thoen (eds.), 1999, pp. 30–64.

Demélas, M.-D. and Vivier, N. (eds.). 2003. *Les propriétés collectives face aux attaques libérales (1750–1914). Europe occidentale et Amérique latine*. Rennes: Presses Universitaires de Rennes.

Devos, L. F. 1937. 'Het Vrijbroek en de "gemeynten" te Mechelen', *Mechelse Bijdragen* 4: 58–72.

1936. 'Het Vrijbroek en de "gemeynten" te Mechelen', *Mechelse Bijdragen* 3: 30–63.

Droesen, W. J. 1927. *De gemeentegronden in Noord-Brabant en Limburg en hunne ontginning. Eene geschied- en landhuishoudkundige studie*. Roermond: Romen.

Dyer, C. 2002. *Making a living in the Middle Ages: the people of Britain 850–1520*. New Haven, CT: Yale University Press.

Easterly, W. 2006. *The white man's burden: why the West's efforts to aid the rest have done so much ill and so little good*. New York: Penguin Press.

Ehmer, J. 2009. 'Rural guilds and urban-rural guild relations in early modern central Europe', in Lucassen, De Moor, and Van Zanden (eds.), 2009, pp. 143–58.

Engel, R. 1956. 'Le partage des biens communaux dans le Duché de Luxembourg depuis Marie-Thérèse jusqu'à la fin de la domination Autrichienne', *Hémecht. Zeitschrift für Luxemburger Geschichte*. 9: 32–55 and 178–205; 10: 72–87; 11: 72–89.

References

Engels, F. 1884. *Der Ursprung der Familie, des Privateigentums und des Staats; im Anschluß an Lewis H. Morgans Forschungen.* Hottingen-Zurich: Schweizerischer Genossenschaftsbuchdruckerei.

Enklaar, D. Th. 1932. *Middeleeuwsche rechtsbronnen van Stad en Lande van Gooiland.* Utrecht: Kemink.

Epstein, S. 1991. *Wage labor & guilds in medieval Europe.* Chapel Hill/London: University of North Carolina Press.

Epstein, S. R. 2004. 'Property rights to technical knowledge in premodern Europe, 1300–1800', *American Economic Review* 94: 382–7.

1998. 'Craft guilds, apprenticeship, and technological change in preindustrial Europe', *The Journal of Economic History* 58: 684–713.

1991. *Wage Labor and Guilds in Medieval Europe.* Chapel Hill, NC: University of North Carolina Press.

Errera, P. 1891. *Les masuïrs. Recherches historiques et juridiques sur quelques vestiges des formes anciennes de la propriété en Belgique.* Bruxelles: P. Weissenbruch.

Ferraris, J. J. F. conte de. 1777. Bruges, fo. 14 of the Kabinetskaart van de Oostenrijkse Nederlanden. Map. Malines: s.e., 1777. From Royal Library of Belgium, Kaarten en plannen [Maps and Plans], signature Ms. IV 5.567.

1777. Damme, fo. 24 of the Kabinetskaart van de Oostenrijkse Nederlanden. Map. Malines: s.e., 1777. From Royal Library of Belgium, Kaarten en plannen [Maps and Plans], signature Ms. IV 5.567.

Fox-Genovese, E. 1976. *The origins of Physiocracy: economic revolution and social order in eighteenth-century France.* Ithaca/London: Cornell University Press.

Galenson, D. W. (ed.). 1989. *Markets in history: economic studies of the past.* Cambridge: Cambridge University Press.

Gilissen, J. 1981. *Historische inleiding tot het recht: overzicht van de wereldgeschiedenis van het recht, de bronnen van het recht in de Belgische gewesten sedert de 13e eeuw, geschiedenis van het privaatrecht.* Antwerpen: Kluwer.

Gilliodts-Van Severen, L. 1880. *De la coutûme de franc de Bruges.* Bruxelles: Commission Royale d'Histoire.

Godding, P. 1987. *Le droit privé dans les Pays-Bas méridionaux du 12e au 18e siecle.* Bruxelles: Palais des Académies.

Goossens, M. 1993. *The economic development of Belgian agriculture: a regional perspective, 1812–1846.* Studies in Social and Economic History. Leuven: Leuven University Press.

Greif, A. 2006a. 'Family structure, institutions, and growth: The origins and implications of Western corporations', *American Economic Review* 96: 308–12.

2006b. *Institutions and the path to the modern economy: lessons from medieval trade.* Cambridge and New York: Cambridge University Press.

Greif, A., Milgrom, P., and Weingast, B. R. 1994. 'Coordination, commitment, and enforcement: the case of the merchant guild', *Journal of Political Economy* 102: 745–76.

References

Gustaffson, B. 1987. 'The rise and economic behaviour of medieval craft guilds. An economic-theoretical interpretation', *The Scandinavian Economic History Review* 35: 1–40.

Hannink, G. 1992. *Het markeboek van de marke Raalterwoold*. Raalte: s.e.

Hardin, G. 1968. 'The tragedy of the commons', *Science* 16: 1243–8.

Haris, C. (ed.). 1979. *The sociology of the family: New directions for Britain*. Keele: University of Keele.

Heringa, J. 1982. *De buurschap en haar marke*. Assen: Provinciaal Bestuur Drenthe.

Hickson, C. R. and Thompson, E. 1991. 'A new theory of guilds and European economic development', *Explorations in Economic History* 28: 127–68.

Hopcroft, R. L. 1999. *Regions, institutions, and agrarian change in European history*. Ann Arbor, MI: University of Michigan Press.

Hoppenbrouwers, P. 2002. 'The use and management of commons in the Netherlands. An overview', in De Moor, Shaw-Taylor, and Warde (eds.), 2002a, pp. 88–112.

Hoppenbrouwers, P. C. M. 2007. 'Meer mythen rond twee meenten: De latere geschiedenis van de meenten het Wijkerzand te Wijk en de Ebbe te Aalburg, 18e t/m 20e eeuw', in Stichting Historische Reeks Land van Heusden en Altena (ed.), *Historische Reeks Land van Heusden en Altena*, Vol. 16 (Heusden: Stichting Historische Reeks Land van Heusden en Altena), pp. 99–134.

   1993. 'Een meent en haar mythen; de vroegste geschiedenis van het Wijkerzand (15de-16de eeuw)', in Stichting Historische Reeks Land van Heusden en Altena (ed.), *Historische Reeks Land van Heusden en Altena*, Vol. 3, *Liber Amicorum C.G. Boender, Burgemeester van Aalburg* 1978–1993 (Heusden: Stichting Historische Reeks Land van Heusden en Altena), pp. 41–63.

Hoyle, R. W. 2010. 'Conclusion: reflections on power and property over the last millennium', in Van Bavel and Hoyle (eds.), 2010, pp. 349–75.

Huff, T. E. 2003. *The rise of early modern science: Islam, China, and the West*. 2nd ed. Cambridge: Cambridge University Press.

Jacquemyns, G. 1929. *Histoire de la crise économique des Flandres, 1845–1850*. Bruxelles: M. Lamertin.

Jager, W. 2000. *Modelling consumer behaviour*. Veenendaal: Universal Press.

Jager, W., Janssen, M. A., De Vries, H. J. M., De Greef, J., and Vlek, C. A. J. 2000. 'Behaviour in commons dilemmas: *Homo economicus and homo psychologicus* in an ecological-economic model', *Ecological Economics* 35: 357–79.

Jorgenson, D. O. and Papciak, A. S. 1981. 'The effects of communication, resource feedback, and identifiability on behavior in a commons', *Journal of Experimental Social Psychology* 17: 373–85.

Kain, R. J. P. 1992. *The cadastral map in the service of the state: a history of property mapping*. Chicago: University of Chicago Press.

Kennedy, D. and Norman, C. 2005. 'What don't we know?', *Science* 309: 75.

Knaepen, R. 1982. *Mol-Baelen-Desschel 1559–1795. De oude Keizerlijke vrijheid en haar voogdijdistrict*. Mol: Lions Mol-Geel.

References

Kohn, M. G. 2003. 'Merchant associations in pre-industrial Europe', Working Paper, Social Science Research Network. Available online at http://www.ssrn.com (Accessed 11 May 2014).

Koninklijke Geschied– en Oudheidkundige Kring van de Antwerpse Kempen (ed.). 2005. *Taxandria: Jaarboek van de koninklijke geschied– en oudheidkundige kring van de Antwerpse Kempen*, Nieuwe Reeks vol. 77. Turnhout: Koninklijke Geschied– en Oudheidkundige Kring van de Antwerpse Kempen.

2004. *Taxandria: Jaarboek van de koninklijke geschied– en oudheidkundige kring van de Antwerpse Kempen*, Nieuwe Reeks vol. 76. Turnhout: Koninklijke Geschied– en Oudheidkundige Kring van de Antwerpse Kempen.

Kos, A. 2010. *Van meenten tot marken. Een onderzoek naar de oorsprong en ontwikkeling van de Gooise marken en de gebruiksrechten op de gemene gronden van de Gooise markegenoten*. Hilversum: Verloren.

Kullmann, W. 1980. 'Der Mensch als politisches Lebenswesen bei Aristoteles', *Hermes: Zeitschrift für klassische Philologie* 108: 419–43.

Kuran T. 2010. *The long divergence: how Islamic law held back the Middle East*. Princeton, NJ: Princeton University Press.

Laborda Pemán, M. and De Moor, T. 2013. 'A tale of two commons. Some preliminary hypotheses on the long-term development of the commons in Western and Eastern Europe, 11th–19th centuries', *International Journal of the Commons* 7: 7–33.

Lana Berasain, J. M. 2008. 'From equilibrium to equity. The survival of the commons in the Ebro Basin: Navarra, from the 15th to the 20th centuries', *International Journal of the Commons* 2: 162–91.

Levi, M. 1988. *Of rule and revenue*. Berkeley: University of California Press.

Lindemans, P. 1952. *Geschiedenis van de landbouw in België*, Vol. 2. Antwerpen-Borgerhout: De Sikkel.

Lindemans, P. 1994. *Geschiedenis van de landbouw in België*, Vol. 2. Antwerpen-Borgerhout: De Sikkel.

Lis, C. and Soly, H. (eds.). 1997. *Werelden van verschil. Ambachtsgilden in de Lage Landen*. Brussel: VUB Press.

1994. 'Corporatisme, onderaanneming en loonarbeid. flexibilisering en deregulering van de arbeidsmarkt in Westeuropese steden (veertiende tot achttiende eeuw)', *Tijdschrift voor Sociale Geschiedenis* 20: 365–90.

Lloyd, W. F. 1833. Two lectures on the checks to population, delivered before the University of Oxford, in Michaelmas term 1832. Oxford, S. Collingwood. Available online at http://www.archive.org/details/twolecturesonch00lloygoog (Accessed 14 August 2014).

Lourens, P. and Lucassen, J. 1997. 'De oprichting en ontwikkeling van ambachtsgilden in Nederland (13de-19de eeuw)', in Lis and Soly (eds.), 1997, pp. 43–77.

Lourens, P., Lucassen, J., and De Munck, B. 2006. 'The establishment and distribution of craft guilds in the Low Countries, 1000–1800', in Prak et al. (eds.), 2005, pp. 32–73.

References

Lucassen, J., De Moor, T., and Van Zanden, J. L. (eds.). 2008. 'The return of the guilds: Towards a global history of the guilds in pre-industrial times', *International Review of Social History* 53, Supplement 16: 5–18.

MacKenney, R. 1987. *Tradesmen and traders: the world of the guilds in Venice and Europe, c.1250–1650*. London and Sidney: Croom Helm.

Maniatis, G. C. 2009. *Guilds, price formation and market structures in Byzantium*. Variorum Collected Studies, Vol. 925. Farnham: Ashgate.

Marx, K. 1867. *Das Kapital, Kritik der politischen Ökonomie*. Hamburg: Meissner.

Mastboom, J. M. 1994. 'Guild or union? A case study of rural Dutch weavers, 1682–1750', *International Review of Social History* 39: 57–75.

McAdam, D., Tarrow, S., and Tilly, C. 2001. *Dynamics of contention*. Cambridge: Cambridge University Press.

McC. Netting, R. 1981. *Balancing on an Alp. Ecological change and continuity in a Swiss mountain community*. Cambridge: Cambridge University Press.

McCloskey, D. 1989. 'The open fields of England: rent, risk and the rate of interest, 1300–1815', in Galenson (ed.), 1989, pp. 5–51.

McCloskey, D. N. 1991. 'The prudent peasant: new findings on open fields', *Journal of Economic History* 51: 343–55.

    1975. 'The economics of enclosure: a market analysis', in Parker and Jones (eds.), 1975, pp. 123–60.

    1972. 'The enclosure of open fields: preface to a study of its impact on the efficiency of English agriculture in the eighteenth century', *Journal of Economic History* 32: 15–35.

McCray, P. 1999. *Glassmaking in renaissance Venice: the fragile craft*. Aldershot: Ashgate.

Merges, R. P. 2004. 'From medieval guilds to open source software: informal norms, appropriability institutions, and innovation', paper presented at Conference on Legal History of Intellectual Property, Madison, WI, 13 November 2004.

Mitterauer, M. 2003. *Warum Europa?: Mittelalterliche Grundlagen eines Sonderwegs*. Munchen: C. H. Beck.

Moeskop, G. 1985. 'Het gebruik van gemene gronden in de Antwerpse Kempen tijdens het Ancien Regime', unpublished PhD thesis, Catholic University of Leuven.

Moll-Murata, C. 2008. 'Chinese guilds, seventeenth through twentieth centuries: An overview', *International Review for Social History* 53, Supplement 16: 213–47.

Neeson, J. M. 2000. 'English enclosure and British peasants: current debates about rural social structures in Britain c.1750–1870', *Jahrbuch für Wirtschaftsgeschichte* 44, 2: 17–32.

    1993. *Commoners: common right, enclosure and social change in England, 1700–1820*. Cambridge/New York: Cambridge University Press.

Ogilvie, S. 2007. ' "Whatever is, is right"? Economic institutions in pre-industrial Europe', *The Economic History Review* 60: 649–84.

    2004. 'Guilds, efficiency, and social capital: evidence from German proto-industry', *The Economic History Review* 57: 287–333.

References

Oliver, P. E. and Marwell, G. 1988. 'The paradox of group size in collective action: a theory of the critical mass. II', *American Sociological Review* 53: 1–8.

Olson, M. 1965. *The logic of collective action: public goods and the theory of groups.* Cambridge, MA: Harvard University Press.

Olsson, M. and Morell, M. 2010. 'Scandinavia 1750–2000', in Van Bavel and Hoyle (eds.), 2010, pp. 315–47.

Ostmann, A. 1998. 'External control may destroy the commons', *Rationality and Society* 10: 103–22.

Ostrom, E. 1990. *Governing the commons: the evolution of institutions for collective action.* The Political Economy of Institutions and Decisions. Cambridge: Cambridge University Press.

Ostrom, E., Janssen, M. A., and Anderies, J. M. 2007. 'Going beyond panaceas', *Proceedings of the National Academy of Sciences of the United States of America,* 104: 15176–8.

Paepen, N. 2005. 'De Aard van de Zes Dorpen 1332–1822. Casusonderzoek naar een Kempische gemene heide (2)', in Koninklijke Geschied– en Oudheidkundige Kring van de Antwerpse Kempen (ed.), 2005, pp. 123–230.

2004. 'De Aard van de Zes Dorpen 1332–1822. Casusonderzoek naar een Kempische gemene heide (1)', in Koninklijke Geschied– en Oudheidkundige Kring van de Antwerpse Kempen (ed.), 2004, pp. 5–78.

Panhuysen, B. 2000. *Maatwerk: Kleermakers, naaisters, oudkleerkopers en de gilden (1500–1800).* Amsterdam: IISG.

1997. 'De Amsterdamse en Haarlemse kleermakersgilden en hun concurrenten. De in– en uitsluiting van mededingers op de lokale afzetmarkt in de 17de en 18de eeuw' in Lis and Soly (eds.), 1997, pp. 127–50.

Parker, W. N. and Jones, E. L. (eds.). 1975. *European peasants and their markets: essays in agrarian economic history.* Princeton/London: Princeton University Press.

Pennisi, E. 2005. 'How did cooperative behavior evolve?', *Science* 309: 93.

Persson, K. G. 1988. *Pre-industrial economic growth: social organization and technological progress in Europe.* Oxford: Basil Blackwell.

Posner, E. A. 2000. *Law and social norms.* Cambridge, MA/London: Harvard University Press.

Poteete, A. R., Janssen, M. A., and Ostrom, E. 2010. *Working together: Collective action, the commons, and multiple methods in practice.* Princeton, NJ: Princeton University Press.

Prak, M. 2006. 'Corporate politics in the low countries: guilds as institutions, 14th to 18th centuries', in Prak et al. (eds.), 2006, pp. 74–106.

2004. 'Moral order in the world of work: social control and the guilds in Europe', In *Social control in Europe, 1500–1800,* in Roodenburg and Spierenburg, (eds.), 2004, 176–99.

1994. Ambachtsgilden vroeger en nu. *NEHA-Jaarboek voor economische, bedrijfs– en techniekgeschiedenis* 58: 10–33.

References

1992. 'Een verzekerd bestaan'. ambachtslieden, winkeliers en hun gilden in Den Bosch (ca. 1775)', in De Vries and Van Tijn (eds.), 1992, 49–79.

Prak, M., Lis, C., Lucassen, J., and Soly, H. (eds.). 2006. *Craft guilds in the early modern low countries: Work, power and representation.* Aldershot, Hants, England/Burlington, VT: Ashgate Pub.

Putnam, R. D., Leonardi, R., and Nanetti, R. Y. 1992. *Making democracy work: Civic traditions in modern Italy.* Princeton, NJ: Princeton University Press.

Quesnay, F. 1972. *Tableau économique* (transl. and eds. M. Kuczynski and R. L. Meek). London: Macmillan.

1958. *François Quesnay et la physiocratie.* Paris: Institut National d'Études Démographiques.

Raub, W., Buskens, V., and Corten, R. 2014. 'Social dilemmas and cooperation', in N. Braun and N. J. Saam (eds.), *Handbuch Modelbildung und Simulation in den Sozialwissenschaften* (Wiesbaden: Springer VS), pp. 597–626.

Recht, P. 1950. *Les biens communaux du Namurois et leur partage à la fin du XVIIIe siècle. Contribution à l'étude de l'histoire agraire et du droit rural de la Belgique accompagnée d'une description des classes rurales à la fin de l'Ancien Régime.* Bruxelles: Bruylant.

Reynolds, S. 1984. *Kingdoms and communities in western Europe, 900–1300.* Oxford: Clarendon Press.

Richardson, G. 2005. 'Craft guilds and Christianity in late-medieval England. A rational-choice analysis', *Rationality and Society* 17: 139–89.

Rodgers, C. P., Straughton, E. A., Winchester, A. J. L., and Pieraccini, M. (eds.). 2011. *Contested common land: environmental governance past and present.* London: Earthscan.

Rommes, R. N. J. and Van der Spek, J. 2004. *Met hand en hart: zeven eeuwen smedengilde en St. Eloyengasthuis in Utrecht 1304–2004.* Utrecht: SPOU.

Roodenburg, H. and Spierenburg, P. (eds.). 2004. *Social control in Europe, 1500–1800.* Columbus, OH: Ohio State University Press.

Roodenburg, M.-C. 1993. *De Delftse pottenbakkersnering in de Gouden Eeuw (1575–1675). De produktie van rood pottengoed.* Hilversum: Verloren.

Ruwet, J. 1943. *L'agriculture et les classes rurales au Pays de Herve sous l'Ancien Régime.* Luik: Bibliothèque de la Faculté de philosophie et lettres de l'Université de Liège.

Schofield, P. and Van Bavel, B. (eds) 2009. *The development of leasehold in northwestern Europe, c.1200–1600.* Turnhout: Brepols.

Shaw-Taylor, L. 2002. 'The management of common land in the lowlands of Southern England circa 1500 to circa 1850', in De Moor, Shaw-Taylor, and Warde (eds.), 2002a, pp. 59–86.

2001a. 'Labourers, cows, common rights and Parliamentary Enclosure: the evidence of contemporary comment, c.1760–1810', *Past and Present* 125: 95–126.

2001b. 'Parliamentary Enclosure and the emergence of an English agricultural proletariat', *Journal of Economic History* 61: 640–62.

References

Simons, W. 2001. *Cities of ladies: beguine communities in the medieval Low Countries, 1200–1565.* Middle Ages Series. Philadelphia: University of Pennsylvania Press.

Slicher van Bath, B. H. 1978. *Bijdragen tot de agrarische geschiedenis.* Antwerpen: Aula.

1960. *De agrarische geschiedenis van West-Europa (500–1850).* Antwerpen/ Utrecht: Het Spectrum.

Slokker, N. 2010. *Ruggengraat van de stedelijke samenleving. De rol van de gilden in de stad Utrecht, 1528–1818.* Amsterdam: Aksant.

Smith, R. M. 1979. 'Some reflections on the evidence for the origins of the 'European marriage pattern' in England' in Haris (ed.), 1979, pp. 74–112.

Steiner, Ph. 2003. 'Physiocracy and French pre-classical political economy', in W. J. Samuels, J. E. Biddle, and J. B. Davis (eds.), *A companion to the history of economic thought* (Chichester: Wiley), pp. 63–77. Available online at http:// onlinelibrary.wiley.com/doi/10.1002/9780470999059.ch5/pdf (Accessed 11 August 2014).

Stiglitz, J. E. 2002. *Globalization and its discontents.* New York: W. W. Norton.

Tan, E. S. 2002. "The bull is half the herd': property rights and enclosures in England, 1750–1850', *Explorations in Economic History* 39: 470–89.

Te Brake, W. 1981. 'Revolution and the rural community in the eastern Netherlands', in Tilly, Tilly, and Social Science History Association (eds.), 1981, pp. 53–71.

Tierney, B. 1982. *Religion, law, and the growth of constitutional thought, 1150–1650.* The Wiles Lectures given at the Queen's University of Belfast. Cambridge/New York: Cambridge University Press.

Tierney, B. and Painter, S. 1983. *Western Europe in the Middle Ages, 300–1475.* New York: McGraw-Hill.

Tilborghs, E. 1988. 'De privatisering van de gemeentelijke heide in de Antwerpse Kempen gedurende de negentiende eeuw', *Tijdschrift van de Belgische Vereniging voor Aardrijkskundige Studies* 2: 303–17.

1987. 'Een nieuwe bestemming voor de woeste gemeentegronden: Een onderzoek naar het lot van de gedurende 1834–1884 geprivatiseerde gemeentegronden in de Antwerpse Kempen', unpublished PhD thesis, Catholic University of Leuven.

Tilly, L. A., Tilly, C., and Social Science History Association (eds.). 1981. *Class conflict and collective action.* Beverly Hills, CA/London: Sage Publications.

Tollebeek, J. 2002. 'De cultus van 1302: twee eeuwen herinneringen', in Van Caenegem (ed.), 2002, pp. 194–239.

Turgot, A. R. J. 1977. *The economics of A. R. J. Turgot* (transl. and ed. P. D. Groenewegen). The Hague: Nijhoff.

Turner, M. 1986. 'English open fields and enclosures: retardation or productivity improvements', *The Journal of Economic History* 46: 669–92.

References

1982. 'Agricultural productivity in England in the eighteenth century: evidence from crop yields', *Economic History Review* 35: 489–510.

1980. *English parliamentary enclosure: its historical geography and economic history.* Folkestone: Dawson.

Van Bavel, B. J. P. 2014. 'History as a laboratory to better understand the formation of institutions', *Journal of Institutional Economics.* First view online-publication, available at http://journals.cambridge.org/abstract _S1744137414000216 (Accessed August 11, 2014).

2011. 'Markets for land, labor, and capital in northern Italy and the Low Countries, twelfth to seventeenth centuries', *Journal of Interdisciplinary History* 41: 503–31.

2008a. 'The emergence and growth of short-term leasing in The Netherlands and other parts of northwestern Europe (eleventh-seventeenth centuries). A chronology and a tentative investigation into its causes', in Van Bavel and Schofield (eds.), 2008, pp. 179–213.

2008b. 'The organization and rise of land and lease markets in northwestern Europe and Italy, c.1000–1800', *Continuity & Change* 22: 13–53.

2006. 'Rural wage labour in the 16th-century Low Countries: an assessment of the importance and nature of wage labour in the countryside of Holland, Guelders and Flanders', *Continuity & Change*, 21: 37–72.

Van Bavel, B. J. P., De Moor, T., and Van Zanden, J. L. 2008. 'The institutional organization of land markets: introduction', *Continuity & Change* 23 (Special issue 01 [The institutional organization of land markets]): 9–11.

Van Bavel, B. J. P. and Hoyle, R. W. (eds.). 2010. *Social relations, property and power. Rural economy and society in north-western Europe, 500–2000.* Turnhout: Brepols.

Van Bavel, B. J. P. and Schofield, P. R. (eds.). 2008. *The development of leasehold in northwestern Europe, c.1200–1600.* Turnhout: Brepols.

Van Bavel, B. J. P. and Thoen, E. (eds.). 2013. *Rural societies and environments at risk: Ecology, property rights and social organisation in fragile areas.* Turnhout: Brepols.

1999. *Land productivity and agro-systems in the North Sea Area (Middle Ages–20th century). Elements for comparison.* Turnhout: Brepols.

Van Bavel, B. J. P., Van Cruyningen, P., and Thoen, E. 2010. 'The Low Countries, 1000–1750', in Van Bavel and Hoyle (eds.), 2010, pp. 169–97.

Van Caenegem, R. C. (ed.). 2002. *1302: Feiten en mythen van de Guldensporenslag.* Antwerpen: Mercatorfonds.

Van der Steur, A. G. 1974. 'Woerdense kleermakers penningen', *Heemtijdinghen: orgaan van de Stichts-Hollandse Vereniging* 10: 2–8.

Van Genabeek, J. 1994. *De afschaffing der gilden en de voortzetting van hun functies.* Amsterdam: Amsterdam University Press.

Van Houtte, J. A. 1977. *An economic history of the Low Countries 800–1800.* London: St. Martin's Press.

1964. *Economische en sociale geschiedenis van de lage landen.* Zeist: W. de Haan.

References

Van Laerhoven, F. and Ostrom, E. 2007. 'Traditions and Trends in the Study of the Commons', *International Journal of the Commons* 1: 3–28.

Van Looveren, E. 1983a. 'De privatisering van de gemeentegronden in de provincie Antwerpen: vier case studies', *Bijdragen Hertogdom Brabant* 66: 189–219.

1983b. 'De gemeentegronden in de provincie Antwerpen: de privatisering van een eeuwenoud gemeenschapsgoed. Een totaalbeeld en vier case studies', unpublished PhD thesis, Catholic University of Leuven.

Van Speybrouck, A. 1884. 'Le Beverhoutsveld', *Annales de la Société d'Émulation De Bruges* 35: 155–83.

Van Uytven, R. 1982. 'Stadsgeschiedenis in het noorden en zuiden', in Blok (ed.), 1982, pp. 188–253.

Van Vleuten, L. and Van Zanden, J. L. 2010. 'Drie golven gilden. Institutionele ontwikkeling van koopliedengilden tot knechtbussen'. *Leidschrift* 25: 59–71.

Van Weeren, R. and De Moor, T. 2014. 'Controlling the commoners. Methods to prevent, detect, and sanction free-riding on the Dutch commons in the early modern period', *Agricultural History Review* 64: 256–77.

Van Zanden, J. 2005. 'De verdeling van de Rosengaerdermarke in 1416', unpublished article, available online at http://www.collective-action.info/sites/default/files/webmaster/CAS_COM_NET_Rosengaerde.pdf (Accessed 11 August 2014).

Van Zanden, J. L. 2009a. *The long road to the Industrial Revolution. The European economy in a global perspective, 1000–1800*. Leiden: Brill.

2009b. 'Why the European economy expanded rapidly in a period of political fragmentation', in Van Zanden (2009a), 32–68.

2008a. 'Economic growth in a period of political fragmentation, western Europe 900–1300', Working Paper, Utrecht University/International Institute of Social History. Available online at http://vkc.library.uu.nl/vkc/seh/research/Lists/Working%20Papers/Attachments/33/VanZanden_EconomicGrowthFragmen tation.pdf (Accessed 11 August 2014).

2008b. 'The road to the Industrial Revolution: hypotheses and conjectures about the medieval origins of the "European Miracle"', *Journal of Global History* 3: 337–59.

2005. 'De timmerman, de boekdrukker en het ontstaan van de Europese kenniseconomie', *Tijdschrift voor sociale en economische geschiedenis* 2: 115–21.

Van Zanden, J. L. and Prak, M. 2006. 'Towards an economic interpretation of citizenship. The Dutch Republic between medieval communes and modern nation states', *European Review of Economic History* 10: 11–47.

Vandenbroeke, C. 1975. *Agriculture et alimentation dans les Pays-Bas Autrichiens*. Gent-Leuven: Belgisch Centrum voor Landelijke Geschiedenis.

Vanhaute, E. 1993. 'Eigendomsverhoudingen in de Belgische en Vlaamse landbouw tijdens de 18de en 19de eeuw', *Belgisch Tijdschrift voor Nieuwste Geschiedenis* 1–2: 185–226.

References

Vanhaute, E. and Thoen, E. 1999. 'The "Flemish husbandry"' at the edge: the farming system on small holdings in the middle of the 19th century', in van Van Bavel and Thoen (eds.), 1999, pp. 271–96.

Verhulst, A. 1980. 'Le paysage rural en Flandre interieure: son évolution entre le IXième et XIIIième siècle', *Revue du Nord* 71: 11–33.

1966. *Histoire du paysage rural en flandre de l'époque romaine au XVIIIe siècle.* Brussel: Coll. Notre Passé.

1957. 'Het platteland', in *Flandria nostra: ons land en ons volk, zijn standen door de tijden heen*, Vol. 1, pp. 11–42. Antwerpen: Standaard.

Verhulst, A., and Blok., D. P. 1981. 'De agrarische nederzettingen', in A. Verhulst and D. P. Blok (eds.), *Algemene geschiedenis der Nederlanden*, Vol. 1 (Haarlem: Fibula-Van Dishoeck), pp. 153–64.

Vivier, N. 2002. 'The management and use of the commons in France in the eighteenth and nineteenth centuries', in De Moor, Shaw-Taylor, and Warde (eds.), 2002a, pp. 143–72.

Vliebergh, E. 1908. *De Kempen in de 19e en 't begin der 20e eeuw.* Ieper: Callewaert-de Meulenaere.

Westlake, H. F. 1919. *The parish gilds of mediaeval England.* London/New York: Society for Promoting Christian Knowledge/Macmillan Company.

Wiesner, M. E. 1991. 'Wandervögels and women: Journeymen's concepts of masculinity in early modern Germany', *Journal of Social History* 24: 767–82.

Willems, H. 1962. 'De ontginningen van de Kempen in de achttiende eeuw', unpublished PhD thesis, Catholic University of Leuven.

Winchester, A. J. L. 2013. 'Property rights, 'good neighbourhood' and sustainability: the management of common land in England and Wales, 1235–1965', in Van Bavel and Thoen (eds.), 2013, pp. 301–29.

2002. 'Upland commons in northern England', in De Moor, Shaw-Taylor, and Warde (eds.), 2002a, pp. 33–58.

Yelling, J. A. 1977. *Common field and enclosure in England, 1450–1850.* London: Macmillan.

Yildirim, O. 2009. 'Ottoman guilds in the early modern era', in Lucassen, De Moor, and Van Zanden (eds.), 2009, pp. 75–95.

Zuijderduijn, C. J. 2009. *Medieval capital markets. Markets for renten, state formation and private investment in Holland (1300–1550).* Global Economic History Series, 2. Leiden/Boston: Brill Academic Publishers.

Archival references

Inventory of the archive of the Gemene and Loweiden, preserved in the City Archives of Bruges (entry nr. X).

1 Copy of the Charter of 1475 of Charles the Bold.
2 Copy (end of the seventeenth century) of the confirmation letters of Charles the Bold (translation of the original French text from 1475): 'Recueil – Fait en 1514, des coutûmes, ordonnances, privilèges, etc'.
3 'Costuymen ende ordonnantien vande ghemeene weede van Assebrouck.' Copy of the original document of 1514, made in January 1887.
4 Extract of 'de costuymen' of the common land of Assebroek of 1514, dating from July 1669.
5 Copy of a fragment of the bylaw (keure) of 1514 regarding the common land of Assebroek (undated).
6 'Octroÿ gemeene weede in Assebroek van den 3en augustii 1553' granted by Emperor Charles in 1553, recognition of full possession of the *aanborgers* of the Gemene weide.
7 Book of resolutions 1672–1787.
8 Book of resolutions 1719–1731.
9 Book of resolutions 1882–1927.
10 Several acts related to the general meetings of the common and the assignation (triennial), and the assignation of user rights (once every nine years).
11 Resolution, undated.
12 'Hoofdboek. Boek van de geslachten van de Gemene en Loweede, 1622–1703'. Main book, containing the families of the Gemene and Lowede, 1622–1703.

Archival references

13 'Hoofdboek. Boek van de geslachten van de Gemene en Loweede, 1718–1767'. Main book, containing the families of the Gemene and Lowede, 1718–1767, copy.

14 'Hoofdboek. Boek van de geslachten van de Gemene en Loweede 1769–1889'. Main book, containing the families of the Gemene and Lowede, 1769–1889.

15 'Hoofdboek van de aanborgers 1889–1981'. Main book of the *aanborgers*,1889–1981.

16 'Hoofdboek 1981 – heden'. Main book, 1981 to present day.

17 Document regarding the registration of *amborgers*, 1667.

18 List of *aanborgers*, 1910.

19 List of *aanborgers*, 1925.

20 List of *aanborgers*, 1931.

21 List of *aanborgers*, 1980s.

22 List of *aanborgers*, 1981.

23 Document regarding the commission of *hoofdmannen* and the transportation of property rights (*verhoofding*) of Maerten Goethals, 1619.

24 Document regarding the election of hoofdmannen for the years 1803–1805.

25 Minutes (*Processen-verbaal*) of the public and general meeting, 1981 and 1937.

26 Account 1573–1575; closed in 1576.

27 Account 1576; part of account.

28 Account 1576–1578; original, severely damaged.

29 Account 1576–1578; duplicate.

30 Account 1579–1581; duplicate.

31 Account 1610–1612; original and photocopy of original.

32 Account 1610–1612; duplicate and photocopy of duplicate.

33 Account 1613–1615; original and photocopy of original.

34 Account 1616–1618; original and photocopy of original.

35 Account 1616–1618; duplicate.

36 Account 1621–1623; closed in 1625; original and photocopy of original.

37 Account 1621–1623; duplicate (incomplete).

38 Account 1625–1627; original and photocopy of original.

39 Account 1625–1627; duplicate and photocopy of duplicate.

40 Account 1628–1630; original copy and photocopy of original copy.

41 Account 1631–1633; original copy and photocopy of original copy.

42 Account 1634–1636; duplicate and photocopy of duplicate.

43 Account 1637–1639; closed in 1640.

44 Account 1661–1664; closed in 1665.

Archival references

45 Account 1667 (incomplete).

46 Account 1670–1671; closed in 1672; fragments of Account (incomplete).

47 Account 1672; fragment.

48 Account 1677–1679; closed in 1680 (incomplete).

49 Account 1680–1682; closed in 1683 (incomplete).

50 Account 1680–1682; duplicate.

51 Account 1684–1686 (only fragment 'ontvang van cijnzen en verpachtingen', receipt of taxes and leasings).

52 Account 1684–1686; closed in 1686.

53 Account 1684–1686; duplicate.

54 Account 1684–1686; fragment of duplicate (incomplete).

55 Account 1693–1695; closed in 1696.

56 Account 1693–1695; duplicate (incomplete).

57 List of payments for cattle grazing, 1698–1701.

58 Account 1698–1699.

59 Account 1699–1702; closed in 1702.

60 Account 1699–1702; duplicate (incomplete).

61 Extract from Account closed in 1699, made in 1757.

62 Account 1704–1706; closed in 1707.

63 Account 1703–1705; duplicate.

64 Account 1707–1709; closed in 1710.

65 Account 1707–1709; duplicate.

66 Account 1710–1712 (incomplete).

67 Account 1712–1717 (incomplete).

68 Account 1718–1720; closed in 1722.

69 Account 1718 (incomplete).

70 Account book 'Handboek vanden ontvanger van 1° de akkoorden over het pastureren van de onvrije beesten 2° de schatgelden gestemd over de beesten der aanborgers, van 1719–1732'.

71 Account 1721–1723; closed in 1725.

72 Account 1721–1723; duplicate.

73 Account 1721–1723; duplicate.

74 Account 1724–1726; closed in 1728.

75 Account 1724–1726; duplicate.

76 Part of an account 1724–26.

77 Account 1727–1729; closed in 1731.

78 Account 1730–1732; closed in 1734.

79 Account 1733–1735; closed in 1737.

80 Part of an account 1734.

81 Account 1736–1738; closed in 1740.

Archival references

82 Account 1739–1741; closed in 1743.
83 Account 1742–1744; closed in 1746.
84 Account 1745–1747; closed in 1749.
85 Account 1748–1750; closed in 1752.
86 Account 1751–1753; closed in 1755.
87 Account 1751–1753; duplicate.
88 Account 1754–1756; closed in 1758.
89 Account 1754–1756; duplicate.
90 Account 1757–1759; closed in 1761.
91 Account 1757–1759; duplicate.
92 Account 1760–1762; closed in 1764.
93 Account 1760–1762; duplicate.
94 Account 1763–1765; closed in 1767.
95 Account 1763–1765 (Account has not been completed, perhaps duplicate).
96 Account 1766–1768; closed in 1770.
97 Account 1769–1771; closed in 1773, copy.
98 Account 1772–1774; closed in 1776.
99 Account 1772–1774; duplicate.
100 Account 1775–1777; closed in 1779.
101 Account 1775–1777; duplicate.
102 Account 1778–1780; closed in 1782.
103 Account 1778–1780; duplicate.
104 Account 1781–1783; closed in 1785.
105 Account 1784–1786; closed in 1788.
106 Account 1787–1789; closed in 1791.
107 Account 1787–1789; duplicate.
108 Account 1811–1813; closed in 1815.
109 Account 1818–1820; closed in 1821.
110 Account 1821–1823; closed in 1824.
111 Account 1824–1826; closed in 1827.
112 Account 1827–1828; closed in 1828.
113 Account 1828–1829; closed in 1831.
114 Account 1831–1832; closed in 1833.
115 Account 1833–1835; closed in 1836; duplicate.
116 Account 1836–1838; closed in 1839.
117 Account 1839–1841: closed in 1842.
118 Account 1863–1868; closed in 1885 (sic!).
119 Account 1868–1882; closed in 1884.
120 Account 1882–1886; closed in 1886.
121 Account 1886–1889; closed in 1889.

Archival references

122 Account 1889–1892; closed in 1892.
123 Account 1892–1895; closed in 1898.
124 Account 1895–1898; closed in 1898.
125 Account 1898–1901; closed in 1901.
126 Account 1901–1904; closed in 1904.
127 Account 1904–1907; closed in 1907.
128 Account 1907–1910; closed in 1910.
129 Account 1922–1925; closed in 1925.
130 Account 1946–1948; closed in 1948.
131 Account 1966–1969; closed in 1969.
132 Account 1969–1972; closed in 1972.
133 Account 1972–1974; no date of closing account mentioned.
134 Account 1975–1978; closed in 1978.
135 Account 1978–1981; closed in 1981.
136 Account 1984–1987; closed in 1985.
137 Fragments of Accounts (including 1672, 1683, 1693, 1699, 1701).
138 Some receipts, seventeenth-eighteenth centuries.
139 Large amount of printed and filled-out receipts, nineteenth–twentieth centuries.
140 Extract of account of barony of Praet and the parish of Oedelem, 1725.
141 Leasing, transport from Clement Neveu to Jacques Gevaert, 1661.
142 Leasing, 1667.
143 Act regarding interest, 1685.
144 Deed of sale, 1687.
145 Taxation (Vercijnsing), 1694(?).
146 Lease, 1698.
147 Leasing to Adriaan de Nolf (for 36 years), 1699.
148 Lease, 1737.
149 Taxation (Vercijnzing), 1757.
150 Leasing of the herding of cows (koewachten), 1788.
151 Leases, 1843–1844.
152 Lease, 1849.
153 Lease, 1849.
154 Lease, 1858.
155 Lease, 1868.
156 Lease, 1871.
157 Lease, 1874.
158 Overview of leaseholders for the years 1868, 1871, and 1874.
159 Lease, 1877.
160 Lease, 1880.

Archival references

161 Lease, 1883.

162 Lease, 1892.

163 Lease, 1910.

164 Lease (hunting privilege), 1912.

165 Lease, 1928.

166 Announcement of leasing of hunting privilege, 1984(?).

167 Public sale of peat, 181(?).

168 Legal proceedings, *hoofdmannen* versus Jan and Joos Yman, 1624–1627 (incl. preceding legal proceedings versus Jan Dysselinck, 1612).

169 Legal proceedings, Chartreusen-klooster versus *hoofdmannen* regarding the course of the St-Trudoledeken, 1669–1735.

170 Amborgerschap Lambrecht van de Kerckhove, 1673–1675.

171 Fragment of legal proceedings versus Antoon Plasschaert, 1670.

172 Legal proceedings, *hoofdmannen* versus seigniory of Sijsele (taxes), 1675.

173 Legal proceedings, G. Hoorickx and Pr. Maeyens versus Maryn van Renterghem, 1704.

174 Legal proceedings, Speliers and inheritants regarding obligation, 1701–1724.

175 Legal proceedings regarding the registration of the cattle on the common (*schatgeld*) at the Council of Flanders.

176 Legal proceedings, seigniory of Sijsele versus Jacob De Budt *et al.*, 1707.

177 Legal proceedings, Gillis Hidde versus Pieter Maeyens, 1707–1709.

178 Legal proceedings, Nicolaeys Maertens, 1717–1718.

179 Legal proceedings versus Father Thiery, 1717.

180 Legal proceedings, *hoofdmannen* versus debtors, 1718–1721.

181 Legal proceedings, Widow of bailiff Schaap versus *hoofdmannen*, 1719.

182 Legal proceedings versus Charles De Brabandere and Jan de Vlieghere (regarding the registration of the cattle on the common (*schatgeld*), 1719 and 1742.

183 Legal proceedings, G. De Vlieghere versus G. Allaert, 1731.

184 Legal proceedings versus abbey of Eeckhoute, 1757.

185 Legal proceedings versus Carel Huys (regarding the Mattemeers).

186 Legal proceedings regarding the cutting down of a linden tree, 1772–1773.

187 Legal proceedings, L.B. Vermeulen, parish priest of Koekelare, versus lawyer Claeyssens, 1789.

188 Legal record, 1884.

Archival references

189–193 Transcripts of documents from the Rijksarchief, having served as legal documents in the legal proceedings of 1863, retrieved by the canon Andries.

194 Legal proceedings regarding the damaging of poplars, 1976.

195 Single documents related to legal proceedings.

196 Testimony, 1757.

197 Announcements, commands issued at church.

198 Several reproductions of maps regarding the Gemene en Loweiden (part of cadastral survey, overview of hamlets and marshes in Section B of the map of Assebroek, . . .).

199 Letter, 1718.

200 Letter, 1722.

201 Articles regarding the Gemene – and Loweide: M. Boussauw, De Amborgers van de Gemeene Weede, Assebroek 1515–1703, Vlaamse Stam, 1974, 10, nr. 1; photocopy of Errera, Les Masuïrs (1891); Booklet 'Procès et jugement tribunal civil de Bruges concernant les Gemeene-& Loo-weiden', 1882.

202 Documents regarding land tax, nineteenth–twentieth centuries.

203 Biographical material regarding canon Andries, composed by J. De Cuyper.

204 Single documents.

Provincial archives of West-Flanders, Modern Archives (2nd series, TB07)

701–708. 'Numerieke staten van het belastbaar vee (hoornvee, schapen en paarden)'. Numeric statements of taxable cattle (horned beasts, sheep, and horses), 1823.

State archives of Bruges, Aanwinsten, 1984

68. 'Bouck van de geslachten van de Gemeene weede. Register van inschrijvingen als aanborger van 1515 tot 1703'. Book of the families of the Gemeene weede, entry register of *aanborgers*, 1515–1703.

Index

aanborgers, 39, 103, 104, 105, 109, 125, 126, 128, 131, 133, 135, 136, 138, 144, 148
aanborgers., 103
aangelanden, 69
aard, 68, 69, 74, 75, 85
Aard van de Zes Dorpen, 37, 44, 67
aardbrieven, 85
aardheide, 68
abbey of Saint Trudo, 101
abundance and scarcity
  laws of, 87
access
  reulation of, 35
access conditions, 88, 89, 90, 93
  basic, 89, 90
  descendance, 82, 90, 103, 104, 143
  financial, 91, 105
  socio-economic, 90
  supplementary, 89, 90
access rights, 90, 98, 143
  limitation of, 9, 14, 35, 37, 98, 103, 104, 105, 111, 121, 143, 144, 152, 157, 162
  regulation of, 105
access rules, 35, 36, 90, 111
account books, 95, 106, 107, 110, 127, 140, 146, 148, 149, 150
active members, 122, 125, 135, 139, 141, 154, 157
active participation, 132, 134, 135
activity rate, 150
adaptation, 155, 157, 158, 167
advantages of scale, 26, 49, 51, 52
affouage, 71
age at marriage, 133, 134

age at *subscription*, 109, 133, 134, 148, 150, 156
aging, 163
agrarian depression of 1650–1750, 78
agreements, 75, 76, 77, 95, 141, 153, 155
agricultural development, 78, 110
  promotion of, 78
agricultural history, 84
agricultural methods, 26
agricultural policy, 78
agricultural produce, 21, 54, 62, 73, 78, 79, 142, 160
  increase of, 21, 73, 78
  prices of, 142
agricultural productivity, 66, 114, 141
agricultural system, 84, 115, 156
  changes in the, 73
agriculture, 21, 26, 61, 63, 64, 65, 66, 73, 78, 81, 84, 87, 109, 110, 112, 115, 117, 135, 136, 139, 153, 156
  intensification of, 78
alliances, 3, 18, 25
Alpertus of Metz, 28
altum dominium, 76, 106
amborchteghe. See aanborgers
ambuerdeghe. See aanborgers
amburger. See aanborgers
Amsterdam, 27
ancien régime, 66, 67, 107, 135
annual meeting, 38, 39, 70, 95, 127, 129, 142, 157, 159
appointed officials, 44
arable land, 26, 54, 67, 68, 72, 74, 78, 102, 135, 139, 150
artificial families, 56

Index

Assebroek, 8, 82, 90, 95, 100, 101, 103, 107, 126, 133, 136, 140, 141, 143
autonomy, 34

balance, 98, 99, 114, 117, 118, 119, 120, 139, 142, 152, 154, 155, 157, 158, 159
bargaining power, 52
Battle of the Spurs, 29, 32
beguinage movement, 23
beguinages, 23, 59
beguines, 23
behavior, 12, 32, 33, 40, 49, 73, 99, 109, 111, 121, 122, 123, 124, 131, 135, 136, 138, 140, 141, 143, 149, 153, 154, 155, 157, 158, 160, 164
  change of, 49, 122
  commoners', 73, 99, 109, 111, 121, 122, 123, 127, 131, 135, 136, 138, 140, 141, 143, 149, 153, 154, 155, 158,
  kinds of, 122
  reciprocal, 141, 164
behavioral strategy, 135
behavioral studies, 6
Belgium, 2, 20, 45, 67, 81, 84, 98, 141, 162
benefits, 34
Beveren-Oudenaarde, 88
Beverhoutsveld, 8, 94, 101, 103, 112
Black Death, 53, 54
bookkeeping, 106, 107, 109, 124, 125, 127, 136, 138, 144, 148, 150
bottom-up movement, 29
bottom-up organization, 18, 121, 162
boundaries, 26, 86, 88, 97, 98, 111
broek, 69, 70, 90
Broodfondsen, 162
brotherhoods. *See* fraternities
Bruges, 28, 35, 39, 53, 82, 91, 103, 111, 113, 144, 149
Brugse Veldzone, 101
Bulskampveld, 8, 101
Bürgerkämpfe, 32
buurtschap, 68
bylaw, 30, 70, 71, 76, 78, 85, 87, 88, 89, 95, 97
Byzantium, 27

cadastre, 66
calengieringen, 96
Campine area, 2, 37, 63, 65, 66, 67, 68, 74, 75, 76, 77, 79, 80, 81, 85, 87, 88, 89, 92, 93, 94, 98, 103

cantonnement, 77
capital goods, 55
  protection of, 54
capital market, 23
care, 164
cartel forming, 41
cattle, 92, 95
  expulsion of, 65
  number of, 54, 109, 139, 142, 144, 145, 146, 147, 150
  possession of, 110
  prices of, 109
cattle pounders. *See schutters*
cattle units. *See* livestock units *and* cattle, number of
cense, 75, 77, 90, 91
censuses, 66, 109, 110, 125, 126, 128, 135, 136, 138
champiage, 71
change, 3, 5, 11, 12, 13, 14, 17, 19, 22, 23, 25, 26, 31, 32, 34, 42, 49, 57, 60, 61, 66, 74, 76, 85, 87, 94, 98, 99, 100, 109, 114, 115, 117, 118, 119, 120, 121, 122, 124, 128, 135, 136, 139, 142, 143, 146, 148, 150, 151, 152, 153, 154, 155, 156, 157, 158, 161, 168
  agricultural, 153
  climate, 117, 161
  economic, 23, 117, 118, 119, 138, 139, 142, 143, 146, 155, 157
  external, 5, 12, 13, 14, 26, 32, 49, 60, 74, 117, 118, 119, 121, 136, 151, 154, 157
  institutional, 16
  intended, 158
  internal, 5, 32, 60, 118, 119, 120, 151
  internalization of, 99
  management, 147, 150
  political, 19, 155
  social, 19, 23, 115, 117, 138, 139, 142, 143, 146, 155, 157
charity, 143, 151
Charles V, 71
charter, 143, 146, 153
cijns. See cense
citizens, 161, 163, 165, 166, 167, 168
citizens' collectives. *See* citizens' collectivities
citizens' collectivities, 161, 163, 164, 165, 166, 167, 168
  conditions for, 168

Index

citizens' cooperatives. *See* citizens' collectivities
citizenship, 36
civil collectives, 166, 168, *See also* citizens' collectivities
civil cooperatives, 164, *See also* citizens' collectivities
civil initiatives. *See* citizens' collectivities
civil society
  construction of, 60
clan holdings, 115
climate, 119
closed commons, 10, 97, 98, 111, 112, 113, 159
clover, 65, 72, 73
Code Civil, 5, 80, 141
collective action, xiii, xv, 3, 4, 5, 6, 8, 11, 12, 13, 15, 16, 17, 18, 19, 20, 23, 30, 31, 32, 33, 34, 35, 38, 40, 46, 47, 48, 49, 50, 52, 54, 55, 56, 57, 59, 60, 67, 77, 83, 86, 98, 121, 150, 159, 161, 166, 167, 168
  conditions for, 58, 60
  debate on, 31
  development of, 55
  emergence of, 56
  motives for, 58, 60
  motors for, 58, 60
collective bargaining power, 52
collective behavior, 12
collective consumption, 165
collective decision-making, 26
collective efforts, 102
collective expression, 31
collective interests, 165
collective management, 24, 67, 83, 102, 158, 168
collective ownership, 152
collective production, 165, 166
collective property, 80, 82, 115, 148, 152, 156
collective provisions, 162
collective resistance, 33
collective resources. *See also* Common-Pool Resources
collective services, 161
collective solutions, 77
collective use, 58, 73, 102, 158, 159
collective-choice arrangements, 141
collectives, 164, 165, 166, 167, 168, *See also* citizens' collectivities
collectivities, 4, 14, 31, 48, 49, 57, 82, 153, 161, 163, *See also* citizens' collectivities
  formation of, 57

collectivization of human capital, 50
collegia, 18, 27,
commercial benefits, 55
commercial survival economy, 65
commercialization, 26, 53, 54, 55, 71, 88, 93, 144, 148, 156, 157, 159, 160, 163
  limitations on, 54, 163
  prevention of, 41, 42, 71, 88, 93, 144
common
  functioning of the, 143
  importance of the, 92, 147, 148, 150, 151, 156
  management of the, 13, 140, 141, 142, 143, 147, 150, 151, 154
  use of the, 139, 140, 141, 142, 143, 145, 147, 149, 150
common arable, 24, 63, 69, 71
  disappearance of, 63
common customs, 114
common knowledge, 52
common land, 1, 2, 63, 66, 67, 68, 74, 75, 76, 77, 78, 79, 80, 81, 87, 97, 141, 148
  availability of, 87
  nature of, 67
  ownership of, 77
  reclamation of, 79, *See also* uncultivated land, reclamation of -
  regulation, 76
  rights to, 75
  sale of, 74, 76, 78, 80, 81, 141, 148, 159
  types of, 66, 68, 97
common management, 68. *See* collective management
common management regimes, 115
common meadows, 69
common pasture, 24, 27, 65, 68, 69, 70, 72, 73
common pool of knowledge, 52
common property, 4, 12, 14, 20, 24, 25, 106, 115, 141, 154
common resources, 111
common rights, 10, 24, 25, 61, 67, 71, 78, 91
  defense of, 95
Common Rules-project, 32, 45
common use, 82,
common waste, 24, 25, 63, 65, 67, 68, 71
common wasteland, 84
common woodland, 24, 70, 82, 84
commoners
  dilemma of the, 159

193

Index

involvement of, 110
motives of, 122, 149
number of, 14
rights of, 30, 141
types of, 110, 120, 124, 131,
Common-Pool Institution, 13, 112, 116,
117, 118, 141, 152, 153, 159
emergence of, 153
Common-Pool Resources, 11, 15, 31, 50,
51, 112, 116, 117, 118, 141, 144, 151
Common-Property Regime, 11, 116, 117,
118, 121
Common-Property Rights, 1, 25, 79, 80
commons
access to, 88, 97, 112
administration of, 95
alienation of, 81
boundaries of, 88,
characteristics of, 98
complexity of, 87, 117
conceptual evolution of, 161
debate on, 116, 161
decline of, 151
development, 58
dissolution of, 2, 4, 17, 20, 46, 57, 81, 82,
83, 84, 112, 114, 115, 121, 122, 141,
151, 154, 156, 159, 161
dynamics of, 100, 153, 158
emergence of, 23, 27, 48, 76
evolution of, 114
external partners of, 40
functioning of, 22, 61, 99, 110, 113, 124,
126, 150, 153, 154, 158, 159
global, 161
governance of, 86, 94
history of, *See* commons, origins of
importance of, 109, 114, 123, 149, 155
internal market of, 42
legal status of, 66
literature on, 7, 114, 115, 117, 121, 122,
123, 154, 155
longevity of, 3
maintenance of, 95
management of, 2, 40, 46, 69, 70, 75, 78,
82, 83, 84, 85, 91, 93, 97, 99, 100, 109,
112, 113, 114, 115, 116, 117, 118,
124, 131, 148, 154, 155, 158
number of, 30
organization of, 87
origins of, 24, 61, 73, 74, 77, 114,
115, 116
protection of, 83
robustness of, 99

sale of, 81
survival of, 82, 83, 99, 112, 113, 117,
120, 141, 148, 151, 152, 153, 154,
155, 156, 165
tragedy of the, 11, 12, 13, 114, 118, 123,
147, 155, 158, 159, 161
typology of, 24, 86, 97
use of, 75, 84, 91, 99, 100, 109, 112,
114, 116, 117, 118, 119, 123,
124, 132, 152, 154, 155,
157, 158
variation of, 87
vulnerability of, 154, 155
Commons Acts, 83
communal property, 50, 141
communal resource management, 5
communal woodland, 70
communalism, 19
communaux, 80
communia, 74
communication strategy, 128
communism, 115
communities, 31
community property, 66
complexity, 160
compliance, 94
conceptual evolution, 161
conditions, 47, 48, 143
economic, 143
legal, 143
political, 143
social, 143
conflicts, 26, 76, 79, 106, 112, 115, 141,
151, 154
consumer initiatives, 167
contentious politics, 31
context, 7, 119, 167
contingency, 94
continuity, 35, 155
control system, 140
cooperation, xv, 1, 2, 3, 5, 6, 11, 12,
15, 20, 43, 45, 49, 52, 56, 60, 67,
120, 151
experiments in, 1
voluntary, 20
cooperative, 1, 2, 6, 12, 17, 19, 33, 45, 49,
50, 163, 166
cooperative behavior, 1, 2, 6, 17,
33, 34
cooperative businesses, 166
cooperative model, 45
cooperative solutions, 50, 166
limitations of, 166

Index

cooperative strategies
  conditions of, 12
cooperatives, 6, 17, 162, 164, 165, 168, *See
  also* citizens' collectivities
  first wave of, 164
  International Year of, 166
  second wave of, 17, 164, 165
CORN-network, 84
corporatism, 22
cost reduction, 26
costs, 94, 121
*Costumen ende Ordonnantien vande
  Ghemeene weede van Assebrouck*, 101
countryside, xiii, 4, 16, 18, 19, 41, 48, 53,
  59, 98, 138, 142, 151, 153
court rolls, 85
Couteberch, Fernane, 101
CPI. *See* Common-Pool Institution
CPR. *See* Common-Property Resources
CPrR. *See* Common-Property Regime
CPRs. *See* Common-Pool Resources
credit exchange, 28
crises, 81, 141, 162, 163, 167
crisis of 1846, 141
critical mass, 27, 30, 121
crops cultivation, 26, 73, 84, 102, 139, 147,
  152, 156
cultivation methods
  intensification of, 64
customary law, 39, 67, 75, 104

Darwin, Charles, 1, 4, 12
De Bie, Floris, 75
De Rijcker, Adriaen, 138
De Rijcker, Andreas, 136, 138
De Rijcker, Bernard, 136
De Rijcker, Bruno, 136
De Rijcker, Félix, 136
De Rijcker, Henri, 136
De Rijcker, Louis, 136
De Rijckere, Adriaen, 138
De Rijckere, Andreas, 136
De Rijckere, Bernardus, 136
De Rijckere, Jan, 136
De Rycker, Henricus, 136
De Rycker, Ludovicus, 136
debate on commons, 116
debtor, 138
decision-making, 3, 13, 26, 45, 98, 124,
  141, 149, 154, 157, 159
decline of the welfare state, 162
*Décret concernant le mode de partage des biens
  communaux*, 80

délivrance, 71
demand, 163
democratization, 19
Dermulle, Bernardus, 125
design principles, 47, 120, 141, 153, 154,
  159, 166
dilemma, 33, 124, 152, 157, 159
disasters, 12, 46
divergence, 4
do-it-yourself-society, 163
domain, 74,
dominium directum, 106
donkmeesters, 94
Drenthe, 165
dries, 64
Dutch Republic, 25

Eastern Netherlands, 32, 40
ecological stability, 119
ecology, 68
economic benefits, 60, 164
economic crisis, xiii, 16, 81, 83, 104, 163
economic development, 3, 20, 21, 22, 32,
  59, 110
economic growth, 21
economic incentives, 60
economic participation, 111, 127, 128, 131,
  133, 150
economic situation, 153
economic strategies, 22
efficiency, 118, 119, 120, 121, 142,
  143, 154
Eighty Years' War, 62
elderly care, 162
Eloy guild, 36
enclosure, 6, 22, 32, 69, 79, 82, 83, 121,
  122, 123, 148, 156
enclosure debate, 123
Enclosure movement, 6, 32, 52, 114, 156,
  See also enclosure
energy cooperatives, 162
energy production, 163
enforcement mechanisms, 38
enforcement tool, 44
England, 30, 32, 45, 82, *See also* Great
  Britian *and* United Kingdom
entitled users, 24
entry rules, 58
environment, xiv, 22, 48, 100, 117,
  124
environmental degradation, 122, 124
equality, 42
equity, 118, 120, 121, 143, 154

195

Index

Erfgooiers, 85
European Marriage pattern, 23, 56
evolutionary process, 153
exclusion, 35, 52, 53, 57, 91, 92, 103, 123, 143
exclusivity, 34
expenditure, 110, 140
exploitation, 51, 87, 94, 144, 145, 146, 147, 148, 149
  level, 144, 145, 146, 147, 148
  mechanisms, 149
expulsion, 44

factor markets, 53
failing markets, 161
fallow periods, 64, 71, 72
family bonds, 55, 60
  disappearance of, 55
family relations, 56
family structure, 23
family support, 59
family ties, 23
farm fragmentation, 65
fertilization, 2, 59, 65, 68, 70, 135, 156
feudalism, 59, 78
feuille, 71
field rotation system, 26
fines, 40, 44, 79, 91, 95, 96, 106
Flanders, 61, 63, 65, 71, 72, 74, 81, 84, 87, 89, 98, 100, 103, 111, 140, 141, 143, 154
flexibility, 153, 157
floodings, 102
fodder crops, 65, 72
four-crop rotation, 64
fragmentation of sovereignty, 56
framework, 47, 99, 111, 113, 114, 116, 119, 120, 154, 168
  conceptual, 114
  institutional analysis and development. *See* IAD-framework
  methodological, 114
France, 32, 84
fraternities, 4, 8, 23, 36
free market, 20, 40, 42
free riding, 2, 10, 13, 14, 39, 44, 51, 60, 70, 155, 164
  prevention of, 39, 44, 52, 60, 70, 87, 155
functional participation, 111, 127, 128, 131, 133, 142, 150

gegildan, 28
Gelderland, 165
Gemene and Loweiden, 8, 9, 10, 14, 39, 69, 82, 90, 95, 100, 101, 102, 103, 104, 105, 106, 107, 108, 112, 113, 126, 128, 130, 135, 138, 139, 140, 141, 143, 144, 147, 149, 154, 156. *See also* Gemene Weide
  origins of, 101, 102
gemene broek, 69, 70
gemene velden, 69
Gemene Weide, 103, 106. *See also* Gemene and Loweiden
gemeynte, 68, 98
general meeting. *See* annual meeting
Genossenschaften, 24
Germanic joint-ownership tradition, 74
Germany, 32, 84, 162
gezworenen. See sworn members
Ghent, 11, 28, 29, 53
glanage. See gleaning ears
gleaning ears, 71
global commons, 161,
goods
  commercialization of, 159
  division of, 159
governance model, 17, 26, 46, 47, 48, 112, 116
governance system, 29, 30, 84, 98, 115
Governing the commons, 47, 119, 123
grain prices, 78, 80
grazing pressure. *See* exploitation, level
grazing rights, 41, 54
Great Britain, 114. *See also* England *and* United Kingdom
Great European Reclamations, 26
Greece, 162
green manuring, 65
group behavior, 124
group composition, 121, 158, *See also* group heterogeneity
  internal, 121
group dynamics, 120
group formation process, 32
group heterogeneity, 109, 110, 121, 122, 124, 150
group identity, 7
group interest, 35
group norms, 38, 60
group size, 33, 35, 110, 121, 122, 150
guild revolutions, 29

Index

guilds, xiii, 4, 5, 8, 11, 12, 18, 19, 20, 21, 22, 23, 24, 25, 26, 27, 28, 29, 30, 31, 32, 34, 35, 36, 38, 39, 40, 41, 42, 43, 44, 45, 46, 47, 48, 50, 51, 52, 53, 54, 55, 56, 57, 59, 60, 82, 104, 113, 114, 150, 163, 164,
  critical mass for, 53
  decline of, 151
  development of, 20, 23
  dissolution of, 4, 20, 57
  evolution of, 27
  growth of, 53
  membership of, 54
  number of, 25, 27, 28, 29
  openness of, 37
  origin of, 28
  revolt of the, 29
  role of, 56
  structure of, 53

Hardin, Garrett, 11, 12, 13, 14, 41, 117, 123, 157, 161
heath, 68, 74, 75, 81, 101
heath land. *See* heath
heide, 75, *See also* heath
Heirnis, 11
heirnismeester, 94
herdgang, 68
heterogeneity
  group, 109
  socio-economic, 109
historical development, 24
historical sources, 100, 107, 125, 135, 136, 141, 143, 144, 146, 150, 152, 153
homo cooperans, 148, 161
homo economicus, 123, 124, 148
homo psychologicus, 124
homo reciprocans, 148
hoofdboeken, 103, 104, 105, 107, 108, 125, 133, 135, 136, 143, 144
hoofdmannen, 92, 94, 96, 105, 106, 113, 127, 138, 142
household, 3, 11, 36, 49, 54, 59, 66, 91, 92, 110, 152, 155, 156, 165
household economy, 11, 155
household needs, 156, 165
household strategies, 49
household use, 55
husbandry, 73

IAD-framework, 47, 119, 154
IASC. *See* Internal Association for the Study of the Commons
IASCP. *See* Internal Association for the Study of the Commons(IASC)
ICA. *See* institutions for collective action
identifiability, 33, 34
incentives, 23, 48, 51, 98, 100, 120, 155
income, 23, 42, 43, 50, 54, 59, 60, 110, 123, 128, 133, 135, 145, 147, 148, 156
  increase of, 54
  security, 23, 50, 60, 102
  strategy, 156
individual benefit, 102
individual choices, 159
individual decisions, 153
individual property, 24
individual responsability, 157
individual strategies, 49
individualism, 20
industrial crops, 65
industrial development, 2
Industrial Revolution, 52
industrialization, 22, 62
inequality, 20
infield, 64
infrastructure, 81
infringements, 96, 140, 159
inheritance system, 89, 103
insecurity, 60
institutional adaptability, 22
institutional analysis and design framework, see IAD-framework
  institutional characteristics, 18, 23
institutional design, 22, 34, 48, 59, 154, 155
institutional development, 61
institutional diversity, 152, 166, 167, 168
institutional revolution, xiii, 18
institutional structure, 19, 29, 151
institutional success, 48
institutional tool-box, 160
institutionalization, 3, 4, 11, 13, 18, 20, 22, 32, 33, 35, 54, 56, 59, 67
institutions, xiii, xv, 3, 4, 5, 6, 8, 9, 11, 13, 14, 15, 16, 18, 19, 20, 21, 22, 23, 24, 25, 27, 29, 30, 31, 33, 34, 35, 36, 37, 38, 39, 40, 44, 46, 47, 48, 51, 52, 53,

197

Index

55, 56, 57, 58, 59, 60, 67, 77, 79, 83, 84, 86, 98, 100, 101, 106, 112, 114, 115, 117, 119, 120, 126, 140, 141, 143, 150, 151, 152, 153, 154, 155, 157, 158, 159, 161, 163, 164, 166, 167, 168,
  causal explanation of, 115, 116
  demise of, 20
  design of, 67, 78
  emergence of, 19
  evolutionary explanation of, 115, 116
  functioning of, 19, 115
  growth of, 55
  life span of, 99
  multi-purpose, 164
  spread of, 59
  structure of, 19
  types of, 168
institutions for collective action, xiii, xv, 3, 5, 6, 8, 11, 15, 16, 17, 18, 19, 22, 23, 31, 32, 34, 38, 40, 46, 47, 48, 52, 56, 58, 60, 67, 74, 77, 83, 98, 104, 115, 116, 119, 120, 150, 153, 155, 158, 160, 161, 163, 164, 166, 167, 168
  characteristics of, 34, 44
  conditions for, 47, 48, 74, 115, 153, 168
  development of, 74
  dissolution of, 156
  dynamics of, 120
  emergence of, 22, 58, 59, 98
  functioning of, 77, 119, 140, 164
  lifespan of, 164
  management of, 48
  motives for, 115, 153
  motors for, 74, 115, 153,
  present day –, 160, 161
  types of, 153
insurance, 151, 157, 162, 164
  companies, 162
  system, 151
intellectual property, 50
interest group, 3
International Association for the Study of Common Property. *See* International Association for the Study of the Commons (IASC)
International Association for the Study of the Commons, 115, 123

International Year of Cooperatives, 166
investment, 34, 52, 55, 59, 68, 81, 100, 102, 131
involvement
  commoners', 118
Ireland, 84
Italy, 32, 60, 103

joint insurance systems, 162
joint ownership, 80, 81
joint welfare, 60

Kempen. *See* Campine Area
kerkgebod, 85
keur, 85, 95, 107
kin-based society, 24, 55, 56, 57
kinship, 18, 25, 60
knowledge, 52
  exchange of, 50
  protection of, 52
  value of, 52
koewachters, 140
Kommunalismus, 19

labor, 21, 43, 53
  demand for, 53
  division of, 52
  input, 65
  market, 23, 53, 55
land lease, 76, 77, 119, 130, 139, 150, 152, 156
land management, 30
land markets, 77
land prices, 80
land productivity, 2, 4, 22, 66
  increase of, 68
land use, 26, 30, 73
  intensification of, 26
land-pasture ratio, 65
Latin America, 25
law, 75, 81, 95
  customary, 75
  written, 75
Law of 25 June 1847 on the reclamation of uncultivated land, 81, 83, 141
lease-holding, 87, 139
leasing-out, 76, 119, 130, 150, 152
legal body, 29
legal changes, 56
legal recognition, 56,
legal security, 80

Index

legislation, 5, 14, 17, 20, 22, 26, 38, 49, 75, 76, 80, 81, 83, 122, 141, 143, 151, 168
  evolution of, 73
  French, 80
Leuven, 28
levancy and couchancy, 54
levy. *See* taxes
lezen van de aren. See gleaning ears
liability, 44, 96
liability clause, 39, 96
liberalism, 1, 2, 4, 5, 81, 162, 163
liberalization, 163
Lier, 29
Limburg, 82, 103
livestock, 66, 144, 145, 146, 147,
  units, 144, 145, 147
loam, 68, 77, 92
local authorities, 38, 48
local conditions, 3
local needs, 3
Loi sur le défrichement des terrains incultes.
  See Law of 25 June 1847 on the reclamation of uncultivated land
longevity, 33, 47, 48, 85, 114, 155
long-term benefit, 33
long-term survival, 33
Lord of Sijsele, 106
Low Countries, 20

Male, 104
Maleveld, 91, 94, 96, 112
management costs, 94
management decisions, 110, 114, 119, 120, 124, 139, 144, 147, 153, 156, 157
management strategy, 87, 124, 147
management structure, 151
management system, 87, 120, 150
managers, 94, 96, 111, 120, 122, 139, 142, 143, 145, 146, 147, 148, 149, 150, 151, 157, 159, *See also hoofdmannen*
  election of, 94
  number of, 94
  protection of, 96
mandatory attendance of meetings, 45
manure production, 65
Maria Theresia, 122
marke. See marken
Marke Exel, 44
Marke Het Gooi, 36, 85
Marke Rozegaarde, 40
markeboeken, 32
markegenootschappen. See marken

marken, 24, 25, 30, 40, 67, 85, 98, 99, 164, 165
Markenwet of 10 May 1886, 83
market development, 49
market economy, 22, 162
market governance, 83
market participation, 54
market protection, 35
market size, 55
market solutions, 12, 15, 46
market system, 4, 41, 54, 163, 165, 166, 167,
marriage, 23, 102, 103, 104, 107, 109, 133, 134, 148, *See also* European Marriage Pattern
marshland, 69, 75
mass movements, 31, 32, 33, 34
masuirs, 98
maximization of output, 65
meadows, 75, 101, 107, 139, 147
meenten, 24, 25, 30, 85, 98
meetings, 39, 70, 95, 122, 124, 127, 128, 129, 157, 159
member lists, 107
members
  active, 110, 111
  number of, 105, 106, 121, 125, 135, 138, 141, 142, 144, 145, 147, 154, 164
  passive, 110, 111
  registration of, 106, 108, 110, 133, 135, 138, 144
  regsitration of, 145
  types of, 150
membership
  advantages of, 109
  conditions for, 85, 89, 103
  obligations of, 21, 36
  restriction of, 100
  right of, 37, 89, 104
membership by inheritance, 37
membership registers. *See hoofdboeken*
methodology, 113, 114, 158
migration, 46, 103
minimum-wage, 42, 43, 50
mixed agriculture, 87
Mondragon Corporation, 166
monitoring, 40, 93, 96, 98, 100, 111, 140, 146, 149, 154, 155, 164, 165
  external, 98, 140, 150, 154
monitoring costs, 94

Index

monopoly, 40
motives, 48, 49
  commoners', 9, 15, 124, 151
motors, 49
movable property
  concept of, 74
Mulle, Bernardus, 125, 126
multi-purpose institutions, 164
mutual agreements, 25
mutual control, 33
mutual dependency, 19
mutual governance, 165

naharking, 71
Napoleon, 62
natural circumstances, 77, 87
natural resources, 26
natural wealth, 20
neighborhood, 68
nested enterprises, 48
Netherlands, 30, 32, 36, 45, 79, 84,
  162, 163
New Institutional Economics, 21
non-commoners
  access for, 35
non-entitled users, 55
non-kin based society, 56
nonmembers
  access for, 42, 88
  access to commons for, 35, 144, 155
  access to guilds for, 35
non-movable goods, 74
norms, 60, 117, 154, 164
  compliance to, 60
Northern Netherlands, 32

occupation, 3, 18, 27, 36, 109, 110, 119,
  123, 128, 135, 136, 138,
Oedelem, 82, 95, 100, 107, 133, 136, 141,
  143, 144
Oliver's paradox, 121
online community, 165
open access, 26, 157
open commons, 97, 98, 111,
  113, 159
openness, 49
Ostrom, Elinor, xiv, 11, 15, 47, 77, 87,
  88, 94, 95, 117, 119, 123, 141, 153,
  154, 159
Ostrom-school, 119
Ouderparticipatiecrèches, 162
outfield, 64

over-exploitation, 2, 10, 11, 12, 13, 14, 35,
  41, 42, 43, 52, 53, 55, 86, 93, 95, 105,
  110, 123, 139, 143, 147, 149, 155, 157
  prevention of, 35, 41, 105, 123, 139, 149,
  157
Overijssel, 165

pacage, 71
pacht. See land lease
paisson, 71
panage, 71
Parent-participation-child-care-centers, 162
participation, xi, 9, 13, 14, 38, 39, 45, 54,
  61, 104, 106, 109, 110, 111, 115, 118,
  123, 124, 125, 126, 127, 128, 131,
  132, 135, 138, 140, 141, 142, 150,
  155, 157, 158, 162
  female, 104
participation intensity, 111, 132, 135
participation level, 106, 115, 125, 128, 135,
  140, 142, 148, 150, 154, 157
participatory behavior, 9, 155
passive members, 125, 127, 139, 147, 149,
  154, 157
pasture, 24, 26, 65, 71, 74, 75, 82, 92, 95,
  101, 102, 105, 122, 125, 127, 130,
  139, 146, 147, 148, 150, 156, 157, 159
  period of, 102
pasture rights, 71, 95, 109, 122, 125
  registration of, 95
Peace Treaty of Münster, 62
peat, 68, 77, 88, 91, 92, 95, 96
personal benefit, 21
Physiocracy, 20, 21, 78, 114
polarization, 131, 139, 149
political institutions, 56
political recognition, 56
political structure, 97
politics, 2, 29, 31, 49, 53, 56, 59, 78, 97,
  143, 158
poor relief, 36, 91, 114, 151
poorter. See citizenship
population aging, 162
population decrease, 53, 162
population density, 35, 74, 87, 98, 146, 162,
  163
population increase, 2, 4, 12, 14, 20, 26, 27,
  49, 53, 59, 64, 73, 75, 76, 78, 82, 93,
  98, 99, 118, 119, 144, 146, 157, 160
  promotion of, 78
poverty, 17, 90, 114, 141, 146, *See also* poor
  relief

200

Index

power balance, 120, 139, 150, 155
power relations, 60, 87, 139
PPP. *See* public-private partnership
prélèvements, 70
price adjustments, 144, 146
price mechanism, 41, 42, 144, 146
price uniformity, 42, 43
private governance system, 26, 152
private property, 1, 2, 4, 12, 20, 21, 24, 25,
    50, 54, 66, 70, 72, 77, 80, 87, 94, 115,
    148, 152, 159
privatization, 4, 5, 10, 14, 17, 26, 68, 73, 78,
    80, 81, 82, 112, 122, 148, 151, 155,
    156, 161, 162, 163, 166
production market, 40
productivity increase, 65
profit, 44, 149, 151, 163, 167
proletarianization, 114, 138, 150, 156
property, 4, 20, 25, 57, 73, 75, 76, 77, 80,
    82, 117, 148
  regimes, 117
  systems, 25
property rights, 57, 73, 75, 76, 77, 80, 82,
    148
  fragmentation of, 82
protectionism, 40, 54
public governance system, 152
public services, 161, 163, 164, 165, 166,
    167, 168
public-private partnership, 162
putting-out system, 41

quality, 42, 43, 50, 155, 163, 166
quality control, 42, 43, 50, 164
quality standard, 42
Quesnay, François, 20
quiritary dominium. See private property

Rabobank, 166
rebellion, 31, 33
reciprocal behavior, 141, 164
reciprocity, 2, 6, 13, 33, 34, 44, 141, 155,
    164,
  double, 164
reclamations, 64, 66, 75, 78, 79, 80, 81,
    105, 141, 147
regeerders, 94
regional agrosystem, 66
regional variations, 68
regulation, 35, 39, 40, 41, 57, 68, 73,
    85, 91, 93, 97, 100, 104, 107, 121,
    124, 140, 143, 149, 151, 153,
    158, 159

regulations, 26, 32, 36, 39, 45, 55, 60, 76,
    85, 88, 90, 94, 95, 101, 106, 121, 140,
    143, 153, 158, *See also* rules
  differentiation of, 87
religion, 44
rendant, 95
representation, 32, 56
residence, 89
resilience, 6, 60, 100, 114, 118,
    119, 120, 154, 155, 158,
    163, 166
resolutieboeken, 85, 107, 124,
    125, 136
resolution books. *See resolutieboeken*
resource units, 67
resources, 1, 2, 3, 4, 5, 11, 12, 13, 14, 15,
    16, 17, 24, 25, 26, 30, 31, 35, 36, 37,
    38, 41, 42, 43, 44, 45, 47, 51, 53, 54,
    55, 57, 58, 67, 70, 73, 83, 84, 86, 88,
    89, 91, 92, 93, 95, 101, 102, 106, 107,
    109, 110, 111, 112, 114, 115, 116,
    117, 118, 119, 120, 121, 122, 123,
    124, 126, 131, 134, 139, 142, 143,
    144, 146, 148, 150, 151, 152, 153,
    154, 155, 156, 157, 158, 159, 160,
    161, 165, 167, *See also* Common-Pool
    Resources
  access to, 121, 153
  accessibility, 159
  appropriation of, 67, 74
  availability of, 114, 118
  collective, 2, 12
  consumption of, 52
  depletable, 91
  exploitation of, 157
  governance of, 16, 30, 54, 58, 112, 116,
    117, 153, 158, 163, *See also* Common-
    Pool Resources
  management of, 9, 24, 26, 30, 32,
    35, 45, 58, 83, 86, 87, 93, 114, 115,
    117, 121, 142, 151, 153, 154, 155,
    157, 167
  natural, 1, 4, 11, 14, 26, 30, 50,
    52, 75, 101, 115,
    123, 139
  non-depletable, 91
  quantity of, 91
  regeneration of, 67
  rural, 26
  sale of, 148
  subsoil, 68
  survival of, 159
  type of, 68

Index

use of, 9, 24, 26, 41, 45, 55, 73, 114, 117, 118, 120, 122, 123, 124, 139, 143, 144, 150, 151, 153, 155, 156, 157, 159, 165, 167
viability of, 143
retreating state, 161
revolts, 32, *See* mass movements
rights
  composition of, 152
  recognition of, 23, 26, 159, 167, 168
riots, 31
Rise of the West, 22
risk avoidance, 26, 51, 59, 102
risk-sharing, 2, 49, 51
robustness, 48, 60, 117, 119, 154, 158
rules, 22, 25, 26, 32, 35, 37, 38, 42, 45, 54, 55, 60, 70, 85, 87, 91, 93, 95, 96, 103, 106, 117, 120, 123, 140, 141, 144, 153, 154, 155, 158, 159
  adaptation of, 153
  changing of, 45, 60, 93, 94, 95, 106, 155, 158
  compliance with, 94
  composition of, 38, 120, 154
  design of, 38
  enforcement of, 39
  implementation of, 85
  internalization of, 45
  self-enforcement of, 25
rural areas. *See* countryside

sanctioning, 2, 8, 32, 38, 39, 44, 45, 60, 87, 88, 91, 95, 96, 123, 140, 155, 164
  graduated, 96
  enhanced, 40
sand, 92
sargant, 96
Scandinavia, 79, 84
scarcity, 53, 59, 87, 149
schutters, 96,
security, 34
seigniorial rights, 76, 78
seigniorial system, 74
seigniory of Sijsele, 101
self-control, 155
self-determination, 48
self-enforcement, 34, 38
self-governance, 3, 15, 22, 38, 60, 150, 151, 155, 157, 158, 161, 167

self-monitoring, 154
self-restrictiveness, 3
self-sanctioning, 3, *See also* sanctioning
self-sufficiency, 55, 65
serfdom, 76
service provision, 83
share, 36
shared goods. *See* Common-Pool Resources
shares, 41
short-term cultivation, 64
short-term investment, 33
Sijsele
  Lord of, 106
  seigniory of, 101
Sijseleveld, 8
silent revolution, 16, 18, 19, 22, 33, 34, 44, 59
single women, 23
Sint-Trudoledeken, 102
Sint-Truiden, 29
skills, 41, 50, 51, 52, 55
Sociaal-ecologisch systeem, 115
social capital, 60
social control, 13, 33, 39, 43, 44, 52, 94, 126, 131, 132, 140, 147, 150, 155, 157, 165, 168
social cost, 60
social crisis, 81
social development, 3
social dilemmas, 12, 23, 33, 35, 49, 59, 100, 153, 159
social organization, 55
social security, 60, 133
social ties, 122
social welfare, 2, 36, 59, 117, 161
socio-economic conditions, 142
socio-economic heterogeneity, 109
solidarity, 60
solutions
  private, 48
  public, 48
Sonderweg, 55
Southern Netherlands, 32, 63, 70, 141, *See also* Belgium
sovereignty
  fragmentation of, 56
Spain, 32, 45
stakeholders, 18, 45, 95, 157
stall feeding, 65
state, 165, 166, 167, 168,
state governance of goods and services, 83
state intervention, 12

Index

state solutions, 12, 15, 46
stoppelgang. See stubble pasture
strategies, 94, 139, 149
stubble pasture, 71, 72
subordination, 20
subsistency, 78, 156
supply and demand, 51, 87
survival strategy, 149
sustainability, 14, 17, 35, 37, 93, 114, 142,
 147, 148, 151, 165, 167
sworn members, 40, 96

Tableau économique, 20
tasks
 division of, 94,
taxes, 66, 67, 76, 80, 91, 105, 106, 109,
 139, 144, 146, 147, 150
 exemption of, 80
technology, 21, 22, 51, 52, 73, 91, 117, 165
temporal dilemma, 34
threats, 157
three-dimensional approach, 113, 118
three-field rotation system, 26, 63, 64, 84
Tiel, 28
tithes, 79
towns. *See* urban settlements
trade, 28
tragedy. *See* commons, tragedy of the
transaction costs
 reduction of, 148
transportation, 79
tribe-based society, 55, 56, 57
trust, 34, 162, 165, 167
turf, 68, 77, 92, 93, 126
Turgot, Anne-Robert Jacques, 20, 21

UK, 84. *See also* United Kingdom, England
 and Great Britain
uncultivated land, 62, 68, 75, 78, 79, 81, *See
 also* wasteland *or* common waste
 reclamation of, 75, 78, 79,
 sale of, 81
under-exploitation, 14, 35, 110, 119, 123,
 126, 143, 145, 146, 147, 155, 157
 prevention of, 145, 146, 157
universitas, 32, 56, 57
United Kingdom, 48. *See also* England,
 Great Britain, *and* UK
urban settlements, 4, 8, 18, 19, 28, 36, 59,
 151, 153
urbanization, 27, 32, 53, 54
use-rights, 2, 24, 35, 41, 53, 67, 69, 71,
 72, 73, 75, 77, 78, 82, 83, 88,

93, 98, 104, 105, 106, 107, 121, 139,
 143, 144, 145, 154, 156
 acknowledgment of, 75
 collective, 70
 definition of, 88
 limitation of, 24, 35, 41, 72, 82, 93, 98,
 105, 121, 139, 152, 165
 obtaining, 104
 recognition of, 78
 regulation of, 71
 transfer of, 76, 77, 89, 156
 use-rules
 supplementary, 92
utility, 118, 119, 120, 121, 131, 134, 142,
 143, 150, 154,
Utrecht, 29

vaine pâture, 72, 73
valuable commodity, 50
Van Belleghem, Laurentius, 126
Van Berchem, Willem, 75
Van Beveren, Isabella, 102, 103
Van den Berghe, Franciscus, 126,
Van Ghistele
 Absoloen, 104
 Mayken, 104
van Metz, Alpertus, 28
veld, 69, 88, 101, *See also gemene veld*
velden, 69
veldwachter, 96
Venice, 50
village autonomy, 26
village economy, 97
voorlijf, 76
vorsters, 96
vreetijd, 72
Vrijbroek of Mechelen, 69, 70, 90,
 143
vrijdom, 89,
Vrijgeweid of Donkt, 88
vrijgeweide, 72, *See also vaine pâture*
vroente, 68, 69, 74, 75, 76, 77
vroentebrief, 76, 85
vulnerability, 14

wage dependency, 126, 136, 150, 156
wage labor, 135, 136, 138, 142, 156
Wallonia, 82
war, 145
wasteland, 25, 30, 63, 65, 66, 71, 72,
 74, 76, 79, 81, 87, 90,
 141, 147
 reclamation of, 66, 141, 147

203

Index

wastina, 74
water boards, 59
wealth, 90
welfare state, 162
  decline of the, 162
widows, 36, 104
Wijkerzand, 41, 83, 99
wildert, 75
William I
  King, 62

woodland, 70, 71, 74, 75, 101
written law, 75

Ypres, 28, 53

zavelmeester, 95
zoon politikon, 4
Zotschore
  seigniory of, 104
ZZP-ers, 162

Other Books in the Series (continued from page iii)

Avner Greif, *Institutions and the Path to the Modern Economy: Lessons from Medieval Trade*

Stephen Haber, Armando Razo, and Noel Maurer, *The Politics of Property Rights: Political Instability, Credible Commitments, and Economic Growth in Mexico, 1876–1929*

Ron Harris, *Industrializing English Law: Entrepreneurship and Business Organization, 1720–1844*

Anna L. Harvey, *Votes without Leverage: Women in American Electoral Politics, 1920–1970*

Murray Horn, *The Political Economy of Public Administration: Institutional Choice in the Public Sector*

John D. Huber, *Rationalizing Parliament: Legislative Institutions and Party Politics in France*

John E. Jackson, Jacek Klich, and Krystyna Poznanska, *The Political Economy of Poland's Transition: New Firms and Reform Governments*

Jack Knight, *Institutions and Social Conflict*

Michael Laver and Kenneth Shepsle, eds., *Cabinet Ministers and Parliamentary Government*

Michael Laver and Kenneth Shepsle, eds., *Making and Breaking Governments: Cabinets and Legislatures in Parliamentary Democracies*

Margaret Levi, *Consent, Dissent, and Patriotism*

Brian Levy and Pablo T. Spiller, eds., *Regulations, Institutions, and Commitment: Comparative Studies of Telecommunications*

Leif Lewin, *Ideology and Strategy: A Century of Swedish Politics* (English Edition)

Gary Libecap, *Contracting for Property Rights*

John Londregan, *Legislative Institutions and Ideology in Chile*

Arthur Lupia and Mathew D. McCubbins, *The Democratic Dilemma: Can Citizens Learn What They Need to Know?*

C. Mantzavinos, *Individuals, Institutions, and Markets*

Mathew D. McCubbins and Terry Sullivan, eds., *Congress: Structure and Policy*

Gary J. Miller, *Managerial Dilemmas: The Political Economy of Hierarchy*

Ilia Murtazashvili, *The Political Economy of the American Frontier*

Douglass C. North, *Institutions, Institutional Change, and Economic Performance*

Elinor Ostrom, *Governing the Commons: The Evolution of Institutions for Collective Action*

Sonal S. Pandya, *Trading Spaces: Foreign Direct Investment Regulation, 1970–2000*

Daniel N. Posner, *Institutions and Ethnic Politics in Africa*

J. Mark Ramseyer, *Odd Markets in Japanese History: Law and Economic Growth*

J. Mark Ramseyer and Frances Rosenbluth, *The Politics of Oligarchy: Institutional Choice in Imperial Japan*

Jean-Laurent Rosenthal, *The Fruits of Revolution: Property Rights, Litigation, and French Agriculture, 1700–1860*

Michael L. Ross, *Timber Booms and Institutional Breakdown in Southeast Asia*

Shanker Satyanath, *Globalization, Politics, and Financial Turmoil: Asia's Banking Crisis*

Norman Schofield, *Architects of Political Change: Constitutional Quandaries and Social Choice Theory*

Norman Schofield and Itai Sened, *Multiparty Democracy: Elections and Legislative Politics*

Alberto Simpser, *Why Governments and Parties Manipulate Elections: Theory, Practice, and Implications*

Alastair Smith, *Election Timing*

Pablo T. Spiller and Mariano Tommasi, *The Instituional Foundations of Public Policy in Argentina: A Transactions Cost Approach*

David Stasavage, *Public Debt and the Birth of the Democratic State: France and Great Britain, 1688–1789*

Charles Stewart III, *Budget Reform Politics: The Design of the Appropriations Process in the House of Representatives, 1865–1921*

George Tsebelis and Jeannette Money, *Bicameralism*

Georg Vanberg, *The Politics of Constitutional Review in Germany*

Nicolas van de Walle, *African Economies and the Politics of Permanent Crisis, 1979–1999*

Stefanie Walter, *Financial Crises and the Politics of Macroeconomic Adjustments*

John Waterbury, *Exposed to Innumerable Delusions: Public Enterprise and State Power in Egypt, India, Mexico, and Turkey*

David L. Weimer, ed., *The Political Economy of Property Rights, Institutional Change, and Credibility in the Reform of Centrally Planned Economies*

For EU product safety concerns, contact us at Calle de José Abascal, 56–1°,
28003 Madrid, Spain or eugpsr@cambridge.org

www.ingramcontent.com/pod-product-compliance
Ingram Content Group UK Ltd.
Pitfield, Milton Keynes, MK11 3LW, UK
UKHW011315060825
461487UK00005B/101